D0447274

A Chanticleer Press Edition

9/2000

To Izzy—
Have fun with trees!
Love,
Marcella

Taylor's Guide to Roses

Houghton Mifflin Company Boston

Library of Congress
Cataloging-in-Publication Data
Main entry under title:
Taylor's guide to roses.
(Taylor's guides to gardening)
Based on: Taylor's encyclopedia of gardening.
4th edition. 1961.
Includes index.
1. Rose culture. 2. Roses. I. Taylor's
encyclopedia of gardening. II. Title: Guide
to roses. III. Series.
SB 411.T33 1986   635.9'33372   85-30492
ISBN 0-395-40450-9 (pbk.)

Prepared and produced by Chanticleer Press,
Inc., New York
Cover photograph: Pascali, by Gillian Beckett
Designed by Massimo Vignelli

Color reproductions by Nievergelt Repro AG,
Zurich, Switzerland
Printed and bound by Dai Nippon, Tokyo,
Japan
Typeset by American–Stratford Graphic
Services, Inc.

First Edition.

DNP   10   9   8   7   6   5

Contents

Contributors

Beverly Dobson, author of the rose accounts, is a well-known figure in rose circles, and member of many rose societies. Mrs. Dobson has served as a Consulting Rosarian and Accredited Judge of the ARS. She publishes an annual booklet, the "Combined Rose List," which provides names, dates, and sources for all roses commercially grown and sold in the United States and in many foreign countries. She also publishes "Bev Dobson's Rose Letter," a periodical that brings rose enthusiasts up to date on the latest developments in breeding, registration, awards, and the like. Mrs. Dobson has received the Silver Honor Medal for the New York State District of the ARS.

Don and Paula Ballin contributed the Rose Calendar and the essay on exhibiting roses. Mr. Ballin has recently been elected President of the American Rose Society. He and his wife Paula, who serves in many capacities for the ARS (including Convention Coordinator for 1985), collaborate in a wide range of articles and projects dealing with roses.

Griffith J. Buck is the author of the essays entitled "Classification of Roses" and "Creating New Cultivars." Recently retired from Iowa State University, where he was a professor of horticulture for 37 years, Dr. Buck is a very well-known specialist in rose breeding. He has been active for many years in the ARS, serving on the Society's committees for Instruction, Classification, and Registration.

Barbara Damrosch is the author of the garden design essay. A landscape designer who has written extensively on the subject for *Horticulture* and other magazines, she is also the author of *Theme Gardens,* published by Workman.

Gordon P. DeWolf, Jr., Ph.D., revised and edited the fifth edition of *Taylor's Encyclopedia of Gardening,* upon which this guide is based. Coordinator of the Horticultural Program at Massachusetts Bay Community College in Wellesley Hills, Massachusetts, he previously served as Horticulturalist at the Arnold Arboretum at Harvard University.

Harold Goldstein, contributor of the essay on The American Rose Society, has been the Executive Director of the ARS since 1970. In that capacity he edits all ARS publications and functions as the World Registrar of Roses. He is a well-known figure in rose circles both in the United States and abroad, having served as a delegate four times to the World Federation of Rose Societies meetings.

The principal contributor of photographs for this book, Pamela Harper has an outstanding library, numbering some 80,000 slides, of photographs of plants and gardens. She is also a well-known horticultural writer and lecturer.

Charles G. Jeremias is the author of the essay "Getting Started." Recently elected Vice President of the American Rose Society, Dr. Jeremias has written several articles for the American Rose Society Annual and *American Rose* magazine. He is a professor emeritus of chemistry of Newberry College in Newberry, S.C.

Betty Pavey wrote the section on flower arranging with roses. A longtime rose enthusiast, Mrs. Pavey is well known in judging circles throughout the rose community. She is the author of "Say It With Roses," a publication of the American Rose Society, and is considered a leading expert on the subject. Mrs. Pavey was awarded the Gold Honor Medal—the American Rose Society's highest honor—and she is the second woman in history to receive this prize.

Holly Harmar Shimizu contributed the Preface and the essay on the history of roses. Curator of the National Herb Garden at the U.S. National Arboretum in Washington, D.C., Holly Shimizu holds an M.S. in horticulture from the University of Maryland. She has worked abroad in many capacities related to horticulture, and is a frequent lecturer on herbs, roses, and other subjects.

Charles A. Walker, Jr. served as a consultant for the rose accounts. Southeast coordinator of The Heritage Roses Group, Mr. Walker is also an Accredited Judge, Consulting Rosarian, and Life Member of the ARS. He writes and lectures frequently specializing in old garden roses, and is pursuing a Ph.D. in horticulture.

Katharine D. Widin wrote the section on rose pests and diseases. Holding an M.S. and Ph.D. in plant pathology from the University of Minnesota, Dr. Widin is a consultant, author, lecturer, and independent research analyst specializing in insects and diseases affecting plant life. She is the founder and operator of a private consulting firm, Plant Health Associates, and a former biology professor.

The ARS

The American Rose Society was started in 1899 by a group of enthusiastic rose growers. Since its inception in Harrisburg, Pennsylvania, it has evolved into one of the premier plant societies in America, with over 30,000 members.

Goals of the Society

The Society's aim is to educate and inform the American public about the pleasures of growing roses. Members enjoy many privileges. They receive the monthly *American Rose Magazine,* devoted to rose culture, history, and information, and the introduction of new varieties. In addition, the *Handbook for Selecting Roses,* compiled by the members, rates most of the roses used in commerce throughout the United States. This is an invaluable small booklet for those planning their gardens. Members also receive *The American Rose Annual,* a yearly publication of approximately 200 pages, full of additional information, lore, and scientific research.

The World of Roses

Although the uninitiated may think of a rose as just one kind of flower, rose hobbyists discover a many-faceted world of interest, and are soon enmeshed in growing one or more of their favorites. There are many rose growers who channel their energies into the art of growing roses for exhibition in shows. Competitions are held around the country and on every level, from local rose shows to district meetings and national rose shows. Show roses require specific care and some expertise in determining when a rose looks its best, when to cut it, how to store roses, and how to transport roses to the show, whether it is held nearby or thousands of miles away.

Consultants and Experts

In addition, the Society has members devoted mostly to creating and perfecting flower arrangements. Some people join the Society to learn how to become judges and apprentice judges for the rose shows. Others are appointed as Consulting Rosarians by their local society, approved by the national organization. These individuals have the expertise to advise other people on how to grow roses in a particular area. A person who has a problem with growing roses can write to the American Rose Society; a Consulting Rosarian will be assigned to help them grow better roses.

The Society sponsors miniature test gardens and conducts experimental tests on new products at the American Rose Center, a 118-acre complex in Shreveport, Louisiana. Open to the public, the Center boasts over 20,000 rosebushes in more than 30 gardens. This makes a fine place for the rose enthusiast to visit and is fast becoming one of the most outstanding gardens in America.

We invite all interested parties, no matter what their particular interest or need, to contact the American Rose Society, P.O. Box 30,000, Shreveport, LA 71130.

Preface

Throughout history, roses have been the most cherished of flowers. They are universally loved for the delicacy of their velvety petals, the exquisite beauty of the unfurling bud, the strength and brilliance of their colorful blooms, their heavenly fragrance, and their pure, unrivaled elegance.

Growing roses will bring you the greatest of pleasures. Whether you select wild roses, old-fashioned roses, or modern types, these glorious flowers will bring you beauty and satisfaction, season after season. This book will dispel the notion that growing roses is the province of a few lucky experts—the splendor of the rose is accessible to everyone.

In contrast to their delicate appearance, roses are long-lived, strong, rugged plants that can bounce back from the rigors of winter. Most blend well into a variety of settings. They can serve as an architectural feature—covering trellises or buildings—or be strictly ornamental. You can add roses to a special fragrance garden, planting them among herbs, or use them as hedges to create privacy and elegance in one stroke. There is a rose for every situation, from the most formal rose garden to the wildest backyard landscape.

This book is a tribute to the queen of flowers. It is designed to encourage the beginner, stimulate the experienced rose enthusiast, and to bring pleasure—through its magnificent color plates—to the armchair gardener.

Acknowledgments

For their valuable assistance in preparing this guide, the contributors and editors would like to extend special thanks to Dr. Henry M. Cathey, Director of the United States National Arboretum; Mr. Harold Goldstein, Executive Director of the American Rose Society; and to Doris Hicks, Peter Haring, and Mrs. Frederic C. Lee.

Illustrators

Mary Jane Spring provided the anatomy drawings and the illustrations of rose pests and diseases, along with the drawings on p. 31 in "Getting Started." Alan D. Singer prepared all the other drawings in "Getting Started"; in addition, he created the drawings for the Visual Key (which are repeated in several places in the book), and the garden design illustration. The drawing on the title pages is the work of Sarah Pletts, and Paul Singer provided the Zone Map.

How to Use

Every garden is individual, reflecting the taste and skill of the person who creates it. Some people prefer the constrained elegance of a formal garden, while others enjoy a wilder kind of beauty in the landscape. But in every situation, and for every kind of garden, roses add a touch of splendor that is found nowhere else in nature. Whether you are an expert gardener or just starting out, this book is for you. To the beginner, it offers encouragement as well as instruction in all phases of growing roses; for the expert, it provides an enormous amount of information on a very wide range of cultivars. This guide will show you how to blend your own talents and imagination with the loveliness of roses to create the ideal rose garden—something you will enjoy for a lifetime.

How the Book Is Arranged
This guide contains three basic kinds of material: color plates, text accounts of rose varieties, and a group of expert articles covering every phase of growing roses. Each section provides valuable assistance for all levels of expertise.

Articles by the Experts
Written by well-known rose authorities, these essays offer advice about every aspect of growing roses—from buying your first rose bush to exhibiting your homegrown masterpieces locally or even at the national level.
In the sections on classification, anatomy, and the history of roses, beginners will find all the botanical facts they need; for more advanced gardeners, there is an article on how to hybridize your own roses.
"Getting Started" spells out, in a convenient, step-by-step fashion, how to purchase, plant, prune, and fertilize rose bushes; what kinds of winter protection they need; and many other aspects of good cultivation.
The zone map and the discussion of hardiness will show you just what kind of impact climate will have on your roses, and what kinds of roses are generally best suited to your area of the country.
"Design for a Rose Garden" is full of straightforward advice about how to make the most of color, what roses work well together, and what other plants will enhance the beauty of your roses.
Also included are informative essays on arranging and exhibiting your roses, and combating pests and diseases.

The Color Plates
The 396 varieties featured in this section bring a bouquet of color right to your fingertips. Chosen with an eye to their practicality for the garden—as well as for their beauty—these roses provide a comprehensive sample of the many varieties that are available to today's rose enthusiast. And when the growing season is over,

This Guide

armchair gardeners will find that browsing through this extensive collection of roses will help to pass the long winter evenings until spring comes again.

The color section includes two special guides. The Color Key presents examples of the enormous range of colors that roses display; the Visual Key shows the organization of the color plates, in eight groups corresponding to eight classes of roses. Within these groups, the photographs are arranged to unfold the magnificent palette of colors available. The captions tell you the size of both the plant and the blossom, as well as when it blooms. There is also information about the fragrance, hardiness, and disease resistance of each variety. Some classes—the climbers, shrub roses, and old garden roses—are made up of smaller subclasses; in these groups, the subclass information is also provided in the captions. Finally, the caption refers you to the page number of the text account, where you will find fuller information about each rose.

Encyclopedia of Roses

Written especially for *Taylor's Guide to Roses,* the rose accounts represent the state of the art in rose literature. This section again organizes the roses into the eight main classes; within those classes, the write-ups are arranged alphabetically, and cross-referenced by page number to the color plates. Short introductions to each section provide a brief history of the classes—their origins and present-day status.

Each rose account tells you the name of the cultivar or species, together with the name of the originator and the date of introduction. In some classes of very ancient roses, this information is not fully known; in these cases, usually just a date is given.

The comments fill you in on the history of the variety, any awards that it may have received, and the uses to which it is best suited in your garden.

Under the heading "Flowers," all the particulars about the color, size, and shape of the blossom, the number of petals, when it blooms, and the fragrance are given. The foliage section tells you about a plant's style of growth, susceptibility to certain diseases and pests, and hardiness.

References and Tips

At the end of the book, special reference sections provide a glossary of rose terms and a list of many nurseries around the country that specialize in selling roses, as well as an index.

A Guide for Everyone

This book will provide you with all the information you need to grow beautiful roses. The color pictures will help you choose what roses to grow, and the articles will be an invaluable tool for the life of your rose garden.

Modern Roses:

Roses are the ultimate plants of legend, romance, and beauty. Throughout history, they have figured prominently in literature, art, and medicine, as well as in horticulture. More than 2000 years have passed since the Greek poetess Sappho christened the rose "queen of flowers"; the course of history clearly bears out this appellation, for their irresistible charm has not diminished over the centuries. Today roses entice the novice gardener with their promise of beauty and bring a special satisfaction to seasoned rosarians.

Ancient Evidence

Fossils found in Europe, Asia, and North America indicate that roses existed approximately 30 million years ago. Among the earliest representations of the flower were decorations on jewelry and ornaments from the early Minoan civilization, which flourished on the island of Crete from about 2800 to 2100 B.C. Approximately 1000 years later, roses began to appear in the paintings and carvings of the later inhabitants of this same island. The first literary reference to the rose is found in the *Iliad;* Homer tells us of the rose oil used by Aphrodite to anoint the fallen Hector.

It appears that the earliest cultivation of roses may have taken place in China; according to Confucius (551–479? B.C.), roses were grown in the imperial gardens of the Chou dynasty. The Greeks also grew roses—particularly around the time of Christ—but not to the extent that the Romans did. In the ancient world, the cultivation of roses reached its peak in the Roman Empire, in the 300 years following the birth of Christ.

The Romans were extravagant in their love of roses. Wealthy citizens used hundreds of thousands of rose petals to carpet their floors. Nets filled with petals were suspended from the ceiling; released during an evening's festivities, they sent down a gentle cascade of color and fragrance onto the guests below. The Romans made beds of rose petals and added the fragrant flowers to their bath water to perfume and preserve their skin.

Supply and Demand

Eventually the clamor for roses became so great that even the huge shipments imported to Rome from Egypt were not sufficient to fill the need. In due course, the Romans began to grow their own roses. Displaying the same ingenuity that had led to the building of impressive networks of aqueducts and the sumptuous pleasure palaces at Pompeii, citizens of the Empire built greenhouses, where piped-in hot water created the warmth necessary for cultivated plants to produce blossoms throughout the winter.

Long an emblem of festivity and luxury, the rose began to signify more than simple pleasure when Roman civic leaders endowed it with political import. A rose hanging from the ceiling during the course of a political meeting signaled confidentiality—those present must never reveal the secrets exchanged *sub rosa.*

A History

Roses in Politics and Art

In more modern times the rose has also had its acolytes among
kings and political leaders. The Wars of the Roses marked a lengthy
period of civil strife in English history during which the houses of
York (the White Rose) and Lancaster (the Red Rose) fought
bitterly for the throne. At the conclusion of the hostilities, the
red-and-white Tudor rose became a symbol of national unity.

The Empress Josephine, first wife of Napoleon Bonaparte,
maintained grand rose gardens at her residence, Malmaison.
Considered to be the first international rose collection, her gardens
were unique because they were designed to show not only the
beauty of the blossoms but also the beauty of the plants themselves.
It is estimated that at Josephine's death in 1814 there were 250
varieties of roses being grown at Malmaison. Fortunately, many of
these have been preserved for us in the paintings of the wonderful
folio edition of *Les Roses,* by Pierre-Joseph Redouté and Claude
Antoine Thory.

The elegance of the rose also inspired architects of the great Gothic
churches of Europe; skilled craftsmen adapted the form of the
blossom to create the beautiful rose windows that adorn many
magnificent cathedrals, such as Chartres. Modern buildings, such as
the National Cathedral in Washington, also show this
influence.

Some varieties of old garden roses have long held a special place in
history. The Provence Rose (*Rosa centifolia*), cultivated in the
Middle Ages, found its way into art, appearing in many Dutch and
Flemish still-lifes of the 17th and 18th centuries. The Damask Rose
(*Rosa damascena*) has a similarly colorful history. The plants were
first brought to Europe in about the 12th century, during the period
of the Crusades, when tremendous breakthroughs in commerce
between East and West were forged. But the first written allusion to
the Damask Rose came from Vergil, who described them in 50 B.C.

Perfume of the Kings

The fragrant oil that roses produce—known as attar of roses—is said
to have been discovered in the mountain kingdom of Kashmir, in
what is now northern India. Legend has it that the wife of the ruler
noticed an oily film on the surface of a stream that ran through her
rose garden. Scooping up some of the petal-laden water, she put her
hand to her face, becoming the first woman to inhale the exquisite
fragrance of attar of roses.

Rose oil has been used by many civilizations as a perfume and to
anoint the dead. In China, where the rose was a royal flower, only
the ruling classes were permitted to use these precious oils. And in
medieval France, commoners were allowed to enjoy this magnificent
fragrance only on their wedding day. At various periods in history,
this oil has commanded huge prices—up to six times its weight in
gold.

Modern Roses: A History

Nutrition from Roses
Even before the earliest cultivation of field crops, roses were valued as a source of food in some primitive cultures. The Romans are thought to have been responsible for introducing the practice of flower-eating into Europe; many peasants living at the time are reported to have thought the practice wrong, because removal of the flower prevented the formation of the fruit.

Fragrant Panacea
In the 18th century, more than one-third of all herbal remedies for various ailments called for the use of roses, and historically the flower has been significant in a wide range of medicinal applications. The healing properties ascribed to the rose were supposed to lie chiefly in the petals—particularly those of *Rosa gallica,* which is widely known as the Apothecary Rose. The petals, which must be thoroughly dried immediately after being picked, are said to be tonic and astringent in their effect.

A conserve made from rose petals was once widely used to strengthen the stomach and to assist in digestion. Syrup of roses, made from the Damask Rose (*Rosa damascena*), was once commonly prescribed as a purgative. Rose vinegar, made by adding dried petals to a distilled vinegar, was given to relieve headaches. And even the fruit of the rose was employed in early medicine. The pulp was separated from the seeds; blended with sugar, it was sold as a curative for numerous ailments.

At present, roses are not so widely used in medicine; nonetheless, rose hips are employed in a large number of commercial products, notably tea and preserves. They are also one of the chief sources of vitamin C today. Some of the better edible hips come from *Rosa rugosa* and *R. canina*. Rose water is also used to make the confection known as Turkish Delight.

Wild Roses and Their Descendants
Most of today's cultivated rose varieties are descended from seven or eight species of wild roses, most of which are in the group that botanists term Gallicanae—*Rosa gallica* and its near relatives.

The wild species or natural varieties of the genus *Rosa* compose a group of extremely beautiful and interesting garden plants. Their potential has, unfortunately, never really been recognized—perhaps because these roses have been eclipsed by the more popular cultivars. For example, the Eglantine Rose (*Rosa eglanteria,* also known as Shakespeare's Rose) should be treasured for the sweet smell of pippin apples given off by the leaves. *Rosa virginiana* puts on a marvelous display of color all year long: the pink flowers of spring are followed by glorious dark red hips; in autumn the leaves turn various shades of red, yellow, orange, and green; and in winter, when the landscape is bare and gray, the arching red canes provide a welcome touch of color.

Notwithstanding the beauty of the wild roses, it is the cultivated varieties that have attracted the most attention and acclaim. The majority of garden roses grown today are derived from two or more of the following species: *Rosa chinensis, R. damascena, R. foetida, R. gallica, R. moschata, R. multiflora, R. odorata, R. rugosa,* and *R. wichuraiana.* All of these species are of Asiatic origin.

A Complex History

Despite this rather limited pool of ancestors, the evolution of our garden roses is complex. When the China Rose (*Rosa chinensis*) was introduced into Europe in 1789, a sort of rose revolution took place. Until that time, the only roses found in Europe were hardy shrubs that bloomed for a short period in late spring or summer. This and other exotic oriental species brought with them a capacity for repeat flowering. Some of them bore yellow flowers—also a novelty—and some had a climbing or trailing habit.

With the introduction of Asiatic discoveries, an increasing number of hybrids began to appear. Throughout the 19th century, which was a very active period in the development of cultivars, it was common practice to plant naturally pollinated seeds; for this reason, the antecedents of many well-known cultivars can be traced only through the maternal side. The hips of some cultivars were gathered at random; for these, the lineage is left to conjecture.

By the late 19th century, the roses of the East and West had been crossed and recrossed many times, creating a range of repeat-flowering roses in many colors and culminating in the creation of the hybrid tea class. Although other classes have come into being since that time, the hybrid teas are still considered to be the most popular of all roses.

Looking Ahead

There is still a great future ahead for those interested in developing and hybridizing roses. Rosarians are becoming increasingly concerned with developing cultivars that are resistant to diseases and insects, as well as improving the fragrance, form, and hardiness of existing varieties. And there are many species that have still never been used for hybridizing. Through our increasing knowledge of roses and our appreciation of them, we can all play a part in their exciting evolution.

Classification

Roses have the distinction of being among the oldest cultivated ornamental plants found in today's gardens. This distinction is in no small part due to the fact that roses grow wild around the globe, from the Arctic Circle to the equatorial zone.

To fully understand the way roses have developed and how new varieties are produced for our gardens, it is helpful to know how plants—especially roses—are classified.

Order, Family, Genus, and Species

Depending upon their stem anatomy, all seed-producing plants are placed in one of two categories, monocots or dicots. Roses are dicots. Dicots are further subdivided into orders, based primarily on their floral traits and plant characteristics. Roses belong to the order Rosales. The orders are then divided into families; roses belong to the Rose family, which is called Rosaceae.

A family is made up of still more narrowly defined groups of related plants that share a certain level of similarity, and often a fairly recent common ancestor. Such a group is called a genus (plural, genera). The rose genus, *Rosa,* like other genera, may include one or more species.

A species is a wild population of plants that can reproduce themselves true to type from seed. Each species has a distinctive name, composed of two parts—the genus name, which is always capitalized, and the species name, which is not. Some examples of species are *Rosa damascena, Rosa multiflora,* and *Rosa gallica.* In addition, each species may have one or more common names, depending on its cultural history.

Naming and Registration of Cultivars

Rose cultivars, because they are not true species, do not have a two-part scientific name. A cultivar can be named to suit the breeder and will carry that name throughout its existence.

The names given to rose cultivars are subject to the restrictions of the International Registration Authority for Roses. Those with potential for international distribution are given a code name, which consists of the first three letters of the breeder's last name plus two or more additional letters. This code name will stay with the rose, even though the cultivar name may be changed. Some roses, in fact, are known by different names in different countries, so the code name given a cultivar serves to standardize the name. Carefree Beauty (Bucbi), Georgie Girl (Dickerfuffle), and Sun Flare (Jacjem) are examples of cultivars and their code names.

Classes of Roses in This Book

A rose is assigned to a particular class on the basis of its ancestry and, in certain cases, on how long it has been in cultivation. These classes are discussed fully in the main text of this book. Before you begin to use the book, it may be helpful to become familiar with the different classes and subclasses of roses included here:

Species roses
These are the naturally occurring roses found in the wild. Most have only five petals. There are about 200 species roses altogether; 24 are included here.

Climbing roses
These are cultivars that can be trained to grow up a trellis, arbor, or building. There are several classes: climbing hybrid tea, hybrid bracteata, large-flowered climbers, kordesii climbers, ramblers, and wichuraiana climbers.

Shrub roses
This is a catch-all class of cultivars that do not belong with either the old garden roses or any of the more modern classes. Subclasses included in this group are: eglantine, hybrid musk, hybrid rugosa, hybrid spinosissima (in part), polyantha, and shrub roses.

Old garden roses
In cultivation since 1867, the old garden roses include the following classes: alba, Bourbon, centifolia, China, damask, gallica, hybrid perpetual, hybrid sempervirens, hybrid spinosissima (in part), moss, Noisette, Portland, and tea.

Floribundas
These are a modern group of roses, the result of crossing hybrid teas with polyanthas. They typically have many blooms per stem.

Grandifloras
Another modern group, the grandiflora class only came into being in the mid-1950s; it was established for the cultivar Queen Elizabeth, which was seen as the first of a class of large-flowered, abundantly blooming roses.

Hybrid teas
This is the most popular class of roses of all. Many familiar long-stemmed varieties are included here, in a very wide range of colors.

Miniature roses
Another popular group, the miniatures look like their larger relatives in every way except for size. Many grow very well in containers; some also do well indoors.

Anatomy

Corolla

Sepal

Peduncle

Bract

Leaf

Bud eye

Petiole

Rhachis

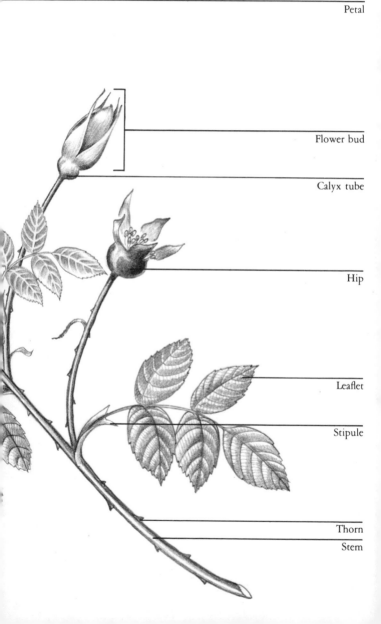

Petal

Flower bud

Calyx tube

Hip

Leaflet

Stipule

Thorn
Stem

Anatomy

In bloom the rose plant has 7 basic parts: blossom or corolla; leaflike sepals; buds; hips; leaflets; stems or laterals; and main shoots or canes. Blossom petals protect reproductive organs inside: Male

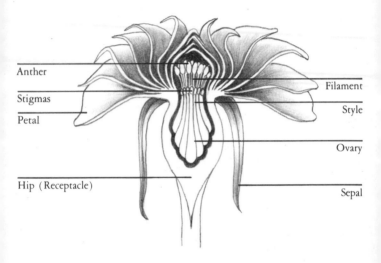

Anther

Stigmas

Petal

Hip (Receptacle)

Filament

Style

Ovary

Sepal

organs, or stamens, con-
sist of round anthers,
containing pollen, and
stemlike filaments; the
female organs, or pis-
tils, consist of the
stigma, which catches
pollen, and the style, in
which tubes develop,

carrying pollen to fer-
tilize eggs in the ovary.

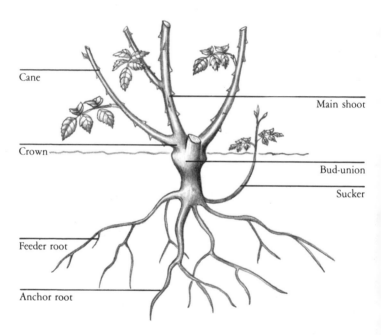

Cane

Main shoot

Crown

Bud-union

Sucker

Feeder root

Anchor root

Getting Started

The first important consideration in growing beautiful roses—and one that is often overlooked by the beginner—is to start out with good plants. To be sure of obtaining good, healthy plants, it is a smart idea to purchase your roses either from a reputable mail-order company or from a local nursery or garden store.

Price *vs.* Value
Don't assume that the price of a rose determines its value. Numerous older hybrid teas, floribundas, and miniatures are less expensive and may also be superior to newer, patented varieties. Many older roses have stood the test of time; still popular with the public, they merit consideration for your garden. The price of a patented rose, however, includes the royalty paid to the hybridizer, and is therefore sometimes much higher than the price of older roses that were never patented or whose patent has expired.
When you order roses through the mail, you will receive dormant, two-year-old, field-grown plants. (This is true for all roses except for the miniatures, which are live potted plants.) The variety, or cultivar, that you choose is budded onto a particular rootstock and provides you with a well-developed root system.

Grades of Rose Bushes
Rose bushes are graded (No. 1, 1½, or 2) in accordance with established standards, first initiated in 1923 and revised when necessary. The American Association of Nurserymen Standards are a sound guide for the commercial rose grower as well as for the amateur. These standards apply to field-grown two-year-old roses, sold either bare-root or packaged. All grades must have a well-developed root system. The commercial growers adhere to these standards to provide their customers with the best possible plants. Some nurseries note the grades of the bushes they sell in their catalogues. If they are out of No. 1 grade bushes, they will substitute No. 1½ grade bushes, if you wish, at a cheaper price. Bushes in each grade must have a well-developed root system in a rounded, well-proportioned pattern so that when the bush is planted in the proper manner, it will grow properly. The canes should show no damage such as blackening or shriveling caused by drying. The bark should be green and the pith should be white or near white, with no sign of shriveling.
Sale or distribution standards have not been established for miniature roses. These little plants grow on their own roots, propagated by rooting cuttings.

Planning the Garden
An important thing to remember, as you prepare to plant your rose bushes, is not to plant them too close to existing trees and shrubs. The roots of these other plants will compete with your roses for food and water. The larger the tree, the farther its roots will extend

from the base. If a tree is not fully grown, attempt to visualize its size in five or ten years before you plant your roses.

Roses need at least six hours of sunlight each day. If there is a choice of morning or afternoon shade, it is better to choose the afternoon shade. Morning shade increases the possibility of mildew and black spot on the bush because it takes longer for the morning dew to dry. Afternoon shade protects the plants from too much summer heat, helping the growth of the plants and retarding the drying out of the soil. As the trees in your garden grow, they will also create more shade, so bear this in mind when you plant.

The next decision you will need to make is how many roses you would like to have in your garden. Beginners should not start on too large a scale. A dozen rose bushes will give you a chance to find out what is involved in growing roses and help you decide if you have the time to care for more.

Selecting Varieties

Choosing your rose varieties, or cultivars, can be difficult, but there are several ways to educate yourself before making a selection. Visit a public rose garden or the gardens of friends and rosarians in your area. Join a local rose society if there is one near you, and attend their rose shows. Obtain catalogues from leading nurseries and mail order rose growers. And by all means consult this book. The varieties included here are widely available and are grown extensively in the United States.

Soil Analysis

After you have determined where to plant your bushes, take a sample of the soil to be analyzed. This analysis can be made by a private laboratory or by a state agricultural college. (Some areas of the country have a county agent, who can supply you with a container for your soil sample and may even send it to a college to be analyzed for you.) To take a soil sample, remove the top two inches of earth and then dig a hole about six inches deep. Take a slice of the soil, running from the top of the hole to the bottom; this gives a representative sample of the six inches of the soil beneath the top two inches—which is where most of a rose's feeder roots grow.

In the report you will find an analysis of the phosphorus and potassium content—two macro nutrients very necessary for plant growth. Other elements reported on will be calcium and magnesium, and possibly iron, manganese, sulfur, and copper, proper amounts of which are also necessary for the growth of the plant.

The Importance of pH

Along with your analysis, there will be a report on your soil's pH—the acidity or alkalinity of the soil. A pH of 7 is neutral—the value for pure water. A higher number (8 or 9) indicates that the soil is alkaline, and a lower number (6 or 5) indicates that the soil is acid. When the pH changes from 7 to 6, the acidity increases tenfold, which means the soil is ten times as acid. Roses prefer a slightly acid soil with a pH of 6.5 to 6.8. They will grow, however, in slightly alkaline soil with a pH of 7.5 or in more acid soil with a pH of 6.

Changing the pH Level

Your local garden center can help you determine what type of soil you have—clay, sandy soil, or sandy loam—and can advise you on how to increase or decrease its pH level to that preferred by roses. To raise the pH level, you can add agricultural lime or dolomitic limestone; to decrease it, you can add sulfur.

Whether you are adding limestone or sulfur to a new bed, be sure to mix it well into the soil—preferably with a garden tiller. Later, when you have established your rose beds, you may find that the pH needs adjusting. Consult your garden center about what amount of limestone or sulfur to use, and try to distribute the material evenly over the beds, scratching it into the soil.

The Size of Your Rose Bed

A rose bed can be almost any size or shape you like—rectangular, square, circular, or curving. Rectangular beds are the most common and probably the easiest to prepare. They will fit into the landscape rather easily as well as into the physical surroundings. A rectangular bed may consist of a single row of bushes, a double row, or three rows. The distance between each bush depends mostly on climate, and somewhat on the bush itself—but be sure you leave enough room to work. Crowding makes it easy for insects and fungus disease to thrive and spread.

In northern states, such as Pennsylvania, Ohio, Illinois, and farther west, rose bushes are usually planted two feet apart. Farther north this distance may be only 18 inches. In the North, the edges of the bed should be at least nine inches from the center of the bush, thus making the bed 18 inches wide.

In the South, where the longer growing season produces larger roses, the bushes are usually planted at least three feet apart (measuring from the center of one bush to the center of the next). The beds should be at least two to three feet wide, according to the space available. Planting bushes at the distances suggested will avoid crowding and ensure free air circulation.

The distances given for planting are for hybrid teas and grandifloras. Floribundas can be planted a little closer if they are the smaller bush type: 18 inches apart in the North, and 30 inches in the South. Shrub roses, old garden roses, and climbers should be planted farther apart than hybrid teas—as much as four to ten feet apart, depending on the growth habit of the plants involved.

Staggering Your Bushes

Staggered planting gives a more solid mass effect, eliminating gaps between the bushes, and allows all the bushes in the bed to be seen from one side. In the North, the bushes should be two feet apart in both directions, in a bed at least 42 inches wide. In the South, plant the bushes three feet apart in a bed at least five feet wide. The distance from the bushes to the edge of the bed is again nine inches in the North, 12 inches in the South.

Preparing the Bed

With the site selected and size of your rose garden determined, you are now ready to prepare the bed. The best time to do this is in the fall, so that the materials added to the soil can begin their work and be settled by spring.

There is no single procedure for preparing a bed, because soil conditions vary throughout the country; the soil may even vary in composition within a small area.

The most common soil is clay. Roses grow well in clay soil, but the clay soil needs to be loosened and kept loose to allow it to breathe and be penetrated by water.

If the soil is sandy, more humus—organic material—needs to be added. Well-rotted cow manure, compost, or peat moss will serve the purpose here. In very sandy soil, you may add humus up to 50 percent by volume, but do not exceed this amount.

If there is grass sod on the surface, remove this two-inch layer and use it where needed in your yard. Now loosen the soil with a spade to a depth of 18 to 20 inches. Some gardeners prefer a depth of 24 inches, but it is harder to loosen the soil at that depth without removing it. Next, work some compost or peat moss into the soil; well-rotted cow manure may also be used. Along with the organic material, add some gypsum. This mineral has the ability to change clay soil from a cohesive substance to a crumbly, easily workable soil. A rotary tiller can be used to turn the earth and churn up this mixture of gypsum, peat moss, and soil. (A word of caution: gypsum will lower the pH of alkaline soil. It should never be used as a top dressing or added to a bed that has been in use for several years and which still has alkaline soil.)

You should use about 15 to 20 pounds of gypsum per 100 square feet. Within these guidelines, the exact amount is not critical because it will not have any adverse effect on the soil and it does not change the pH. Neither is the amount of peat moss or compost critical. The recommended ratio is one shovelful of peat moss to three shovelfulls of soil. This works out to be about 12 cubic feet of peat moss per 100 square feet of soil. The same amount of compost is used in place of the peat moss.

Other Additives

Depending on the soil, other materials—such as sharp sand or vermiculite—may be added. If the soil has less than the required amount of phosphorus, then bone meal (15 pounds per 100 square feet) or 20 percent super phosphate (three to four pounds per 100 square feet) may be mixed into the bed. Phosphorus helps a rose bush to produce a strong root system.

An Easy Method of Soil Preparation

To a beginner, all of this may seem like a lot of work, but the results pay off handsomely. However, if you are not sure of your ability as a rose grower, here is a procedure that is somewhat simpler.

This method of preparing a bed should be started in July or August. After you have determined the size of your bed, cut the grass and weeds but do not dig them up. If you have clay soil, cover the grass and weeds with gypsum until the ground looks white and then cover it with three to four sheets of newspaper. (If the soil is sandy, leave out the gypsum.) Now cover the newspapers with any kind of organic material available—leaves, decomposable kitchen garbage, grass clippings, or chopped up weeds. To speed up decomposition, sprinkle a little commercial fertilizer, such as 10–10–10 or 8–8–8, over the surface.

As the weather becomes cooler, turn the compost under, digging it into the soil and dead grass. After spading or tilling the bed, continue to add leaves and other organic matter. In the North, nothing much can be done in winter, so before the ground freezes add manure—about 150–200 pounds of manure per 100 square feet. In the South, this can be done in January or February by spading or tilling the whole bed once more. By spring, you will have a bed in which roses will grow well, and it will have been done with a minimum of work.

Raised or Sunken Beds

You have probably concluded at this point that the soil level in your bed will be much higher than the surrounding area. Most rosarians prefer raised beds, but some maintain a bed three inches below the grade level to make it easier to mow the grass around the beds. Sunken beds, however, are not recommended for beginners; they must have well drained soil and are generally quite tricky. They must also be very carefully protected in the winter.

The Importance of Good Drainage

Roses will tolerate many kinds of soil, but poor drainage and lack of aeration—problems encountered by many beginners—will cause your plants to weaken and die.

If winters in your area are usually damp and the soil very wet in the spring, you may have a problem at planting time. Consider covering your rose bed with plastic in the fall. Doing so will keep the bed dry enough for easier planting in the spring.

Preparing Rose Bushes for Planting

Rose bushes are sold either in pots or with bare roots. Plants ordered by mail from a catalogue are normally bare-root plants. The bushes will be shipped to you at the time designated on the order blank or at a time the nursery judges best for your geographical location. As soon as you receive the shipment, open the carton and check to see that the roots are still damp. If a shipment is delayed or if the carton has been stored near heat, the roots may have dried out. In any event you should soak the roots in water before planting, at least overnight or up to 24 hours.

Storing Your Rose Bushes

If for some reason you cannot plant immediately, then there are several ways to store your roses. Moisten the bush (especially the roots) and wrap it in the plastic shipping bag. Place the bag in the shipping carton and store in a cool, dark place, preferably at a temperature of 35°–40° F (2°–5° C). Check the bushes every two or three days and dampen them whenever necessary; they can be kept for as long as two weeks in this manner.

If for any reason you need to store the roses longer before planting them, the best thing you can do is to put them in a trench and then cover them with soil. The trench should be at least a foot deep; place the roses close together, lying at a 45° angle. Covering the plants with soil will keep them from drying out, but it is all right for the canes to protrude above the soil. If a hard freeze is forecast, cover the bushes with leaves and plastic, but be sure to remove the plastic if the temperature rises above freezing.

Planting

At planting time, place your rose bushes in a tub of water that covers the canes as well as the roots and let them soak for a couple of hours. When you are ready to plant them, remove the bushes from the water; examine the roots and remove any broken ones, using pruning shears to cut the broken roots just above the break.

Digging the Holes

For each bush, dig a hole in your new bed at least 18 inches in diameter and 18 inches deep. If the hole is a little wider, it does not matter. If a plant proves to be too large for the hole, enlarge the hole. If the roots are too long, cut them back so that they fit easily in the hole, but retain as much of the root system as possible. Before you plant the bush, inspect the canes and be sure to cut off any split or broken ends or any canes broken in shipment. In the North, canes longer than 12 inches are pruned back to 10 or 12 inches before planting. Make the cut approximately one-fourth inch above a bud eye, at a slight downward angle away from the bud eye. In the South, the canes do not need pruning, but broken canes must be trimmed.

Drainage

Roses do not grow well on steep slopes; but it is easy to convert a slope into a series of raised beds by terracing. As a rule, terracing will promote good drainage and retard or eliminate the problems of erosion.

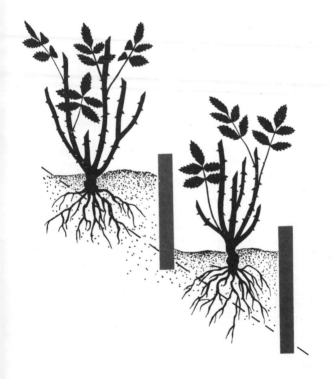

Roses need soil that is very well drained. Some gardeners choose to install a drainage pipe in the soil, several inches below the roots of their rose bushes, to make sure that any excess water in the soil is carried away to a lower level.

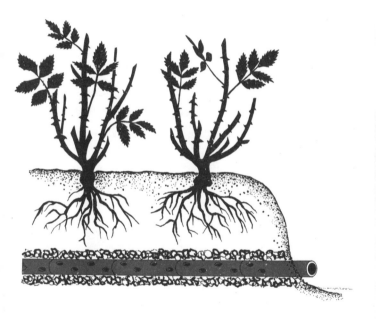

Getting Started

Orienting Your Bushes

Replace most of the soil into the hole, forming a mound or pyramid. Place the plant on this mound, spreading the roots as evenly as possible. The crown, or bud union—the knot of wood between the canes and the roots—should be one or two inches below the level of the bed in the North, where temperatures fall below zero during the winter, and one or two inches above the level of the soil in southern climates. The bud union is usually on the side of the root cane, although it may completely surround the root cane. When planting the bush, place it in the hole so that the sides of the bud union from which most of the canes grow will face north. Orienting the plant this way will help the bud union to cover the root cane completely, causing new canes to form on the south side and producing a more rounded bush.

Fill in the hole until it is about three-fourths full, tamping or firming the soil with your hands so that the soil is packed firmly around the roots. Do not use your feet for this procedure. Tamping with the feet causes the soil to pack so tightly that it becomes difficult for food and water to easily pass through the plant and will destroy the porosity of the soil—which you have worked so hard to achieve.

With the garden hose or a bucket add water to the hole, filling it to the top and letting it soak into the soil. The soil particles will be packed around the roots as they are carried down by the water, helping to anchor the roots and removing any air pockets in the soil around the roots. If the bed is too dry, thoroughly but gently water the entire bed. When the water has completely soaked in, fill the rest of the hole with the remaining soil.

Protecting Bushes

If you live in the North, build a mound of soil over the newly planted bush to a height of 10 to 12 inches (less if the canes are short). If there is not enough soil mixture left, use a mulching material. The mound should be thoroughly drenched so that it is damp all the way through.

Usually in three or four weeks—sometimes less, depending on the weather—the bud eyes begin to swell on the canes, producing new and tender canes and leaves. The protection can then be removed over a week's time by gently washing the plant down with water. In the South, after the bush is planted, it should be left as is. However, if it has not broken dormancy—that is, if the bud eyes do not swell—you can cover the bush with a plastic bag; a milky white, tan, or light brown bag will do. These bags will also protect the bush if a light freeze occurs. In the deep South, the early spring is sometimes very warm, so make three or four tiny holes or slits in the top of the plastic so that some of the heat can escape.

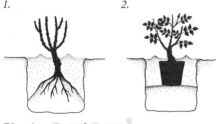

1.   2.

Planting Potted Roses

For potted roses, prepare the planting site, protect the canes, and water as you would for a bare-root plant. Because the roots are already in soil you will have a head start over a bare-root plant. The pots that these roses come in are usually made of plastic, paper-coated plastic, or biodegradable paper. If the rose bushes have been started in a greenhouse during the fall, they may have a well-established root system. But in many instances a nursery does not pot its roses until spring. These roses are usually in a very porous planting mixture, and therefore only feeder roots have begun to develop. Removing the plant from the pot causes the mixture to fall from the roots; this may damage the feeder roots, and the shock of transplanting may be too much for the rose. Thus it is better to place a potted rose—pot and all—in the hole to the desired depth. Next, fill in around the pot with the soil mix; then remove the plant—pot and all—from the hole. Cut the bottom out of the pot, leaving it momentarily in place. Make two slits in the pot, on opposite sides, starting at the bottom and extending three-quarters of the way to the top. Holding the bottom of the plant with one hand, place it carefully in the fitted hole, removing the bottom piece. Then finish the side cuts, gently removing the two sides of the pot, firming the loose soil around the potted soil. Now add the remaining soil to bring the hole up to bed level.

Planting Miniatures

Outdoors in prepared beds, miniatures may be planted as close as 12 inches apart in northern areas and from 14 to 18 inches apart in southern areas. Since miniatures grow on their own roots, they should be planted in the ground slightly deeper than they were in the pots that they arrive in from the nursery. If the soil in the pot is dry, soak each plant thoroughly for several hours before transplanting. If the leaves turn yellow and drop off, this does not necessarily mean that the plant is dead. Placed in the growing environment, the miniature will recover.

Pruning

To have strong, healthy bushes, it is essential to learn how to prune your roses. Pruning is a process that continues throughout the growing season. With newly planted rose bushes, pruning should be kept to a minimum. Many rosarians remove the first blooms, allowing only the second cycle of bloom to develop to maturity. Doing this gives the bush more canes and stronger growth for the summer as well as for the remainder of the year.

Everyone needs a good pair of pruning shears; do not stint on the price, as poor-quality shears can damage your rose bushes. Do not buy anvil shears, which crush the cane. Other pruning shears go by several names: scissors-type, hook-type, or secateurs. The secateur type, if kept sharp, will give a clean cut. Hold the hook edge above the cutting blade, so if there happens to be a little crushing of the cane, it will be on the part of the cane that is being cut off.

Treating New Canes

On the bud union or crown, a new cane, called a basal break, may form. This can occur throughout the year, but generally happens in the spring when the bush breaks dormancy. Then the question is how to treat the new basal breaks. On some bushes the basal breaks may only grow two feet tall, while on others they may grow to four feet. (The tall ones may break off in a wind storm, so it is not a bad idea to tie them to a stake.) You may prefer to pinch the top out when the cane has reached a certain height—12 inches in the North and 15 to 18 inches in the South. Doing so should make the cane stouter and encourage it to put out two or three new canes.

Special Techniques

On hybrid teas, a cluster of blooms forms from the basal breaks as well as from the new canes that break from older canes, forming what is known as a candelabra. Flowers produced from these canes are small and usually have short stems. You can prevent a candelabra from forming by removing the side buds, which appear below the top terminal bud, just as the buds begin to grow. Grasp the bud between the thumb and forefinger and snap it off at the leaf axil, while holding the cane just below this point with the other hand. On grandifloras, the side buds may be on full-length mature canes, growing above the center or terminal bud. These side buds can be stronger and have larger flowers if the terminal bud is removed early. Floribundas produce a cluster of blooms when left to grow naturally.

Deadheading

After a bush has bloomed, the next step is to remove the spent blooms. This is called "deadheading." On a new bush, the process of removing the first blooms is a little different from what is done on an older bush. Cut the bloom (using pruning shears) at the stem, about one-quarter inch above the first pair of five-leaflet leaves. (Some rose bushes may have two or three pairs of three-leaflet leaves below a five-leaflet leaf; where this is so, cut off the stem above the second pair of these leaves.) If you want more blooms, continue this practice as your bushes grow older. However, if you want longer stems—particularly on hybrid teas—then you should cut the stem back to the second set of five-leaflet leaves after the first cycle of blooms.

Pruning Older Bushes

All the following information on pruning two-year-old or older bushes is for hybrid teas and grandiflora roses. Depending on where you live, the average heights are also given.

Pruning is essential to rejuvenate two-year-old or older bushes. Dead

Cut at a 45° angle above a bud eye

canes or dead wood caused by winter freezes, dying canes, or diseased wood should be removed. You will also want to remove damaged or broken stems, along with stems that have crossed through the center of the bush and are rubbing against another cane. First remove weak canes and any that are less than 3/16 of an inch in diameter. Stems growing from pruned canes will grow no larger than the cane from which they have been cut, and are usually smaller.

Pruning of the remaining larger canes depends on whether you live in the North or the South. In the North, the canes are cut back to 12 to 14 inches or less, depending on the amount of winter damage. In the South, the plants are left higher—18 to 24 inches.

Cutting to an Outside Eye

When a leaf drops off or is removed from a cane, it leaves a crescent-shaped scar. The area above the scar will produce a swelling, from which a new cane will form; such a swelling is known as an "eye" or "bud eye." These eyes can be found all around the cane where foliage has grown. The first cut should be made as high as possible above an outside, or outward-facing, eye. Cutting to an outside eye gives the bush a better shape: It keeps canes from growing in the center of the bush, helps sun to get to the bud union, and helps keep fungus diseases away from the plant. Depending on a bush's vigor and the number of healthy canes, you will want to retain three to six young canes. Where winter damage has been severe, you will be in good shape if you are able to keep at least three canes with three to four bud eyes each.

Examining the Pith

As you prune the cane, be sure to examine the color of the center, or pith. If the pith is white, you have a good live cane. If you have cut it to the desired height, go to the next cane. However, if the cane has a brown pith, cut a little more off the top, continuing to snip off a little at a time until you have located the white center. If this seems drastic, it is—and some rosarians will not cut all the way to a white center, particularly after a severe winter. Instead, they cut back to a bud eye where the center is slightly colored or is a very light tan. The theory is that these canes can produce new wood, helping to keep the bush more productive.

Protecting Cut Canes

It is advisable to seal all cut canes. Some sort of compound should be used to seal the cut against borers—various types of insects that drill holes in the center of the cane. If borers attack more than one cane the bush will be weakened and flower production will fall off drastically. Several materials may be used to seal the cut: fingernail polish, Elmer's Glue, carbolated vaseline, or a tree-wound compound.

Pruning

After the first cycle of blooms, you can increase the number of blossoms produced by a bush if you cut back to the first bud eye below the topmost five-leaflet leaf.

When a few weeks have passed, a new stem will grow from the bud eye, and another flowering stem may appear at the base of the lower leaf.

Cut here

Second bloom cycle

In spring, remove any old, weak canes that did not produce good blooms last season; also cut away any canes that cross through the center of the bush.

When pruned, the bush has 3 or 4 healthy, strong canes that will soon produce a bounty of colorful blossoms.

Before pruning

After pruning

Pruning Climbers

Climbers are of two types and are pruned differently. The ramblers bloom once during a season with small, clustered flowers. They may be allowed to spread and may even be used as a ground cover by pruning only weak or diseased canes. The ends of the long canes can be snipped to produce more lateral stems and blooms next year. Some rosarians prefer to cut ramblers back to the ground as soon as the bush has finished blooming. Doing this allows new canes to grow during the summer from which blooms are produced during the next year. Nearly all the ramblers produce flowers only on second-year wood.

Large-flowered climbers may be once-bloomers or repeat bloomers. They need pruning only of old, nonproductive canes of winter die-back. The repeat bloomers should have the short flowering stems cut back to the first set of five-leaflet leaves as soon as the flowers are spent. Because most climbers set hips to produce seed, most of the food and energy goes to producing the seed rather than more flowers. Thus, be sure this deadheading is taken care of, or there will be very little repeat blooming. Don't be surprised if some climbers do not bloom until the third year.

Shaping a Bush

When the pruning is finished, the bush should form a bowl, with the canes radiating from the center like the spokes of a wheel. This leaves the center open to sunlight during the year and encourages basal breaks from the bud union. During the growing season, check the basal canes; if they are growing poorly, prune them out. Canes that form on the inside can be left as long as they are not crossing or rubbing other canes. Weak or small canes should be pruned out. It is best to keep the center open throughout the growing season. If a bush has a spreading habit and takes up too much space, then you can prune back to an inner eye. This causes the new canes to grow straight up, keeping the bush in bounds so that it does not encroach on a neighboring bush. The center will remain open.

In the South and the West, young, green basal canes that grew late during the previous year often survive the winter. Only the flower buds should be removed from these canes. Removal of these buds allows the wood to harden, but cutting into the soft green cane will usually cause it to die. In the following spring, after the lateral stems have grown and bloomed, you may cut this basal cane back to just above the lateral growing canes.

Preventing Disease

After pruning, clean up all debris and old leaves to keep diseases from spreading. It is a good idea to spray the bushes and ground with a fungicide at this time, to kill any dangerous fungus spores that may be present.

Thumb Pruning

The removal of unwanted eyes from rose stems, laterals, and canes with the thumb (instead of shears) is called thumb pruning. This process removes problem stems early; once a stem has produced a bud, it is very hard for most gardeners to remove it.

Unwanted eyes may grow in the wrong place, the wrong direction, or too close together. If you remove them early enough, you can rub them off with your thumb. If the bud eye has already produced a short stem, you can use your thumb and forefinger.

Remove any eyes growing low down on the inside of a cane or bud union; this will keep the center open and prevent large scars. Frequently a bud eye produces two or three stems, which will become weak as they grow. Thumb prune the excess stems, removing the weakest and leaving the strongest stem—usually the center one—to develop. This process will leave the bush with stronger stems and larger flowers. Sometimes the center eye dies and one stem develops on each side. Thumb prune the weaker one when their comparative strength is evident; should the eyes appear equal, leave the one that will give your bush a better shape.

Winterizing

The removal of a spent bloom is also considered pruning. Therefore in the fall, three to five weeks before the first hard frost in your area, you should refrain from cutting the spent heads or blooms on your bushes. Leaving the spent blooms in place is part of winterizing your plants before cold weather arrives. Even though roses in the Deep South may not go dormant, leaving the spent blooms on in November gives the plants a rest from blooming. In the South, the plants retaining spent blooms form seed pods, thereby becoming semidormant. In January, you can begin pruning for the coming year.

You should also withhold any nitrogen-containing fertilizer six to ten weeks before the last blooming cycle. The last blooms could appear by the end of July in the extreme north or the end of September in the extreme south.

The most common way to protect roses is to take soil from a location other than the rose bed and make a mound around the base of the plant to a height of 10 to 12 inches. Where temperatures remain below freezing for some time and the weather becomes stabilized, additional protection is needed. Materials on hand that you can use include leaves, wood chips, pine needles, bark, sawdust, and ground-up corn cobs. Do not apply the protective material too early, as it could cause a late soft growth that will hinder dormancy. Since white and yellow roses suffer winter damage the most, they should be given extra winter protection.

Cones and Collars

One successful protection device is a rose cone, made of foam plastic, which covers the base of the rose bush. Cones are practical only for growers with just a few bushes, since they are expensive and pose storage problems. Cones must be weighted down to keep them in place during strong winds. You must also prune the bush and tie the canes to fit inside the cones. Provide adequate ventilation, because unseasonable warm spells cause sweating in the containers, and mildew and insects will appear if the cones are not ventilated. Collars can be made from cardboard, metal, plastic-covered wire mesh, plastic, tar paper, or layers of newspapers, folded and stapled. The collar encircles the base of the plant; to hold it in place and permit air to circulate freely, you can fill the collar with soil, leaves, straw, pine needles, and other matter. To accommodate sprawling plants, collars can be contoured, simply by pinning two sections together.

Roses grown in containers, including miniatures, can be buried in soil to the top of the container and treated in the same way as roses growing in beds. Potted roses can be brought indoors and handled like indoor miniatures. Larger plants should be exposed to the outdoors long enough to begin dormancy. Do not allow them to completely dry out because this will cause permanent damage to the plant. If the plants go into active growth indoors without enough light, they will become twiggy or leggy, with light green foliage that will readily be attacked by aphids.

Tree roses that remain outdoors require protection, too. After the bush has been pruned, remove the soil from one side of the roots to allow the plant to be bent. Dig a trench large and deep enough to completely accommodate the plant and lie it down in the trench; cover it entirely with soil.

Protecting Climbers

Climbing roses need extra protection, at least in the North. Mounding soil on the base will help, and wrapping the canes in burlap will protect them from the drying effect of winter winds. You may also dig a trench next to the bush and bend the canes into the trench, covering them with soil or other material.

Mulching

Another rose growing practice that you should consider is mulching. Some rosarians do not use mulch; those who live in cool climates maintain that mulching is unnecessary, and that mulch harbors insects and disease. They prefer the soil to be left bare so there can be light cultivation (no more than one and one-half inches deep), because deeper cultivation will injure the feeder roots of the rose bush. Some people also feel that without mulch there is less incidence of crown gall and that fertilizer may be worked into the soil more easily. But keeping unmulched beds free of weeds and grass requires constant care.

If you have less time to devote to weeding, then you will need to

Mound soil at the base of your bushes to a height of about 12 in. Tying the canes will keep them from breaking in strong winds.

In especially cold weather you may want to use straw, leaves, or another mulch to provide insulation.

Protect a tree rose by first digging up half the roots; this will enable you to lie the plant down on its side. Now cover the plant with a large mound of soil, and you will have complete protection.

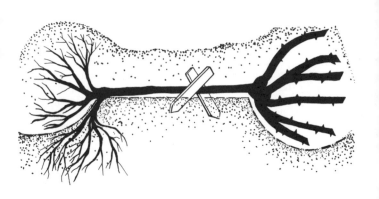

consider mulching. Mulching is a convenient way to keep weeds under control, insulate the soil against summer heat, and conserve moisture by slowing down evaporation.

The real value in using mulch is found in the soil itself. The humus resulting from the mulches make the nutrients already found in the soil more readily available to the roots of the roses, improving the soil structure while at the same time adding trace elements. Soil temperature and moisture are consistent, providing favorable conditions for a continuous growth of fine roses.

The best time to apply mulch is after the soil has warmed and before bushes start growing. Before you mulch, the soil should be soaked by a good rain or water from the garden hose.

Mulching Materials
Many materials have been used and tested for use as mulch. It has been found that a depth of four inches is necessary for most mulches to give the desired results. Cost and availability also determine which mulch to use. So that grass and weeds can be easily removed by hand, mulch should be placed no closer to the bush than six inches. Consult your local garden center to determine which mulches will suit you best.

Controlling Weeds in Your Rose Garden
If by the end of the growing season the weeds are out of hand and you did not use mulch, there is help available. There is a product called Casoron, which comes in two strengths—Casoron 4G and Casoron 10G. It is a winter herbicide that is applied after there have been two killing frosts (temperatures below freezing). Casoron should be applied one foot away from any plant that is only one year old.

Casoron, a pre-emergent herbicide, will not kill Johnson grass or wild onions. These weeds can be removed by hand, before making the bed or by digging them up later. You may also use Poast, a post-emergent grass herbicide. Use Poast with a liquid oil emulsion; it will not harm your bushes, although leaves and flowers may become slightly speckled.

Fertilizer
Beginners will find that there are many materials and methods of fertilizing. What constitutes the best method is a matter of opinion, but it certainly depends on the type of soil and climate. A group of researchers in England has found that a combination of organic fertilizer and chemical fertilizer will grow better roses than either by itself.

When you buy fertilizer, three numbers are printed on the bag or container. The first number indicates the percentage, by weight, of nitrogen included. The second number gives the percentage of phosphorus available as phosphoric acid or P_2O_5 (phosphorus pentoxide). The third number is the percentage of potassium or soluble potash, usually represented by the chemical formula K_2O (potassium oxide). There are many types of formulations: 8–8–8, 10–10–10, 0–20–20, 20–20–20, 18–6–12, 5–10–10, and so on. A soil analysis will tell you what formulation of fertilizer will be best.

When to Feed Your Roses

For newly planted rose bushes, add fertilizer only after the first blooming cycle and thereafter only once a month. Stop feeding your roses by six weeks before the last bloom cycle. Scatter the fertilizer evenly around the bush, at least six inches from the base. Scratch it lightly into the soil, and then water it in. If your soil is dry, water the ground soil the day before you feed your roses.

On two-year-old or established rose bushes, feeding should start in the spring about four to six weeks before the first cycle of blooms, with continued feeding as discussed above.

Other Kinds of Fertilizer

You may want to take advantage of various other products available, including slow-release fertilizers and water-soluble fertilizers. Be sure to read and follow label directions carefully. Or you may want to make your own organic fertilizers, using a blend of products that are easy to get hold of. Some rosarians like to use a solution of Epsom salts to induce more basal breaks. In the summer, if your roses need an extra boost, consult your local garden center about how to apply fish emulsion.

Creating New

Wild roses respond very gradually over time to the demands and pressure of the situation, or ecological niche, in which they grow. Adapting to survival in a dynamic environment is a lengthy process, full of changes so subtle and slow that they may be very nearly impossible for a person to detect. This process of change has come to be known as selection.

Unlike wild roses, most roses in cultivation are bred with the intention, on the part of the breeder, of enhancing or minimizing certain inherited traits—such as color or fragrance—that may have no bearing on the plant's survival. Gardeners want flowers with many petals, blooms of different colors, and a variety of growth habits and sizes. These different forms may be the result of seedling variability, intentional and accidental hybridization, or mutation. Variant forms are produced in the wild, too, but plants under cultivation are subjected to more critical observation, and the variant, if it is desirable, is more likely to be bred again and again. These selected variants are called *cultivars,* because they develop under cultivation; they are also commonly referred to as varieties.

Mutation

New rose cultivars come about through one of two processes—either mutation or hybridization. Mutation is spontaneous; relatively uncommon, it occurs in the meristem (which is inside the developing stem tip) when a gene in one cell changes, or mutates. The affected cell develops and divides, producing a relatively large body of cells. When these cells mature, the change in traits becomes evident. The most common mutations produce changes in flower color or growth habit; for example, a pink rose may produce red flowers or a bush rose may develop a climbing form. A more rare mutation is the change from once-flowering to repeat-flowering. Most mutations, often called "sports," are relatively unstable and may change back, either partially or completely, to the parental form. Almost always, only one trait is involved.

Hybridization

Whether intentional or accidental, hybridization is the principal way to create rose cultivars. The species in the genus *Rosa* are remarkably uniform. The five-petaled flowers have many pistils at the center; the pistils (made up of the stigma, style, and ovary) are surrounded by many stamens—the pollen producers. Each pistil is attached to the inside wall of the receptacle. When fertilization occurs and the resulting egg cell matures, it becomes an achene—a seed enclosed in a woody coating. The receptacle, with its enclosed achenes, enlarges as it matures and, when ripe (a "hip"), turns from green to yellow, orange, orange-red, or purplish black.

A factor complicating hybridization in roses is the varying number of chromosomes in the different species. It is the interplay among these chromosomes that determines the appearance and other traits

Cultivars

of the offspring. Rose chromosomes are divided into groups called genomes, with seven chromosomes each. Hybridization between cultivars with the same number of genomes is relatively uncomplicated and usually produces fertile progeny. Hybridization between cultivars with different numbers of genomes usually succeeds, but the progeny will be relatively infertile.

Artificial Pollination

Once you have learned to grow roses, you may discover that you are interested in cross-breeding some of your own varieties. The techniques you need to master in order to produce seeds by artificial pollination are relatively simple.

To provide the pollen, choose a flower that is just starting to open. Remove the sepals and petals. Examine the stamens to be sure they have not started to shed pollen; if they have, choose a younger flower. With a pair of small scissors or forceps, remove the stamens and place them on a small sheet of wax paper. Put the wax paper and stamens in a shaded, calm place, where the stamens will ripen and shed pollen (which looks like fine yellow dust).

Now select a flower to pollinate. Choose one at the same stage of development as the rose you have selected to be the pollen parent. With a pair of scissors, a small knife, or forceps, remove the sepals, petals, and stamens. Using a small brush, place pollen on the pistils. Cover the pollinated flower with a small paper bag, secured to the stem with a twist-tie; this will prevent unwanted pollination by insects and keep it from drying out.

If you are attempting to make more than one cross, it is vital to use a clean brush when changing pollen parents. You can sterilize a pollen brush by dipping it in ethanol and then drying it. Put a label on the pollinated flower showing the name of the seed and pollen parents—for example, Crimson Glory × Peace. (It is customary to list the seed parent first.) Pollen may not be available when the seed parent flower has been prepared, but if the prepared flower has been protected from drying out, it should remain usable for two to three days. Discard it if the pistils begin to discolor.

If your attempt has been successful, you will begin to see the effects in about two weeks. The receptacle, or hip, will start to enlarge; when it is ripe and ready to harvest, it will have changed color—usually about three months after pollination. Remove the ripe hips before the first frost sets in; cut them open and remove the seeds. If you have a warm greenhouse or other suitable facility, you can plant the seeds at this time. Otherwise, keep them in a cool place (at a temperature of 35–40° F.), make sure they stay moist, and plant them when spring comes.

It is a good practice to keep a permanent record of one's hybridizing work. Such a record should include not only the names of the parents but also the number of flowers pollinated, the dates of pollination, and the number of seeds obtained.

Zone Map

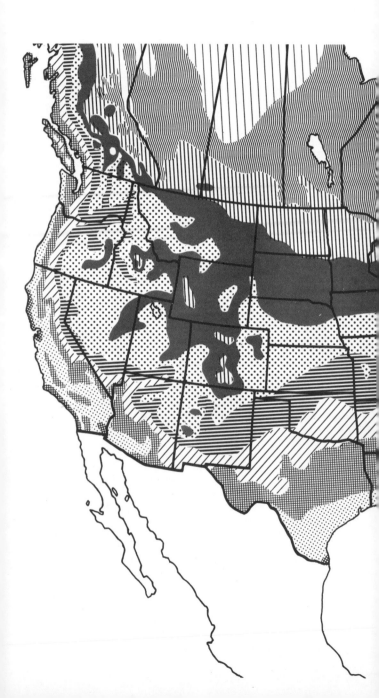

This map was compiled by the United States Department of Agriculture as a broad guideline to temperature extremes in your area.

The key below gives you the average minimum temperatures of the ten zones. Determine if your area corresponds to its zone allocation by comparing your coldest temperatures with those given in the key.

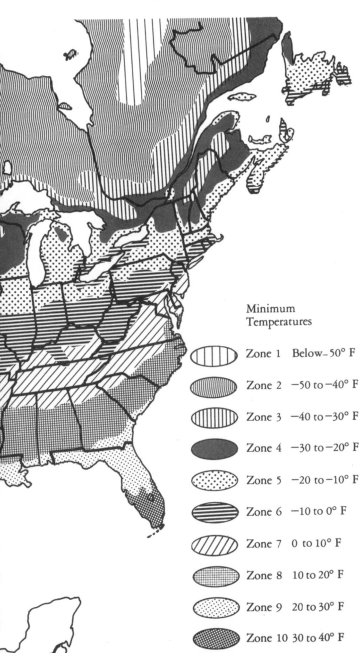

Minimum Temperatures

Zone 1 Below –50° F

Zone 2 –50 to –40° F

Zone 3 –40 to –30° F

Zone 4 –30 to –20° F

Zone 5 –20 to –10° F

Zone 6 –10 to 0° F

Zone 7 0 to 10° F

Zone 8 10 to 20° F

Zone 9 20 to 30° F

Zone 10 30 to 40° F

Hardiness

The Plant Hardiness Zone Map was prepared by the U.S. National Arboretum, Agriculture Research Service, U.S. Department of Agriculture in cooperation with the American Horticultural Society. It shows 10 different zones for the United States and Canada, each representing 10° differences in average minimum annual winter temperatures. Although many factors—such as rainfall, duration and intensity of sunlight, and soil conditions—contribute to winter hardiness in plants, minimum temperatures are considered to be of prime importance in plant survival over winter conditions. Within zones, there are islands of different temperatures; indeed, this can readily be seen on the map. But smaller differences and local variations also contribute to winter hardiness.

Other Important Considerations

It is undeniably useful for gardeners to be aware of their winter hardiness zones, but this information is of less use in growing roses than in growing most other ornamental plants. The main reason is that the actual degrees of cold are less important to roses than such factors as the drying effects of wind and sun and wide temperature fluctuations.

Different Hardiness in Cultivars

Among roses, winter hardiness varies with each different rose cultivar, and is related to the ability of each rose to manufacture its own "anti-freeze." This is a genetic trait, and it varies enormously within each group or classification or roses. It is certainly possible to make generalizations; for example, certain species roses and old garden roses, and most modern shrub roses, are extremely winter hardy, while only a few of the modern hybrid teas, grandifloras and floribundas can survive in severe winter climates. Nonetheless, there are many exceptions.

Nurserymen do not relate varieties of roses to the plant hardiness zone map. Standards have never been established, and reports are contradictory and inconsistent. It is easy to see why, when one's microclimate is so much more important than the zone one is in. One factor that helps roses—even modern roses—through a severe winter is the presence of a good snow cover the whole winter long. Rose gardens in such regions have fewer winter losses than others in a milder zone that has snow alternating with a lack of snow.

Building Protection

In areas where freezes and thaws alternate, some gardeners use foam rose cones or build foam housing over their rose beds. A less expensive method, and one that does not require storage space, is to staple layers of newspaper around the rose bush to make a tight-fitting collar. Whatever winter protection is used, it is critical that the timing be right. It must not be applied too soon. The time of removal is a little less critical, but still very important.

What Roses Need

Roses will grow almost anywhere, in any kind of soil. They will come through very low temperatures if the change is gradual. All but a very few require good drainage; to bloom profusely, they must have at least a half day, and preferably more, of sunlight. In general one can say that the tender varieties will do well in zones 8, 9, and 10, and that the hardy kinds will do well in zones 5, 6, and 7. Only the extremely hardy roses will perform well in zones 2 and 3, and probably only two or three species will thrive in zone 1.

Special Exceptions

Being in one zone or another does not tell the whole story. In Florida, for example, roses require a special understock (*Rosa fortuniana*) for long life; but in other regions of zone 10 this is not the case. Some of the extremely tender kinds thrive in certain areas in zones 4 and 5. These may be exceptional cases—but, with roses, the exception does not prove the rule! It just leads the mind on to ever more cases of unusual instances where rose varieties are blooming abundantly, in unexpected places.

Hardiness by Class

The species roses vary from very hardy to very tender. *Rosa sempervirens,* the Evergreen Rose, and *Rosa gigantea,* from southwestern China and Burma, are extremely tender. The hardiest of all roses is probably *Rosa acicularis,* the Polar Rose, found growing around the Arctic Circle and over wide areas of Asia and North America.

Most old garden roses, such as the gallicas, the damasks, and the albas, are extremely hardy, as are many of the modern shrub roses and old climbers and ramblers.

Old garden roses go into a very deep dormancy and they hold that dormancy through alternating spring thaws and freezes. In modern roses, hardiness varies greatly. In general, the floribundas are hardier than hybrid teas and grandifloras. But you can encourage all your roses to get into a deeper dormancy by refraining from cutting flowers or deadheading bushes in the fall. Allow the hips to form. Withhold fertilizers in the fall, but never withhold water. The real winter enemy of roses is dessication, not cold temperatures.

Good Culture and Hardiness

It is not even practical for gardeners to organize their winter protection according to hardiness zones, although as a general guideline the information provided on the map will prove useful. But planting according to zones is no guarantee of survival. Rely on methods used by others in your local area, and their observable results. Rose growers will tell you that good cultural practices during the growing season are your best winter protection, and that choosing hardy varieties is your best insurance of winter survival.

Calendar

Taking care of roses is not just a summertime activity: there is plenty to do year-round for the person who loves roses. The year in a rose garden, at least in the upper Midwest, begins in April—the time when the plants first break dormancy. In the Deep South or Southern California, however, the year begins much earlier, so the accurate timing of different gardening procedures will depend on your location. This calendar will help you plan your activities for a satisfying year with your roses.

Month 1
Remove any winter protection from your garden. This is the time to prune existing rose plants, removing all dead wood down to where the pith in the middle is white. Remove all weak canes.
Before planting new bare-root rose bushes, soak them in a bucket of water; prune them and check the roots, removing broken ones.
Once about two inches of growth is evident on your new roses, begin removing the soil mounds around the bushes. If it doesn't rain one inch per week, begin watering, soaking the beds deeply.
When the foliage starts to grow, begin spraying with insecticide and fungicide. If using a systemic insecticide, spray once every two weeks, as long as temperatures remain under 85° F. Apply fungicide weekly for both black spot and mildew.
Toward the end of the month, give your roses their first fertilizer. Water before spraying, as well as before and after fertilizing.

Month 2
Continue your weekly watering and spraying programs. One month after you first apply fertilizer, reapply a well-balanced rose food.

Month 3
Your roses are blooming! Remove spent blooms down to the first five-leaflet leaves, retaining as much foliage as possible. Continue to water weekly, spray regularly, and feed monthly. This is also the time to mulch your beds.

Month 4
Continue watering, removing spent blooms, and feeding your roses monthly. Your spray program becomes critical now. Hot weather brings black spot and mildew, so apply fungicide faithfully.
If temperatures are running in the range of 85° F. or higher, reduce the amount of insecticide and fungicide you are using by one-fourth to one-third to avoid foliage burn.

Month 5
Give your roses their last complete application of fertilizer no later than six weeks before the first frost. Continue watering and spraying as you did in the very warm summer days.

Month 6
Maintain your spraying schedule, reverting to full-strength doses as the weather becomes cooler. Regular watering is vital as the plants begin to prepare for dormancy.

Month 7
You can now eliminate the insecticides, but continue to use fungicides. Also continue watering if the weather is very dry. Evaluate your bushes, noting which did well and which were weak, and eliminate the weaklings. If you are going to expand your garden, this is also the time to build beds and order bushes. Test the soil in all your beds, taking a sample in four or five places to get an average. The results will tell you what fertilizers and soil amendments you need for next season.

Month 8
If you live in an area with cold winter climate, this is the time to organize your winter protection. Many people choose to build soil mounds around each plant, up to a height of 12 inches (30 cm), although other methods are popular in some regions.

Month 9
Complete your winter protection by applying leaves over the entire bed; the branches from Christmas trees make good added protection against wind damage and freezing temperatures.

Month 10
While winter prevents outdoor gardening work, it is an excellent time to clean your garden tools and sharpen your pruning shears. During thaws, check to see if you provided adequate winter protection for your plants—make sure they are not heaving out of the ground from the freeze/thaw cycles. If they are, replace as much soil as possible around the roots and bud union.

Month 11
Make maps of your new beds, assigning the plants you have ordered to specific areas to make planting easier.

Month 12
Check your supply of fertilizers and spray materials; replace anything that you need. Label and date insecticides and fungicides (these materials generally have a shelf life of only two or three years).

Month 1
You're now back to the beginning of the year, ready to start again. If you have followed this calendar, your rose garden in the coming year should be ready—healthier, more productive, more satisfying, and the envy of the neighborhood.

Showing Roses

While many people are content to grow roses simply for their own pleasure, others feel the urge to take their flowers out of the backyard and into the spotlight. One of the most interesting ways to do this is to take part in a rose show, where participants from all walks of life meet to admire each others' achievements.

Judging Standards

A complete program on training and accrediting judges has been developed by the American Rose Society in the basic text *Guidelines for Judging Roses*. If you are serious about exhibiting, you should obtain a copy of this book from the American Rose Society. Judges award points based on six different elements: form; color; substance; stem and foliage; balance and proportion; and size. Judging each of these characteristics involves a detailed understanding of roses in general, and of each kind of rose in particular; but these are the basic elements that a judge will look for.

Form

The many-petaled hybrid tea is at its most perfect phase of beauty when the bloom is from one-half to three-fourths open; at this time, the form should be "gracefully shaped with sufficient petals, symmetrically arranged in an attractive circular outline, and tending toward a high center." A judge views the specimen from both the top and the profile, and also turns it to get an overall view of its symmetry. The center of the blossom should be high and pointed, show little or no evidence of confusion or splitting, and be sufficiently open so judges can examine it; the outer petals should be at a horizontal plane.

Color

The color of the specimen should be typical of the variety; the color should be clear and bright, with no evidence of streaking or blotching.

Substance

The term "substance" actually refers to the amount of moisture contained within the petals. Good substance is evidenced by a sheen on the petals, a crisp, fresh look, and the feeling—although touching is not allowed—that if you broke a petal it would snap like fresh lettuce. Color and substance are closely related: A rose can lose its color for many reasons (such as having been refrigerated) without losing substance; but once a flower begins to lose substance, it loses color. Loss of substance diminishes the vibrancy of the color.

Stem and Foliage

The stem of an exhibition specimen should be straight, well clothed in foliage, and long enough to complement the bloom. The foliage should be free of dirt or spray residue, unmarred by damage from insects and disease, and be "stacked" so that when you look at the specimen from the top, the foliage presents a circular framing effect.

Blossom Size
The size of the flower should be typical of the variety or larger; a rose that exceeds typical size is given extra points. A judge will normally award 7 points out of a possible 10 to a bloom that is normal in size, reserving the right to confer the extra few points on blooms that are larger than usual.

Balance and Proportion
The relationship among the bloom, the stem, and the foliage determines the balance and proportion of a rose. The size of the bloom must be in proportion to the size of the foliage; foliage that is too large, dominating the specimen over and above the bloom, would lower the number of points awarded. Points awarded in this category are affected also by how the exhibitor stages the specimen in the vase—a stem that is too short or too long will destroy the balance and proportion.

Special Rules for Clusters
The information above applies specifically to one-bloom-per-stem hybrid teas, floribundas, grandifloras, and miniatures. The regulations for sprays are somewhat different. In judging a spray, or cluster of blooms, form is broken down into three categories.
The first and most important is the overall appearance of the inflorescence; it should be symmetrical in outline without uneven gaps between the florets. The next most important feature, at least for floribunda and miniature sprays, is evidence of stages of bloom. The ideal spray would have some buds, some blooms one-quarter open, some in exhibition form, and some fully opened with fresh stamens showing. The final consideration is the form of those individual florets that, in the exhibition stage, have a form similar to that of hybrid teas.
Balance and proportion are judged differently for sprays. Because inflorescences can be quite large, it is frequently impossible to get a stem long enough to balance the spray. A shorter stem must enhance the exhibit. In all respects but those mentioned here, sprays are judged like hybrid teas.

Culture for Exhibition Roses
To grow exhibition roses, gardeners deviate somewhat from normal cultural procedures, beginning with the fertilization program. Many gardeners simply fertilize monthly, using a well-balanced commercial food; exhibition roses, however, require soil analysis so that optimal growing conditions can be provided. Based on the analysis, you should provide your soil with the nutrients it requires, plus whatever other material is needed to bring it to the proper pH. More frequent

Showing Roses

feeding—perhaps every three weeks, rather than monthly—is encouraged. When feeding more frequently, cut down on the recommended monthly amount and apply smaller doses more often. The last application of fertilizer should occur approximately three weeks before the fall rose shows.

As stems progress, be on the lookout for side growth. Hybrid teas are exhibited with one bloom to a stem; there is a penalty for scars left by disbudding, and a specimen is disqualified if side buds are evident. Inspect stems daily, and when evidence of side growth appears, remove it cleanly, leaving no stubs; do so as early as possible to prevent unsightly scars.

Staking

While some growers consistently produce straight, long, strong stems, not everyone is so lucky. What's more, some varieties produce crooked stems because of their genetic breeding. You can straighten a stem by placing a bamboo garden stake as close to it as possible and securing the stem to the stake with plastic ties. Once the stem is staked, you must watch the developing stem carefully and prevent the plastic tie from cutting into it; you must also be sure a portion of the stem doesn't "belly" out between the ties. You must adjust the ties frequently, especially in the area just below the calyx tube.

Watering

Approximately three weeks before the first show date, begin watering frequently and deeply, at least twice a week, more often if the weather is very hot. This additional water will improve the substance of your specimens and will give them an added edge in sustaining the rigors of exhibition.

Protection

Once the sepals have come down from the bloom, protect the blooms from sun scalding, insect damage, rain, and heavy dew. There are many forms of bloom protection. One that often works well is a waxed-paper sandwich bag placed over the bloom and secured at the neck with a twist tie. These bags can be left on during the day, but they are most effective at night, when they prevent dew from spotting the blooms.

Cutting

The most difficult decision you will have to make is when to cut a specimen bloom. Much depends upon the number of petals—the greater the number of petals, the longer you leave the bloom on the plant to develop. As a general rule of thumb, test by squeezing the fullest part of the flower gently between your thumb and middle finger. If it feels soft, cut the bloom; but if it feels as if there were a small marble in the center, the bloom is not ready. You should be able to feel the petals move, but remember to be gentle.

Category	Points
Form	25
Color	20
Substance	15
Stem and foliage	20
Size	10
Balance and proportion	10

The six categories on which roses are judged, and the maximum possible points awarded for each:

When you determine it is time to cut, the next question is how long you should leave the stem. As a general guideline, take a stem that is too long, not too short. You can always cut off some of the stem if it is too long, but you can't add stem if you leave it too short. To ensure adequate stem length without depriving your plant of its needed foliage, measure your bloom from top to bottom, then multiply this figure by seven; this will give you the length of stem that will protrude from the top of your container. Allow another five inches, at least, below this point. Thus, if your bloom is one and a half inches, you should cut a stem of 15½ inches.

Once you have cut the specimen and placed it in water, you should recut it under water and remove half an inch to an inch of stem. The reason for this is that cutting the stem on the bush creates tension, which pulls as much as half an inch of air into the stem, leaving an air bubble at the base. Recutting under water eliminates this air bubble and thus will prevent the rose from wilting prematurely.

Storage

Once the bloom is cut, it must be refrigerated, assuming there are still several days until the actual show date. Refrigerator temperature should range between 36° and 40° F, and no fresh food should be stored with the roses. Before placing the blooms in the refrigerator, decide what type of container you will use. It should be able to hold enough water to supply the bloom, and if it is to hold more than one specimen, it should be able to safeguard them against foliage damage. Some exhibitors make cones of waxed paper, wrapping them around each stem and thus forcing the foliage up (it straightens easily when the paper is removed). In addition, plastic sandwich bags should be placed over the blossoms to prevent deterioration and damage. These can be secured with a twist tie.

Cleaning

Remove your blooms from the refrigerator the night before the show (unless they are the light-petaled varieties), so that they can warm up and begin to open into perfect exhibition form. At this point, clean the foliage and stem, making sure that all spray residue has been eliminated. Do not use houseplant foliage cleaners on your roses, as these products are considered foreign substances employed to improve the appearance of the specimen; if detected, they can lead to disqualification. The same rule holds for milk, lanolin, or any material not native to roses, so it is best to use water and a soft cloth to clean the foliage, allowing the natural sheen to come through.

Show Schedules and Rules

Obtain a rose-show schedule in advance of the show date and read it carefully. All the rules governing the show will be in the schedule provided by the host society. Being conversant with these rules will help you avoid some common pitfalls. Most shows sanctioned by the American Rose Society permit the exhibitor to show only one specimen of a specific named variety. There are also challenge classes, requiring multiples of roses, sometimes of the same variety, sometimes of different varieties.

Identifying Your Entry
The night before the show is a good time to make out entry tags for each specimen you have. If you think you may have difficulty identifying your blooms once you remove them from refrigeration, attach a label to the neck of each rose, removing it at the show site once the entry tag has been placed on the vase. Roses must be accurately named, or they will be disqualified.

By determining in advance which classes you may wish to enter, you can avoid cutting too many blooms of the same variety. The show schedule will tell you when you can begin to make entries and when the show committee ceases to accept entries. It's a crying shame to have excellent roses to exhibit, and then arrive too late to enter them in the show.

Transportation
Another thing for you to consider is how you will get your blooms to the show. Many different types of contraptions are used to bring roses in a car, each designed to incorporate the types of containers used to store the blooms in the refrigerator. Some people use large buckets to hold the cones of waxed paper accommodating each bloom. Although this is perhaps the easiest method, serious exhibitors find it chancy. For transporting blooms a long distance, custom-designed polystyrene boxes with refrigerated cold packs seem to be most common. Whatever method you devise, there should be an ample water supply for the blooms, and protection against breezes or inclement weather.

Grooming
Once at the show, the process of grooming each individual bloom begins. The first step is to place each bloom in the individual container (supplied at the show), staging the specimen so that the stem is the proper length for the bloom. Some shows will allow you to use materials such as foil, plastic wrap, or foam wedges to prop the stem upright and hold it as straight as possible. Check the show schedule carefully to determine if such propping is allowed.

At this point, you can begin the process of opening the bloom to the proper exhibition stage for the variety. Opening a bloom takes a great deal of skill, so try practicing during the growing season. Move the petals with a finger, cotton swab, or a smooth-surfaced implement, pushing them back around other petals to see how to improve the configuration of the flower. Remove unsightly guard petals by gently moving them back and forth at the petal hinge until they come free. Similarly, remove any petals on the outer perimeter that have unsightly streaks or that have dropped below the horizontal to a distracting degree. Not every bloom needs to be groomed—some open properly as a matter of course. But a little assistance for those flowers that appear lopsided or irregular doesn't hurt.

A Rewarding Endeavor

Exhibiting roses can be a very satisfying adjunct to the hobby. It takes practice, work, and—as with most competitions—an element of luck. Learning to time your roses to bloom when there is a rose show is an inexact science; it depends upon the weather, so the timing varies each year. If you calculate 50 days for the heavy-petaled varieties, and 40 to 45 days for the light- to moderately-petaled types, you should be able to obtain at least some exhibition flowers. If you become a dedicated exhibitor, keeping records—of when you cut back a variety, when it bloomed, how well it took to refrigeration, and how it held up during show conditions—will be crucial to your success.

If you are exhibiting just for the fun of it, take your chances on what is available when the show day arrives, then cut your blooms, bring them in, and hope for the best. No matter what else you achieve, you'll develop a camaraderie with the other exhibitors, learn more about roses, and have fun in the process.

Design for a

Many people consider a rose garden to be the ultimate garden, the way a diamond is the ultimate gem. Fortunately, it is an ultimate within reach—a jewel of a garden that can turn an ordinary yard into a pocket of old-fashioned grace, fragrance, and glowing color. Rose gardens are probably the only single-flower gardens that people commonly attempt. In a time and place of large estates, one might have had a primrose garden, an azalea garden, a chrysanthemum garden, and even several others. But normally a homeowner will not limit a garden to a single flower that blooms at only one time in the season, unless he or she is particularly attached to that flower. A properly designed rose garden, on the other hand, can be versatile and long-blooming, and often the only garden you need.

Good planning right from the beginning will pay off throughout the life of any garden, making it more beautiful and easier to take care of. Many factors go into that planning, chiefly the needs of the specific plants involved—how much room they will need, what kind of site, how much sun, from which direction they will be viewed, and so on. Roses are no exception. But with roses especially, the style of the garden is the first thing to consider. A plant as rich in history as the rose deserves a special setting, as if it were a painting being set in a frame.

Garden Styles

Roses have been grown for so many centuries, and by such diverse civilizations, that surely there is no one style of rose gardening. Yet if you review some of the ways they have been grown, certain practices recur over and over. The ancient Romans grew roses in their enclosed courtyards (as well as in vast fields, for their petals) and trained them to climb on walls. The castle dwellers of medieval Europe also placed them within enclosures, in small square beds with railings around them. The ancient and medieval gardens of the Middle East also had enclosed gardens filled with small plots of fragrant roses. These too were thought of as little paradises, shut away from the more violent world outside for the purposes of enjoyment, meditation, music, poetry, and romance. So closely is the idea of the rose garden associated with romantic love that in literature the rose is often identified with the lady herself—wooed, captured, and then protected within an enclosed garden.

Oddly enough, this strong emotional tradition has influenced the way we grow and display roses. We still think of a rose as the queen of flowers, something to be enclosed, protected, and displayed by herself in a formal setting, with no distractions. Common wisdom has it that roses demand to be treated in this way, that isolating them is not only the loveliest way to set them off, but is also essential to their delicate health. Most people believe that extraordinary measures must be taken to dig rose beds several feet deep, spray the plants all summer against all ills, and mulch or mound them heavily each fall. Unarguably, extra care like this will

Rose Garden

give you a more spectacular rose garden than that of your neighbor, but it is a mistake to think of all rose bushes as delicate damsels; they are actually sturdy shrubs. Recognizing this might encourage the fainthearted and give a wider range of design options to braver souls.

One good antidote to an excess of rose caution is to read Gertrude Jekyll, particularly her book *Roses*. The robust and independent Miss Jekyll was a great English gardener and garden designer who lived from 1843 to 1932; her writings are an inspiration in the multifarious ways to grow roses. She practiced all the traditional rose arts, and her ideal rose garden, as she described it, was a rather formal one. In it small beds were neatly laid out with paths, steps, balustrades, and backdrops of stately dark evergreens. But she was also expert in the informal use of roses, particularly the climbers, ramblers, and species roses, sometimes training them on arches, pillars, and pergolas, but often as not letting them have their own way. When Miss Jekyll spoke of roses "foaming" up over a wall, or "finding their way" into the upper branches of trees, or the way a rose will "rush up to clothe" an unsightly shed, she was talking about something with a will as strong as hers was, not a fragile maiden.

What Style Is for You?
In the end, of course, the style of rose garden you adopt will depend on what you like. If you like precision and old-world elegance, divide it into parterres with one variety in each, and place a marble statue in the center. If you like natural abandon, cover your house and outbuildings with old-fashioned climbers, and mix your roses with other flowers, cottage-garden style.

You will want to decide how large a garden you have space for, and how much time you will realistically have to tend it. Your design may also depend on what sorts of roses you *can* grow. In very cold or very hot climates your choice may be limited to a few varieties known to withstand local conditions. And you may find that the availability of plants is a factor. Sometimes all you can find locally are hybrid teas, floribundas, and a few climbers. If you are set on including old-fashioned roses or some of the species roses, you may have to go to some lengths to acquire them. You will undoubtedly, however, find that your trouble was well worth it.

Site and Exposure
The next practical decision to make about your garden is where to put it. You may not have much choice. If there is only one sunny, open place on your property, that is where the garden will have to go. Five to six hours of sun is crucial, and good circulation of air is almost as important. Roses do not like stagnant pockets of air that yield fungus diseases in hot summer and harsh freezes in winter. A flat place is usually preferable too, but if this is not to be found you

can terrace a hilly site and grow roses on the terraces, with steps leading up to each.

If you have a choice of exposures, the southern (the sunniest) is prime. The northern will be the least protected and most shaded. Eastern or western exposures are acceptable, depending on where the harshest wind and weather come from in your particular area.

Choose a site with good deep soil. Planting roses on ledge or hardpan is asking for trouble. Avoid also a site where tree roots will encroach.

Roses and Other Plants

Do you want just roses, or do you want to combine them with other plants? There is a wide range of possibilities here. You might want to focus on the roses alone, with the only contrast between different rose colors, flower forms, and growth habits. This is very often done, with wonderful results.

Sometimes the only additional plant in a rose garden is a hedge of dark evergreens, for roses seen against a background of this kind stand out beautifully—the bright colors appear all the more vibrant and the pale colors all the more delicate. Trees often used are yew, hemlock, arborvitae, holly, and Hinoki cypress. Arborvitae is particularly good because its roots keep to themselves. If your garden is small, or if it needs to be seen from a distance, the hedge should be pruned low. If it is large, and viewed from within, a taller hedge is possible. Sometimes the individual beds are edged in some evergreen such as boxwood or germander, clipped as low as eight inches.

You may want to use various foliage plants as accents for rose beds. White-leaved plants make attractive foils that do not detract from the bright rose colors. You can choose among the low-growing artemisias such as *Artemisia stellerana* or *A. schmidtiana nana* (silver mound); other possibilities include lamb's ears (*Stachys lanata*), annual dusty miller (*Cineraria maritima*), the perennial *Centaurea cineraria*, or lavender cotton (*Santolina chamaecyparis*). These would all be planted in front of the roses, as a border. You might also try a dark-foliaged plant, such as *Hosta sieboldiana* or, in an informal garden, a dark ground cover such as ajuga, periwinkle, violets, or wild ginger (*Asarum canadensis*). All are shallow-rooted enough so as not to interfere with the growth of the roses.

As for flowering perennials, there are many ways in which these might be combined with roses. How and whether this is done depends partly on what kind of roses you are growing. If you are using the old varieties that bloom once in June and rarely if ever repeat, you will look for complements among spring-blooming flowers and simply construct a June garden (or else plant some things to lend color later, after the roses are finished). Alternating peonies with roses would be an interesting idea, because the dark, lush mounds of peony foliage would remain after the flowers have bloomed, as a nice contrast to the stiff, open rose bushes. Bulbs and irises could also serve as preludes to roses.

In Bethlehem, Connecticut, Miss Caroline Ferriday has a magnificent collection of historical roses. It is so much a June garden that its owner can pinpoint, each year, the exact date on which it will be at its absolute best. And with all those old varieties, from the white Madame Hardy to the dark maroon Cardinal de Richelieu, the garden is as fragrant as it is colorful.

On the other hand, if you prefer a garden of modern roses with all-summer bloom, you would also demand a long succession of bloom from whatever companion perennials you choose as well. Delphiniums, liatris, lilies, phlox, various campanulas and veronicas, coral bells, the softer-colored chrysanthemums, baby's breath, pansies, heather, lavender, sea lavender (*Limonium latifolium*), sea holly (*Eryngium amethystinum*), and mountain bluet (*Centaurea montana*) would all be sufficiently delicate. But they must be planted in such a way that they do not block, crowd, or distract attention from the roses. Careful dividing and thinning must be practiced. Annuals such as bachelor's button, alyssum, and love-in-a-mist would also look well. But avoid large annuals with very strong colors, such as gloriosa daisies or giant zinnias. Old-fashioned flowers with muted colors and spiky flower shapes are ideal rose companions.

Planning for Harmonious Color

Even if you use roses alone, you will need to give some thought to balancing the colors. All rose colors look pretty together, from the palest shell pinks to the brightest red-oranges. But I would not put all the oranges together; a balanced look is best.

Rose foliage can also be a factor in design, if you are familiar with the different species. The old albas, for example, have a wonderful dark blue-green leaf, while the rugosas have a lighter, apple-green one. Contrasts such as these add further interest to the garden.

Shape of the Garden

Most traditional rose gardens are geometrical and symmetrical. They may be laid out in all straight lines and right angles, or they may have curved parterres, but there is usually a regularity to them. You do not have to stick to this pattern, but you should bear in mind the kind of plant you are trying to display. Large shrub roses, or some of the historical ones, will need a good deal of space, and are appropriately grouped in wide borders.

Climbers also need space, either on a wall or a trellis, or in a wide place where they can spill out, fountainlike. "Pillar" roses, which are just climbers that rarely exceed ten feet, can be trained upward on tall posts of wood, metal, or masonry. Often these posts are connected at the top in parallel rows to form a pergola, with roses climbing over the top. For a beautiful old-fashioned effect you can even connect the posts with garlands of roses, by hanging chains

Design for a Rose Garden

between them and training the roses to climb along the chains. Other good traditional ways to deal with climbers, ramblers, and shrub roses are pegging them at intervals along the ground, or training them laterally along a fence.

When using the smaller upright bushes, such as hybrid teas and floribundas, you want smaller, narrower beds so that you can see each bush and its blooms clearly. Bear in mind that most hybrid teas grow three to five feet tall, most floribundas about two to four, and most grandifloras about three to six. Within these groups, the individual varieties vary greatly, and heights will also depend on the growing conditions within your own garden. It is safest to plant your borders to a width of no more than two or three bushes. The very small roses—polyanthas and miniatures—can be planted in beds of their own or as foreground for the larger kinds.

Types of Rose Gardens
The following list suggests just some of the different kinds of rose gardens that you might choose from.

A Large Formal Rose Garden
This might extend over a broad expanse of lawn, with many beds set into it, as well as arbors, trellises, and even a gazebo. A long walkway might run through the center with a rose-covered pergola over it. The view through this long vista could end in a fountain, statue, or other focal point.

A Small Formal Rose Garden
Individual plots of roses with walkways between them make up the entire garden, with a small ornament in the center.

An Informal Rose Border
A wide expanse of lawn could have large rose bushes all along its sides, some of them in great mounds, or climbing up into the trees; smaller bushes would be planted in front of them.

A Miniature Rose Garden
This would consist of miniatures and polyanthas, with perhaps a few small floribundas in the center. Such a garden lends formality and charm to a small, sunny yard.

Roses Along a Walk
Roses can be beautifully arrayed in rows beside a path, either alone or with an edging of alyssum or lavender.

Island Rose Beds With Paths
Paths meander through large foliage shrubs and various roses arranged in free-form, curving beds, so that the different parts of the garden are seen separately as you stroll through it.

A Rose Collector's Garden
This garden would have many different kinds of roses. There would be both large and small beds, and structures to display the climbing varieties.

Garden Ornaments
In addition to the arbors and other frameworks on which roses are actually grown, there are many artifacts that look well in rose gardens. Fountains, statues, birdbaths, and sundials contribute to the nostalgic quality that rose gardens can have, but these ornaments should be tasteful and not overdone. You do not want a cluttered look. Nor is nostalgia everything; a contemporary rose garden with a redwood arbor and modern garden sculptures would not be inappropriate.

Paths and Edgings
Stone, brick, and grass paths look the best in rose gardens, but gravel, bark mulch, and wooden paths can also be used to good effect. A rose bed always looks better if it is defined by some kind of edging, whether a row of bricks or flagstones, or just a metal strip. One of the nicest solutions is to plant some low-growing flowering annuals or perennials along the front of the bed, where they will not interfere with the roses, but will spill over onto the paths.

A Sample Rose Garden
The design that follows suggests a garden for an average-size yard, combining many rose garden features without trying to cram too much into one concept. The garden itself is 29 feet wide and 38 feet long. Beyond these perimeters it is bordered on the two long sides by a yew hedge, pruned to no higher than eight feet, and at the far end a row of arborvitae, allowed to grow as high as they like. The garden faces south, southwest, or southeast, so that the tall hedge will not shut out any sun. (A larger garden could have a taller hedge on all of its sides.) At the front end is a low stone wall, either mortared or dry, with an open entrance in the middle; an iron gate would also be attractive here. At the far end, in the center, is an arbor with a stone or wooden bench under it, and trellises extending to either side, in front of the arborvitae.

The garden is designed to be a fairly formal and private pocket of fragrance and color. When you walk into the garden, the roses are arranged in diminishing height from the far sides to the center of the garden, accenting the central vista. The focal point is the bench under the arbor, which could house a fountain or statue instead. It should be a carefully tended garden, framed in dark green, and treated as a living work of art—one where your own imagination can paint the picture that to you is a perfect one.

Design for a Rose Garden

Below is a key to the illustration, listing the name and the page number of the color plate.

Hybrid Teas
1. Charlotte Armstrong, p. 223.
2. Christian Dior, p. 236.
3. Chrysler Imperial, p. 235.
4. Mister Lincoln, p. 235.
5. Miss All-American Beauty, p. 239.
6. Tiffany, p. 222.
7. Duet, p. 220.
8. Dainty Bess, p. 223.
9. Tropicana, p. 239.
10. Fragrant Cloud, p. 238.
11. Mojave, p. 241.
12. Eclipse, p. 242.
13. Oregold, p. 243.
14. Peace, p. 217.
15. Honor, p. 214.

Grandifloras
16. Comanche, p. 207.
17. Camelot, p. 210.
18. Queen Elizabeth, p. 208.

Floribundas
19. Fashion, p. 195.
20. Iceberg, p. 186.
21. Gruss an Achen, p. 188.
22. Betty Prior, p. 194.

Climbers
23. New Dawn, p. 97.
24. America, p. 103.
25. Golden Showers, p. 94.
26. Blaze, p. 105.

Species roses, old garden roses, and shrub roses
27. Cécile Brunner, p. 114.
28. The Fairy, p. 115.
29. Madame Hardy, p. 138.
30. Pink Grootendorst, p. 115.
31. Blanc Double de Coubert, p. 108.
32. Sarah Van Fleet, p. 113.
33. Reine des Violettes, p. 169.
34. Common Moss, p. 154.
35. *Rosa rugosa rubra,* p. 82.

The illustration shows the plan of a sample rose garden. All the varieties shown are included in this book.

The numbers in the drawing below refer to the key on the opposite page.

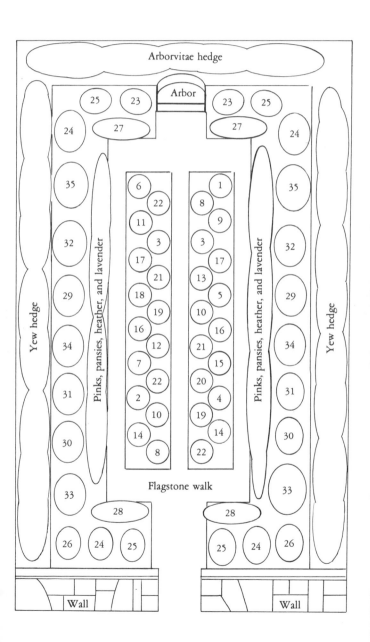

The Color Plates

Color Key

White
White
White
White
White blush

Light yellow
Medium yellow
Deep yellow
Apricot blend
Apricot blend

Yellow blend
Yellow blend
Pink blend
Striped pink and
blush

Light pink
Blush pink
Medium pink
Medium pink
Deep pink

Both mauve

Experts assign roses to a color class, based on the colors or combinations of colors present in the bloom. Within each color class there can be a wide range of shades.

The photographs below present a sampling of this magnificent palette of colors.

Color Key

Left to right

Coral-pink
Coral-salmon
Coral
Coral

All orange blend

Orange-red
Light red
Medium red
Medium red
Deep red

All red blend

Purple
Maroon

Roses are found in an astounding array of colors—not only solid tones, but stripes and blends as well. Some of these hues are found in nature, while others have been created deliberately by crossing certain varieties with others.

Visual Key

Species Roses

These are the roses found in the wild. The ancestors of all our cultivars, they have 5 to 12 petals.

After blooming, they set brightly colored hips.

Climbers

Climbing roses have long canes and can be trained up a trellis or wall. Some are forms of bush roses.

There are 7 groups, each with a different heritage.

Shrub Roses

The shrub roses comprise 6 groups. They include neat little bushes with clusters of flowers;

tall, arching plants; and large, billowy bushes that are perfect for hedges.

Old Garden Roses

The old garden roses are a very large class, made up of 10 groups of roses that have been in cultivation since before 1867. Their flowers are typically large, globular, and very full—some with as many as 200 petals. Old garden

varieties are among the most fragrant of all roses. Many of these roses bloom only once, while others—notably the teas and Chinas—are dependable repeat bloomers.

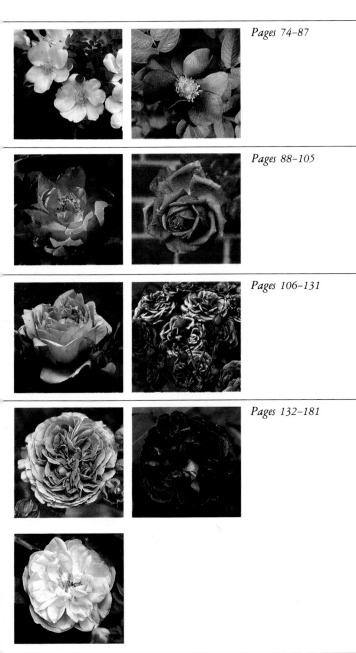

Pages 74–87

Pages 88–105

Pages 106–131

Pages 132–181

Floribundas

With their abundant large blossoms, borne singly or in clusters, the floribundas were developed by crossing repeat-blooming hybrid teas with many-flowered polyanthas, which are one group of shrub roses.

Grandifloras

A recently established class, the grandifloras are the result of a cross between hybrid teas and floribundas. These big, vigorous plants bear large, fine flowers.

Hybrid Teas

A product of crossing 2 old garden types—hybrid perpetuals and teas—hybrid teas are the most popular of all roses. Grown today almost everywhere in the world, these hardy roses bloom early in the season and continue to produce flowers until fall. The blossoms are borne singly on long stems; they have a classic spiral shape, with the petals unfurling evenly from a high center. Some are very fragrant.

Miniatures

Perfect for small gardens, terraces, and indoor pots, these petite plants are uncannily like their large relatives. They are tremendously popular today.

Pages 182–203

Pages 204–211

Pages 212–245

Pages 246–287

Species Roses

76

Rosa laevigata

Plant height: 6–20 ft.
Blossom width:
2½–3½ in.
Blooms early in season
with no repeat
p. 295

Fragrant
Not winter hardy
Disease resistant

Rosa rugosa alba

Plant height: 3–5 ft.
Blossom width:
2½–3½ in.
Blooms continuously
p. 299

Strong clove fragrance
Winter hardy
Disease free

Rosa multiflora

Plant height: 7–12 ft.
Blossom width: ½ in.
Blooms early to
midseason with no
repeat
p. 296

Honey fragrance
Winter hardy in all
but severe climates
Disease free

Rosa soulieana

Plant height: to 12 ft.
Blossom width: 1½ in.
Blooms early to
midseason with no
repeat
p. 300

Little or no fragrance
Not reliably winter
hardy
Disease free

Rosa wichuraiana

Plant height:
10–20 ft.
Blossom width:
1½–2 in.
Blooms late in season
with no repeat
p. 301

Fragrant
Hardy in all but severe
climates
Disease free

Rosa carolina

Plant height: 3–6 ft.
Blossom width: 2 in.
Blooms in midseason
p. 292

Fragrant
Winter hardy except in
severe climates
Disease free

Rosa spinosissima
Plant height: 3–4 ft.
Blossom width:
1¼–2 in.
Blooms very early in
season with no repeat
p. 300

Light, sweet fragrance
Winter hardy
Disease resistant

sa palustris
Plant height: 6–12 ft.
Blossom width: 2½ in.
Blooms late in season
with no repeat
p. 296

Very sweet fragrance
Winter hardy
Disease free

Rosa roxburghii normalis

Plant height: 7–9 ft.
Blossom width:
3½–4 in.
Blooms early in season
with no repeat
p. 298

Light, sweet fragrance
Not entirely winter
hardy
Disease free

Rosa rubrifolia

Plant height: 4–8 ft.
Blossom width: ½ in.
Blooms early in season
with no repeat
p. 298

Fragrant
Winter hardy in all
but severe climates
Disease free

Rosa pendulina   Plant height: to 4 ft.   Light, sweet fragrance
Blossom width: 2 in.   Winter hardy
Blooms in midseason or   Disease free
later
p. 297

Rosa eglanteria   Plant height: 8–10 ft.   Light, sweet fragrance
Blossom width: Winter hardy
1–1½ in.   Disease free
Blooms early in season
with no repeat
p. 293

Rosa pomifera

Plant height: 5–7 ft.
Blossom width: 2 in.
Blooms early in season
with no repeat
p. 297

Fragrant
Winter hardy
Disease free

Rosa rugosa rubra

Plant height: 3–5 ft.
Blossom width:
2½–3½ in.
Blooms continuously all
season
p. 300

Strong fragrance
Winter hardy
Disease free

Rosa rugosa Plant height: 3–5 ft. Strong fragrance
Blossom width: Winter hardy
2½–3½ in. Disease free
Blooms continuously all
season
p. 299

Rosa roxburghii Plant height: 6–7 ft. Slight fragrance
Blossom width: Not winter hardy
2–2½ in. Disease resistant
Blooms in midseason
with no repeat
p. 297

**Rosa ×
highdownensis**

Plant height: 9–12 ft.
Blossom width: 1½ in.
Blooms early in season
p. 294

Fragrant
Winter hardy
Disease resistant

Rosa foetida bicolor

Plant height: 4–5 ft.
Blossom width:
2–2½ in.
Blooms early in season
with no repeat
p. 293

Heavy fragrance
Not reliably winter
hardy
Susceptible to black spot

Rosa moyesii

Plant height: to 10 ft.
Blossom width:
1¾–2½ in.
Blooms early in season
with no repeat
p. 295

Slight fragrance
Winter hardy
Disease free

**Rosa foetida
persiana**

Plant height: 4–5 ft.
Blossom width:
2½–3 in.
Blooms early with no
repeat
p. 294

Little or no fragrance
Not winter hardy
Susceptible to black spot

Rosa hugonis

Plant height: to 6 ft.
Blossom width:
1½–2 in.
Blooms early in season
with no repeat
p. 294

Little or no fragrance
Winter hardy except in
extreme climates
Disease free

**Rosa chinensis
viridiflora**

Plant height: 3–4 ft.
Blossom width:
1½–2½ in.
Blooms all season
p. 292

Not fragrant
Not winter hardy
Disease resistant

Rosa spinosissima altaica

Plant height: to 6 ft.
Blossom width:
1½–2½ in.
Blooms very early in
season with no repeat
p. 301

Slight fragrance
Winter hardy
Disease resistant

Rosa banksiae lutea

Plant height:
20–30 ft.
Blossom width: 1 in.
Blooms very early in
season with no repeat
p. 292

Slight fragrance
Not winter hardy
Disease free

Climbers

Albéric Barbier

*Wichuraiana Climber
Plant height: to 20 ft.
Blossom width:
3–3½ in.
Blooms late in season
with no repeat
p. 304*

*Green-apple fragrance
Winter hardy
Disease free*

Elegance

*Large-flowered Climber
Plant height:
12–15 ft.
Blossom width:
4½–5½ in.
Blooms abundantly in
midseason with no
repeat
p. 310*

*Fragrant
Winter hardy
Disease resistant*

City of York *Large-flowered Climber* *Strong fragrance*
Plant height: to 20 ft. *Winter hardy*
Blossom width: *Disease free*
3–3½ in.
Blooms in midseason
for long period with no
repeat
p. 306

Paul's Lemon Pillar *Climbing Hybrid Tea* *Strong lemon*
Plant height: *fragrance*
10–12 ft. *Not winter hardy*
Blossom width: *Disease resistant*
3½–4 in.
Blooms well all season
p. 314

Leverkusen

Kordesii Climber
Plant height: 8–10 ft.
Blossom width:
3–3½ in.
Blooms well in
midseason with good
repeat
p. 312

Slight fragrance
Winter hardy
Disease free

Silver Moon

Wichuraiana Climber
Plant height: to 20 ft.
Blossom width:
3½–4½ in.
Blooms in midseason
for long period with no
repeat
p. 315

Fragrant
Winter hardy
Disease free

Mermaid

Hybrid Bracteata
Plant height: to 20 ft.
Blossom width:
4½–5½ in.
Blooms in midseason
for long period with no
repeat
p. 313

Fragrant
Not winter hardy
Disease resistant

High Noon

Climbing Hybrid Tea
Plant height: 8–10 ft.
Blossom width: 3–4 in.
Blooms well all season
p. 311

Spicy fragrance
Winter hardy
Disease resistant

Golden Showers

Large-flowered Climber
Plant height: 8–10 ft.
Blossom width:
3½–4 in.
Blooms abundantly all
season
p. 310

Fragrant
Winter hardy except in
severe winter climates
Disease resistant

Joseph's Coat

Large-flowered Climber
Plant height: 8–10 ft.
Blossom width: 3–4 in.
Blooms well in
midseason with fair
repeat
p. 312

Slight fragrance
Not dependably winter
hardy
Disease resistant

Lawrence Johnston
Large-flowered Climber
Plant height: to 20 ft.
Blossom width:
3–3½ in.
Blooms in early to
midseason with no
repeat
p. 312

Fragrant
Winter hardy
Disease resistant

Handel
Large-flowered Climber
Plant height:
12–15 ft.
Blossom width: 3½ in.
Blooms well in
midseason with good
repeat
p. 311

Slight fragrance
Winter hardy
Disease resistant

Veilchenblau

Rambler
Plant height: to 12 ft.
Blossom width: 1¼ in.
Blooms midseason to
late season with no
repeat
p. 315

Green-apple fragrance
Winter hardy
Disease resistant

Blossomtime

Large-flowered Climber
Plant height: 7–9 ft.
Blossom width:
3½–4 in.
Blooms well in
midseason with sparse
repeat
p. 306

Strong fragrance
Winter hardy
Disease resistant

American Pillar

Rambler
Plant height:
15–20 ft.
Blossom width: 2–3 in.
Blooms very
abundantly late in
season for long period
p. 305

Little or no fragrance
Winter hardy
Disease resistant

New Dawn

Wichuraiana Climber
Plant height:
12–15 ft.
Blossom width:
3–3½ in.
Blooms well in
midseason with good
repeat
p. 313

Fragrant
Winter hardy
Disease resistant

Baltimore Belle

Large-flowered Climber
Plant height: 8–10 ft.
Blossom width:
2–2½ in.
Blooms late in season
with no repeat
p. 305

Little or no fragrance
Winter hardy
Disease resistant

May Queen

Wichuraiana Climber
Plant height: 15 ft.
Blossom width:
3–3½ in.
Blooms in midseason
for long period with no
repeat
p. 313

Green-apple fragrance
Winter hardy
Disease free

Dr. J. H. Nicolas

Large-flowered Climber
Plant height: 8–10 ft.
Blossom width:
4½–5 in.
Blooms profusely in
midseason with good
repeat
p. 309

Strong fragrance
Winter hardy
Disease resistant

Clair Matin

Large-flowered Climber
Plant height:
10–12 ft.
Blossom width:
2½–3 in.
Blooms profusely in
midseason for long
period with no repeat
p. 307

Fragrant
Winter hardy
Disease resistant

Aloha

Climbing Hybrid Tea
Plant height: 8–10 ft.
Blossom width: 3½ in.
Blooms well all season
p. 304

Strong fragrance
Winter hardy
Disease resistant, but
slightly susceptible to
mildew

Viking Queen

Large-flowered Climber
Plant height:
12–15 ft.
Blossom width: 3–4 in.
Blooms in midseason
with good repeat
p. 315

Strong fragrance
Winter hardy
Disease resistant

Dorothy Perkins
Rambler
Plant height:
10–12 ft.
Blossom width: ¾ in.
Blooms late in season
with no repeat
p. 308

Little or no fragrance
Winter hardy
Disease resistant, but
susceptible to mildew

Coral Dawn
Large-flowered Climber
Plant height: 8–12 ft.
Blossom width:
4½–5 in.
Blooms well in
midseason with fair
repeat
p. 307

Fragrant
Winter hardy
Disease resistant

Excelsa

Rambler
Plant height:
12–18 ft.
Blossom width: ¾ in.
Blooms late in season
with no repeat
p. 310

Little or no fragrance
Winter hardy
Disease resistant, but
susceptible to mildew

Dr. Huey

Large-flowered Climber
Plant height:
12–18 ft.
Blossom width:
3–3½ in.
Blooms in midseason
for long period with no
repeat
p. 309

Fragrant
Winter hardy
Disease resistant

America   *Large-flowered Climber*   *Fragrant*
                     Plant height: 9–12 ft.   *Winter hardy*
                     Blossom width: *Disease resistant*
                     3½–4½ in.
                     Blooms well in
                     midseason with fair
                     repeat
                     p. 304

Don Juan   *Large-flowered Climber*   *Strong fragrance*
                     Plant height: 8–10 ft.   *Not reliably winter*
                     Blossom width: *hardy*
                     4½–5 in.   *Disease resistant*
                     Blooms profusely in
                     midseason with good
                     repeat
                     p. 307

Paul's Scarlet Climber

Large-flowered Climber
Plant height:
12–15 ft.
Blossom width:
3–3½ in.
Blooms profusely in
midseason with no
repeat
p. 314

Slight fragrance
Winter hardy
Disease resistant

Dublin Bay

Large-flowered Climber
Plant height: 8–14 ft.
Blossom width: 4½ in.
Blooms profusely in
midseason with good
repeat
p. 309

Fragrant
Winter hardy
Disease resistant

Blaze
Large-flowered Climber
Plant height: 7–9 ft.
Blossom width:
2½–3 in.
Blooms well in
midseason with
excellent repeat
p. 306

Slight fragrance
Winter hardy
Disease resistant

Dortmund
Kordesii Climber
Plant height:
10–12 ft.
Blossom width:
3–3½ in.
Blooms profusely in
midseason with good
repeat
p. 308

Fragrant
Winter hardy
Disease free

Shrub Roses

Penelope

Hybrid Musk
Plant height: 5–7 ft.
Blossom width: 3 in.
Blooms in midseason
with good repeat
p. 332

Very fragrant
Winter hardy
Disease resistant

Blanc Double de
Coubert

Hybrid Rugosa
Plant height: 4–6 ft.
Blossom width:
2½–3 in.
Blooms early to
midseason with fair
repeat
p. 320

Very fragrant
Very winter hardy
Disease free

Schneezwerg

Hybrid Rugosa
Plant height: to 5 ft.
Blossom width:
3–3½ in.
Blooms abundantly
early to midseason with
good repeat
p. 334

Slight fragrance
Winter hardy
Disease free

Sea Foam

Shrub
Plant height: 8–12 ft.
Blossom width:
2–2½ in.
Blooms in midseason
with excellent repeat
p. 334

Slight fragrance
Winter hardy
Disease resistant

Hebe's Lip
Eglanteria
Plant height: to 4 ft.
Blossom width: 3 in.
Blooms early in season
with no repeat
p. 329

Moderately strong
fragrance
Winter hardy
Disease free

Frau Dagmar
Hastrup
Hybrid Rugosa
Plant height: 2½–3 ft.
Blossom width:
3–3½ in.
Blooms early to
midseason with good
repeat
p. 325

Very strong clove
fragrance
Winter hardy
Disease free

Nevada

Shrub
Plant height: 6–8 ft.
Blossom width:
3½–4 in.
Blooms in midseason
with excellent repeat
p. 331

Little or no fragrance
Winter hardy
Disease resistant

Frühlingsmorgen

Hybrid Spinosissima
Plant height: 5–7 ft.
Blossom width:
3–3½ in.
Blooms profusely, early
in season, with no
repeat
p. 326

Slight, sweet fragrance
Winter hardy
Disease free

Ballerina

Hybrid Musk
Plant height: 3–4 ft.
Blossom width: 2 in.
Blooms in midseason
with good repeat
p. 319

Slight sweet-pea
fragrance
Winter hardy
Disease resistant

Cornelia

Hybrid Musk
Plant height: 6–8 ft.
Blossom width: 1 in.
Blooms in midseason
with good repeat
p. 323

Fragrant
Winter hardy
Disease resistant

Sarah Van Fleet

Hybrid Rugosa
Plant height: 6–8 ft.
Blossom width:
3–3½ in.
Blooms early to
midseason with good
repeat
p. 334

Very fragrant
Winter hardy
Disease resistant

Conrad Ferdinand Meyer

Hybrid Rugosa
Plant height: 9–12 ft.
Blossom width:
3½–4½ in.
Blooms early to
midseason with no
repeat
p. 322

Strong fragrance
Not reliably winter
hardy
Disease free

Cécile Brunner

Polyantha
Plant height: 2½–3 ft.
Blossom width: 1½ in.
Blooms profusely late
in season with excellent
repeat
p. 321

Slight fragrance
Not reliably winter
hardy in severe climates
Disease resistant

Sparrieshoop

Shrub
Plant height: to 5 ft.
Blossom width: 4 in.
Blooms well in
midseason with fair
repeat
p. 335

Very fragrant
Winter hardy
Disease resistant

Pink Grootendorst   *Hybrid Rugosa*   *Not fragrant*
                        Plant height: 5–6 ft.   *Winter hardy*
                        Blossom width: 1½ in.   *Disease resistant*
                        Blooms profusely in
                        midseason with good
                        repeat
                        p. 333

The Fairy   *Polyantha*   *Little or no fragrance*
                        Plant height: 1½–2 ft. *Winter hardy*
                        Blossom width: *Disease resistant*
                        1–1½ in.
                        Blooms late in season
                        with excellent repeat
                        p. 335

La Marne

Polyantha
Plant height: 1½–2 ft.
Blossom width:
1½–2 in.
Blooms in midseason or
later with good repeat
p. 329

Little or no fragrance
Winter hardy
Disease resistant

Constance Spry

Shrub
Plant height: 5–6 ft.
Blossom width:
4½–5 in.
Blooms in midseason
with no repeat
p. 322

Strong myrrh scent
Winter hardy
Disease resistant

Nymphenburg   *Hybrid Musk*   *Very fragrant*
                   Plant height: to 8 ft. *Not reliably winter*
                   Blossom width: 4 in.   *hardy in severe climates*
                   Blooms in midseason   *Disease resistant*
                   with good repeat
                   p. 331

China Doll   *Polyantha*   *Slight fragrance*
                   Plant height: to 1½ ft. *Winter hardy*
                   Blossom width: 1–2 in. *Disease resistant*
                   Blooms late in season
                   continuously until frost
                   p. 321

Robin Hood

*Hybrid Musk
Plant height: 5–7 ft.
Blossom width: ¾ in.
Blooms in midseason
with excellent repeat
p. 333*

*Moderate fragrance
Winter hardy
Disease resistant*

Marguerite Hilling

*Shrub
Plant height: 6–8 ft.
Blossom width: 4 in.
Blooms in midseason
with excellent repeat
p. 331*

*Little or no fragrance
Winter hardy
Disease resistant*

Erfurt

Hybrid Musk
Plant height: 5–6 ft.
Blossom width: 3½ in.
Blooms well all season
p. 324

Strong fragrance
Winter hardy
Disease resistant

Belinda

Hybrid Musk
Plant height: 4–6 ft.
Blossom width: ¾ in.
Blooms in midseason
with good repeat
p. 319

Light fragrance
Winter hardy
Disease resistant

Baby Faurax

Polyantha
Plant height: 8–12 in.
Blossom width: 2 in.
Blooms in midseason or later
p. 318

Little or no fragrance
Winter hardy with some protection
Disease resistant

Birdie Blye

Shrub
Plant height: 4–5 ft.
Blossom width: 3½–4 in.
Blooms in midseason with fair repeat
p. 320

Slight fragrance
Winter hardy
Disease resistant

Delicata

Hybrid Rugosa
Plant height:
3½–4½ ft.
Blossom width:
3–3½ in.
Blooms abundantly in
early to midseason with
good repeat
p. 323

Very strong clove
fragrance
Winter hardy
Disease free

Belle Poitevine

Hybrid Rugosa
Plant height: 7–9 ft.
Blossom width:
3½–4 in.
Blooms profusely in
early season with good
repeat
p. 319

Strong clove fragrance
Winter hardy
Disease resistant

Hansa

Hybrid Rugosa
Plant height: to 5 ft.
Blossom width:
3–3½ in.
Blooms early to
midseason with good
repeat
p. 327

Clove fragrance
Winter hardy
Disease resistant

Gartendirektor
Otto Linne

Shrub
Plant height:
3½–4½ ft.
Blossom width:
1½–2 in.
Blooms in midseason
with good repeat
p. 326

Little or no fragrance
Winter hardy
Disease resistant

Roseraie de l'Haÿ   *Hybrid Rugosa*   *Strong fragrance*
Plant height: 7–9 ft.   *Winter hardy*
Blossom width: *Disease free*
4–4½ in.
Blooms very early in
season with occasional
repeat
p. 333

Lavender Lassie   *Hybrid Musk*   *Strong fragrance*
Plant height: 5–7 ft.   *Winter hardy*
Blossom width: 3 in.   *Disease resistant*
Blooms in midseason
with good repeat
p. 329

124

Elmshorn   *Shrub*   *Slight fragrance*
Plant height: 5–6 ft.   *Winter hardy*
Blossom width: 1½ in.   *Disease resistant*
Blooms in midseason
with good repeat
p. 323

F. J. Grootendorst   *Hybrid Rugosa*   *Not fragrant*
Plant height: 6–8 ft.   *Winter hardy*
Blossom width: 1½ in.   *Disease resistant*
Blooms profusely in
midseason with good
repeat
p. 324

Orange Triumph

Polyantha
Plant height: 1½–2 ft.
Blossom width:
1–1½ in.
Blooms late in season
with good repeat
p. 332

Little or no fragrance
Winter hardy
Disease resistant

Happy

Polyantha
Plant height: 1½–2 ft.
Blossom width:
1½–2 in.
Blooms in midseason
with good repeat
p. 328

Little or no fragrance
Winter hardy
Disease resistant

Will Scarlet *Hybrid Musk* *Moderately strong*
Plant height: to 6 ft. *fragrance*
Blossom width: 3 in. *Winter hardy*
Blooms in midseason *Disease resistant*
with good repeat
p. 336

Margo Koster *Polyantha* *Slight fragrance*
Plant height: to 1 ft. *Winter hardy*
Blossom width: *Disease resistant*
1–1½ in.
Blooms late in season
with excellent repeat
p. 330

Fred Loads

Shrub
Plant height: 4½–5 ft.
Blossom width:
3–3½ in.
Blooms well all season
p. 325

Little or no fragrance
Winter hardy
Disease resistant

Alchymist

Shrub
Plant height: 8–12 ft.
Blossom width:
3½–4 in.
Blooms early to
midseason with no
repeat
p. 318

Fragrant
Winter hardy
Disease resistant

Buff Beauty

Hybrid Musk
Plant height: to 6 ft.
Blossom width: 3 in.
Blooms in midseason
with good repeat
p. 321

Fragrant
Winter hardy
Disease resistant

Westerland

Shrub
Plant height: 5–6 ft.
Blossom width: 3 in.
Blooms in midseason
with no repeat
p. 336

Strong fragrance
Winter hardy
Disease resistant

Agnes

Hybrid Rugosa
Plant height: to 5 ft.
Blossom width:
3–3½ in.
Blooms early to
midseason
p. 318

Strong fragrance
Winter hardy
Disease resistant

Goldbusch

Shrub
Plant height: to 5 ft.
Blossom width:
2½–3 in.
Blooms midseason or
later with good repeat
p. 327

Fragrant
Winter hardy
Disease resistant

Maigold

Shrub
Plant height: to 5 ft.
Blossom width: 4 in.
Blooms early to
midseason with no
repeat
p. 330

Strong fragrance
Winter hardy
Disease resistant

Golden Wings

Shrub
Plant height:
4½–5½ ft.
Blossom width: 4–5 in.
Blooms profusely all
season
p. 327

Slight fragrance
Winter hardy except in
very severe climates
Disease resistant

Harison's Yellow   *Shrub*   *Light, sweet fragrance*
                        Plant height: 5–7 ft.   *Winter hardy*
                        Blossom width: *Disease resistant*
                        2–2½ in.
                        Blooms very early in
                        season with no repeat
                        p. 328

Frühlingsgold   *Hybrid Spinosissima*   *Fragrant*
                        Plant height: 5–7 ft.   *Winter hardy*
                        Blossom width: *Disease free*
                        3–3½ in.
                        Blooms early in season
                        with no repeat
                        p. 325

Old Garden

Roses

Rosette Delizy

Tea
Plant height: 3½–4 ft.
Blossom width:
3½–4 in.
Blooms in midseason
with good repeat
p. 375

Spicy fragrance
Not winter hardy
Disease resistant

Lady Hillingdon

Tea
Plant height: 2½–3 ft.
Blossom width: 3½ in.
Blooms early in season
with good repeat
p. 361

Fragrant
Not winter hardy
Disease resistant

Gloire de Dijon

Tea
Plant height:
10–12 ft.
Blossom width: 4 in.
Blooms early in season
with good repeat
p. 355

Fragrant
Not winter hardy
Disease resistant

Celine Forestier

Noisette
Plant height:
10–15 ft.
Blossom width:
2–2½ in.
Blooms in midseason
with excellent repeat
p. 347

Very fragrant
Not winter hardy
Disease resistant

Madame Alfred Carrière

Noisette
Plant height:
10–15 ft.
Blossom width:
2½–3 in.
Blooms in midseason
with excellent repeat
p. 363

Fragrant
Moderately winter
hardy
Disease resistant

Madame Legras de St. Germain

Alba
Plant height: 6–7 ft.
Blossom width: 3½ in.
Blooms early in season
with no repeat
p. 365

Very sweet fragrance
Winter hardy
Disease free

Frau Karl Druschki *Hybrid Perpetual*
Plant height: 5–7 ft.
Blossom width:
4–4½ in.
Blooms in midseason
with good repeat in
fall
p. 354

Little or no fragrance
Winter hardy
Disease resistant

Maxima *Alba*
Plant height: 6–8 ft.
Blossom width:
2½–3 in.
Blooms profusely, early
to midseason with no
repeat
p. 369

Very fragrant
Winter hardy
Disease free

Madame Hardy
Damask
Plant height: 5–5½ ft.
Blossom width:
3–3½ in.
Blooms in midseason
with no repeat
p. 364

Fragrant
Winter hardy
Disease free

Sombreuil
Tea
Plant height:
12–15 ft.
Blossom width:
3½–4 in.
Blooms early to
midseason with good
repeat
p. 376

Fragrant
Moderately winter
hardy
Disease resistant

Boule de Neige   *Bourbon*   *Fragrant*
                     Plant height: 4–5 ft.   *Winter hardy*
                     Blossom width: *Disease resistant*
                     2½–3½ in.
                     Blooms in midseason
                     with good repeat
                     p. 346

Madame Plantier *Alba*   *Very fragrant*
                     Plant height: 5–6 ft.   *Winter hardy*
                     Blossom width: *Disease free*
                     2½–3 in.
                     Blooms profusely in
                     midseason with no
                     repeat
                     p. 367

Mabel Morrison
Hybrid Perpetual
Plant height: 4–4½ ft.
Blossom width:
3½–4 in.
Blooms well in
midseason with good
repeat in fall
p. 363

Fragrant
Winter hardy
Disease resistant

Champneys' Pink Cluster
Noisette
Plant height: 8–12 ft.
Blossom width: 2 in.
Blooms in midseason
with excellent repeat
p. 348

Very fragrant
Not winter hardy
Disease resistant

Félicité et Perpétue   *Hybrid Sempervirens*   *Fragrant*
                           Plant height: to 20 ft.   *Not winter hardy*
                           Blossom width: 1½ in.   *Disease free*
                           Blooms long, late in
                           season, with no repeat
                           p. 353

Blush Noisette   *Noisette*   *Very fragrant*
                           Plant height: 8–12 ft.   *Not winter hardy*
                           Blossom width: 2 in.   *Disease resistant*
                           Blooms in midseason
                           with excellent repeat
                           p. 345

Mary Washington
Noisette
Plant height: 8–12 ft.
Blossom width: 2½ in.
Blooms in midseason
with good repeat
p. 369

Fragrant
Winter hardy with
protection
Disease resistant

Stanwell Perpetual
Hybrid Spinosissima
Plant height: to 5 ft.
Blossom width: 3½ in.
Blooms early in season
with good repeat
p. 376

Fragrant
Winter hardy
Disease resistant

Souvenir de la Malmaison

Bourbon
Plant height: to 2 ft.
Blossom width:
4½–5 in.
Blooms sparsely in midseason or later with sparse fall repeat
p. 376

Strong, spicy fragrance
Winter hardy with some protection
Disease resistant

Alfred de Dalmas

Moss
Plant height: 2½–3 ft.
Blossom width:
2½–3 in.
Blooms in midseason with fair repeat
p. 342

Fragrant
Winter hardy
Disease resistant

Duchesse de Montebello

Gallica
Plant height: to 5 ft.
Blossom width:
2½–3 in.
Blooms midseason or later with no repeat
p. 352

Fragrant
Winter hardy
Disease resistant

Général Kléber

Moss
Plant height: to 5 ft.
Blossom width:
2½–3 in.
Blooms midseason or later with no repeat
p. 354

Very fragrant
Winter hardy
Disease resistant

Maiden's Blush
Alba
Plant height: 5–6 ft.
Blossom width:
2½–3 in.
Blooms very profusely,
early to midseason,
with no repeat
p. 367

Very fragrant
Winter hardy
Disease free

York and Lancaster
Damask
Plant height: 3–4 ft.
Blossom width:
2½–3 in.
Blooms in midseason
with no repeat
p. 380

Fragrant
Winter hardy
Disease free

Chloris

Alba
Plant height: 5–6 ft.
Blossom width: 3½ in.
Blooms early in season
with no repeat
p. 349

Intense, sweet fragrance
Winter hardy
Disease free

Gloire de Guilan

Damask
Plant height: 3–5 ft.
Blossom width: 3 in.
Blooms profusely, early
to midseason, with no
repeat
p. 356

Intensely fragrant
Winter hardy
Disease free

Marchioness of Londonderry

Hybrid Perpetual
Plant height: 5–7 ft.
Blossom width:
4½–5 in.
Blooms profusely in
midseason with
occasional repeat in fall
p. 368

Very fragrant
Winter hardy
Disease resistant

Gloire des Mousseuses

Moss
Plant height: 2½–3 ft.
Blossom width: 3 in.
Blooms in midseason
with no repeat
p. 356

Very fragrant
Winter hardy
Disease resistant

Belle Amour

Alba
Plant height: 5–6 ft.
Blossom width: 3½ in.
Blooms profusely, early
in season
p. 344

Intense, spicy scent
mixed with a faint
bitterness
Winter hardy
Disease free

Ispahan

Damask
Plant height: 3–4 ft.
Blossom width:
2½–3 in.
Blooms for long period
in midseason with no
repeat
p. 359

Very fragrant
Winter hardy
Disease free

Belle Isis

Gallica
Plant height: 2½–3 ft.
Blossom width:
2½–3 in.
Blooms in midseason
with no repeat
p. 345

Fragrant
Winter hardy
Disease resistant

Rose des Peintres

Centifolia
Plant height: 5–7 ft.
Blossom width:
3–3½ in.
Blooms in midseason
with no repeat
p. 374

Fragrant
Winter hardy
Disease resistant

Duchesse de Brabant

Tea
Plant height: 3–5 ft.
Blossom width: 4–5 in.
Blooms early to midseason with excellent repeat
p. 352

Very fragrant
Not reliably winter hardy
Disease resistant

Madame Pierre Oger

Bourbon
Plant height: 4½–5½ ft.
Blossom width: 3–3½ in.
Blooms abundantly in midseason with good repeat in fall
p. 366

Very fragrant
Winter hardy
Disease resistant

Georg Arends

Hybrid Perpetual
Plant height: 4–5 ft.
Blossom width:
4–4½ in.
Blooms in midseason
with good repeat in
fall
p. 355

Very fragrant
Winter hardy
Disease resistant

Louis Gimard

Moss
Plant height: 4–5 ft.
Blossom width:
3–3½ in.
Blooms in midseason
with no repeat
p. 362

Very fragrant
Winter hardy
Disease resistant

Gloire de France

Gallica
Plant height: 2–2½ ft.
Blossom width:
2½–3 in.
Blooms in midseason
with no repeat
p. 356

Fragrant
Winter hardy
Disease resistant

Salet

Moss
Plant height: 4–5 ft.
Blossom width:
2½–3 in.
Blooms in midseason
with fair repeat in fall
p. 375

Fragrant
Winter hardy
Disease resistant

Madame Louis Lévêque

Moss
Plant height: 4–5 ft.
Blossom width: 3–3½ in.
Blooms in midseason; some repeat in fall
p. 366

Very fragrant
Winter hardy
Disease resistant

Celestial

Alba
Plant height: 4½–5 ft.
Blossom width: 3½ in.
Blooms early in season with no repeat
p. 347

Very sweet fragrance
Winter hardy
Disease free

Celsiana

Damask
Plant height: 3½–4 ft.
Blossom width:
3½–4 in.
Blooms for long period
in midseason with no
repeat
p. 348

Intensely fragrant
Winter hardy
Disease free

Common Moss

Moss
Plant height: 5–7 ft.
Blossom width: 3 in.
Blooms in midseason
with no repeat
p. 350

Very fragrant
Winter hardy
Disease resistant

Baroness Rothschild

Hybrid Perpetual
Plant height: 4–6 ft.
Blossom width:
5½–6 in.
Blooms profusely in
midseason with fair
repeat in fall
p. 344

Very fragrant
Winter hardy
Disease resistant

Old Blush

China
Plant height: 3–4 ft.
Blossom width: 3 in.
Blooms well all season
p. 370

Little or no fragrance
Not winter hardy
Disease resistant

Fantin-Latour

Centifolia
Plant height: 5–6 ft.
Blossom width:
3–3½ in.
Blooms profusely in
midseason with no
repeat
p. 353

Very fragrant
Winter hardy
Disease resistant

Petite de Hollande

Centifolia
Plant height: 3½–4 ft.
Blossom width:
2–2½ in.
Blooms in midseason
for a long period with
no repeat
p. 371

Very fragrant
Winter hardy
Disease resistant

Comte de Chambord	*Portland* *Plant height: 3½–4 ft.* *Blossom width: 3 in.* *Blooms in midseason* *with good repeat* *p. 351*	*Very fragrant* *Winter hardy* *Disease resistant*

La Ville de Bruxelles	*Damask* *Plant height: to 5 ft.* *Blossom width:* *3½–4 in.* *Blooms abundantly in* *midseason with no* *repeat* *p. 361*	*Very fragrant* *Winter hardy* *Disease free*

158

Louise Odier
Bourbon
Plant height:
4½–5½ ft.
Blossom width: 3½ in.
Blooms abundantly in
midseason with good
repeat
p. 363

Very fragrant
Winter hardy
Disease resistant

Archduke Charles
China
Plant height: 2–3 ft.
Blossom width:
2½–3 in.
Blooms well all season
p. 342

Fruity fragrance
Not winter hardy
Disease resistant

Empress Josephine   *Gallica*   *Slight fragrance*
Plant height: 3–4 ft.   *Winter hardy*
Blossom width: *Disease resistant*
3–3½ in.
Blooms in midseason
with no repeat
p. 352

Maman Cochet   *Tea*   *Fragrant*
Plant height: 3–3½ ft.   *Not winter hardy*
Blossom width: *Disease resistant*
3½–4 in.
Blooms in midseason
with excellent repeat
p. 368

Königin von Dänemark

Alba
Plant height: to 6 ft.
Blossom width: 3½ in.
Blooms early in season
with no repeat
p. 360

Intense, sweet fragrance
Winter hardy
Disease free

Hermosa

China
Plant height: 3–4 ft.
Blossom width: 3 in.
Blooms well all season
p. 358

Fragrant
Not winter hardy
Disease resistant

La Reine Victoria
*Bourbon
Plant height:
4½–5½ ft.
Blossom width:
3–3½ in.
Blooms abundantly in
midseason with good
repeat in fall
p. 360*

*Very fragrant
Winter hardy
Disease resistant*

Maréchal Davoust
*Moss
Plant height: to 5 ft.
Blossom width: 3 in.
Blooms in midseason
with no repeat
p. 368*

*Very fragrant
Winter hardy
Disease resistant*

Madame Lauriol de Barny

Bourbon
Plant height: to 6 ft.
Blossom width:
3½–4 in.
Blooms in midseason
with occasional repeat
p. 365

Fruity fragrance
Winter hardy
Disease resistant

La Noblesse

Centifolia
Plant height: to 5 ft.
Blossom width:
3–3½ in.
Blooms profusely,
midseason or later,
with no repeat
p. 360

Extremely fragrant
Winter hardy
Disease free

Little Gem

Moss
Plant height: to 4 ft.
Blossom width: 2 in.
Blooms in midseason
with no repeat
p. 362

Fragrant
Winter hardy
Disease resistant

Crested Moss

Moss
Plant height: 5–7 ft.
Blossom width:
3–3½ in.
Blooms in midseason
with no repeat
p. 351

Very fragrant
Winter hardy
Disease resistant

Madame de la Roche-Lambert

Moss
Plant height: 4–5 ft.
Blossom width: 3 in.
Blooms in midseason
with no repeat
p. 364

Very fragrant
Winter hardy
Disease resistant

Madame Isaac Pereire

Bourbon
Plant height: 5–6 ft.
Blossom width:
3½–4 in.
Blooms profusely in
midseason with fair
repeat
p. 365

Intense fragrance
Winter hardy
Disease resistant

Baronne Prévost   *Hybrid Perpetual*   *Fragrant*
Plant height: 4–6 ft.   *Winter hardy*
Blossom width: *Disease resistant*
3½–4 in.
Blooms well in
midseason with good
repeat in fall
p. 343

Ulrich Brunner Fils   *Hybrid Perpetual*   *Very fragrant*
Plant height: 5–7 ft.   *Winter hardy*
Blossom width: *Disease resistant*
3½–4 in.
Blooms in midseason
with occasional repeat
in fall
p. 379

Rosa gallica officinalis

Gallica
Plant height: 3–3½ ft.
Blossom width:
3–3½ in.
Blooms in midseason
with no repeat
p. 373

Fragrant
Winter hardy
Disease resistant

Zéphirine Drouhin

Bourbon
Plant height: 8–12 ft.
Blossom width:
3½–4 in.
Blooms well all season
p. 381

Very fragrant
Winter hardy
Disease resistant

Complicata

Gallica
Plant height: to 5 ft.
Blossom width:
4–4½ in.
Blooms in midseason
with no repeat
p. 350

Fragrant
Winter hardy
Disease resistant

American Beauty

Hybrid Perpetual
Plant height: 5–6 ft.
Blossom width: 5–6 in.
Blooms in midseason
with fair repeat in fall
p. 342

Very fragrant
Winter hardy
Disease resistant

Paul Neyron
Hybrid Perpetual
Plant height: 5–6 ft.
Blossom width:
4½–5½ in.
Blooms in midseason
with fair repeat in fall
p. 370

Fragrant
Winter hardy
Disease resistant

Tour de Malakoff
Centifolia
Plant height: 6–7 ft.
Blossom width:
3–3½ in.
Blooms in midseason
with no repeat
p. 378

Very fragrant
Winter hardy
Disease free

Reine des Violettes   *Hybrid Perpetual*   *Very fragrant*
Plant height: 5–6 ft.   *Winter hardy*
Blossom width: 3 in.   *Disease resistant*
Blooms profusely in
midseason with
occasional sparse repeat
p. 371

Cardinal de   *Gallica*   *Fragrant*
Richelieu   *Plant height: 2½–3 ft.*   *Winter hardy*
Blossom width: *Disease resistant*
2½–3 in.
Blooms in midseason
with no repeat
p. 347

The Bishop

Centifolia
Plant height: 4–5 ft.
Blossom width:
2½–3 in.
Blooms early to
midseason with no
repeat
p. 377

Fragrant
Winter hardy
Disease resistant

Rose du Roi

Portland
Plant height: 3–4 ft.
Blossom width: 2½ in.
Blooms in midseason
with good repeat
p. 374

Very fragrant
Winter hardy
Disease resistant

Belle de Crècy

Gallica
Plant height:
3½–4½ ft.
Blossom width:
2½–3 in.
Blooms for long period
in midseason with no
repeat
p. 344

Very fragrant
Winter hardy
Disease resistant

Tuscany Superb

Gallica
Plant height: 3–4 ft.
Blossom width:
3½–4 in.
Blooms in midseason
with no repeat
p. 379

Very fragrant
Winter hardy
Disease resistant

Tuscany
Gallica
Plant height: 3–4 ft.
Blossom width:
3–3½ in.
Blooms in midseason
with no repeat
p. 378

Very fragrant
Winter hardy
Disease resistant

Roger Lambelin
Hybrid Perpetual
Plant height: 2–2½ ft.
Blossom width:
2½–3 in.
Blooms in midseason
with fair repeat in fall
p. 372

Fragrant
Winter hardy
Disease resistant

Nuits de Young
Moss
Plant height: to 5 ft.
Blossom width: 2½ in.
Blooms in midseason
with no repeat
p. 370

Very fragrant
Winter hardy
Disease resistant

Baron Girod de l'Ain
Hybrid Perpetual
Plant height: 4–5 ft.
Blossom width: 4 in.
Blooms well in
midseason with fair
repeat in fall
p. 343

Fragrant
Winter hardy
Disease resistant

Gloire des Rosomanes

China
Plant height:
3½–4½ ft.
Blossom width: 3 in.
Blooms well all season
p. 357

Little or no fragrance
Moderately hardy
Disease resistant

Rose de Rescht

Damask
Plant height:
2½–3½ ft.
Blossom width:
2–2½ in.
Blooms in midseason
with good repeat
p. 374

Very fragrant
Winter hardy
Disease resistant

Gruss an Teplitz

Bourbon
Plant height: 5–6 ft.
Blossom width:
3–3½ in.
Blooms profusely in
midseason with good
repeat
p. 357

Strong, spicy fragrance
Winter hardy
Disease resistant

Henry Nevard

Hybrid Perpetual
Plant height: 4–5 ft.
Blossom width:
4–4½ in.
Blooms well in
midseason with good
repeat in fall
p. 358

Very fragrant
Winter hardy
Disease resistant

Henri Martin

Moss
Plant height: to 5 ft.
Blossom width: 2½ in.
Blooms midseason or
later with no repeat
p. 358

Fragrant
Winter hardy
Disease resistant

John Hopper

Hybrid Perpetual
Plant height: 5–7 ft.
Blossom width: 4 in.
Blooms well in
midseason with
occasional repeat in fall
p. 359

Very fragrant
Winter hardy
Disease resistant

William Lobb   *Moss*   *Very fragrant*
                   Plant height: 4–5 ft.   *Winter hardy*
                   Blossom width: 3 in.   *Disease resistant*
                   Blooms in midseason
                   with no repeat
                   p. 380

Charles de Mills   *Gallica*   *Fragrant*
                       Plant height: 4½–5 ft.   *Winter hardy*
                       Blossom width: *Disease resistant*
                       3–3½ in.
                       Blooms in midseason
                       with no repeat
                       p. 349

Ferdinand Pichard   *Hybrid Perpetual*   *Fragrant*
Plant height: 4–5 ft.   *Winter hardy*
Blossom width: *Disease resistant*
3–3½ in.
Blooms well in
midseason with fair
repeat
p. 354

Rosa Mundi   *Gallica*   *Fragrant*
Plant height: 3–3½ ft.   *Winter hardy*
Blossom width: *Disease resistant*
3–3½ in.
Blooms in midseason
with no repeat
p. 373

Commandant Beaurepaire

*Bourbon
Plant height: 4–5 ft.
Blossom width:
3–3½ in.
Blooms in midseason
with sparse repeat
bloom
p. 349*

*Fragrant
Winter hardy
Disease resistant*

Camaieux

*Gallica
Plant height: 3–3½ ft.
Blossom width:
3–3½ in.
Blooms in midseason
with no repeat
p. 346*

*Fragrant
Winter hardy
Disease resistant*

Striped Moss

Moss
Plant height: 5–6 ft.
Blossom width:
1½–2 in.
Blooms in midseason
with no repeat
p. 377

Fragrant
Winter hardy
Disease resistant

Rosa centifolia
variegata

Centifolia
Plant height: 5–7 ft.
Blossom width:
3–3½ in.
Blooms profusely in
midseason with no
repeat
p. 372

Fragrant
Winter hardy
Disease resistant

Variegata di Bologna	*Bourbon*	*Fragrant*
	Plant height: 5–7 ft.	*Winter hardy*
	Blossom width:	*Disease resistant*
	3½–4 in.	
	Blooms in midseason	
	with no repeat	
	p. 379	

Leda	*Damask*	*Fragrant*
	Plant height: 2½–3 ft.	*Winter hardy*
	Blossom width:	*Disease free*
	2½–3 in.	
	Blooms in midseason	
	with no repeat	
	p. 362	

Floribundas

Goldilocks

Plant height: 3½–4 ft.
Blossom width: 3½ in.
Blooms abundantly in
midseason with good
repeat
p. 391

Little or no fragrance
Not winter hardy
without protection
Disease resistant

Apricot Nectar

Plant height: 4–5 ft.
Blossom width:
4–4½ in.
Blooms abundantly in
midseason with good
repeat
p. 384

Fruity fragrance
Very winter hardy
Disease resistant

Sun Flare

Plant height: 2–2½ ft.
Blossom width: 3 in.
Blooms well all season
p. 398

Slight, licorice
fragrance
Winter hardy
Disease resistant

Ivory Fashion

Plant height: 3½–4 ft.
Blossom width: 3½ in.
Blooms abundantly in
midseason with good
repeat
p. 393

Fragrant
Winter hardy
Disease resistant

French Lace

Plant height: 3–3½ ft.
Blossom width:
3½–4 in.
Blooms well in
midseason with good
repeat
p. 390

Moderate fragrance
Winter hardy
Disease resistant

Iceberg

Plant height: to 4 ft.
Blossom width: 3 in.
Blooms early to
midseason with
continuous repeat
p. 392

Fragrant
Winter hardy
Disease resistant, but
susceptible to black spot

Saratoga

Plant height: 4–4½ ft.
Blossom width: 4 in.
Blooms profusely in
midseason with fair
repeat
p. 397

Strong fragrance
Winter hardy
Disease resistant

Summer Snow

Plant height: 2½–3 ft.
Blossom width:
2½–3 in.
Blooms well all season
p. 398

Little or no fragrance
Not winter hardy
Disease resistant

Evening Star

Plant height: 3–3½ ft.
Blossom width:
4–4½ in.
Blooms in midseason
with fair repeat
p. 388

Slight fragrance
Not winter hardy
Disease resistant

Gruss an Aachen

Plant height: 2–2½ ft.
Blossom width:
3–3½ in.
Blooms early to
midseason with good
repeat
p. 391

Fragrant
Winter hardy
Disease resistant

Lavender Pinocchio   *Plant height: 2½–3 ft.*   *Fragrant*
Blossom width: *Winter hardy*
3–3½ in.   *Disease resistant*
Blooms well in
midseason with fair
repeat
p. 393

Poulsen's Pearl   *Plant height: 2½–3 ft.*   *Fragrant*
Blossom width: *Winter hardy*
2½–3 in.   *Disease resistant*
Blooms in midseason
with good repeat
p. 395

Escapade   *Plant height: 2½–3 ft.*   *Fragrant*
Blossom width: 3 in.   *Winter hardy*
Blooms very well in   *Disease resistant*
midseason with
excellent repeat
p. 387

Rose Parade   *Plant height: 2½–3 ft.*   *Fragrant*
Blossom width: 3½ in.   *Winter hardy*
Blooms abundantly in   *Disease resistant*
midseason with good
repeat
p. 396

Gene Boerner   *Plant height: 4–5 ft.*   *Little or no fragrance*
                     Blossom width: *Winter hardy*
                     3–3½ in.   *Disease resistant*
                     Blooms very well in
                     midseason with
                     excellent repeat
                     p. 390

Angel Face   *Plant height: 2½–3 ft.*   *Strong fragrance*
                     Blossom width: *Winter hardy*
                     3½–4 in.   *Disease resistant*
                     Blooms in midseason
                     with good repeat
                     p. 384

Simplicity

Plant height:
2½–3½ ft.
Blossom width: 3–4 in.
Blooms abundantly all
season
p. 398

Little or no fragrance
Winter hardy
Disease resistant

Little Darling

Plant height:
2½–3½ ft.
Blossom width:
2½–3 in.
Blooms abundantly,
early to midseason,
with continuous repeat
p. 394

Spicy fragrance
Winter hardy
Disease resistant

Vogue
Plant height: 2½–3 ft.
Blossom width:
3½–4½ in.
Blooms well all season
p. 399

Slight fragrance
Winter hardy
Disease resistant

Sea Pearl
Plant height: 3–3½ ft.
Blossom width: 4½ in.
Blooms profusely, early
to midseason, with good
repeat
p. 397

Moderately strong
fragrance
Winter hardy with
protection
Disease resistant

Betty Prior

Plant height: 5–7 ft.
Blossom width:
3–3½ in.
Blooms abundantly in
midseason with
excellent repeat
p. 385

Fragrant
Winter hardy
Disease resistant

First Edition

Plant height: 3½–4 ft.
Blossom width:
2½–3 in.
Blooms well in
midseason with fair
repeat
p. 389

Slight fragrance
Not winter hardy
without protection
Disease resistant

Fashion

Plant height:
3½–4½ ft.
Blossom width:
3–3½ in.
Blooms in midseason
with excellent repeat
p. 389

Slight fragrance
Winter hardy
Disease resistant

Circus

Plant height: 2½–3 ft.
Blossom width: 3 in.
Blooms in midseason
with good repeat
p. 386

Spicy fragrance
Winter hardy
Disease resistant, but
needs protection from
black spot

Masquerade

Plant height: 2½–3 ft.
Blossom width: 2½ in.
Blooms profusely in
midseason with good
repeat
p. 394

Slight fragrance
Winter hardy
Disease resistant

Charisma

Plant height: 3–3½ ft.
Blossom width:
2½–3 in.
Blooms well in
midseason with good
repeat
p. 386

Slight fragrance
Winter hardy
Disease resistant

Redgold   *Plant height: 3–3½ ft.*   *Slightly fruity*
               Blossom width: *fragrance*
               2½–3 in.   *Winter hardy*
               Blooms well in   *Disease resistant*
               midseason with fair
               repeat
               p. 395

Orangeade   *Plant height: 2½–3 ft.*   *Slight fragrance*
                 Blossom width: *Not winter hardy*
                 3–3½ in.   *without protection*
                 Blooms abundantly in   *Disease resistant, but*
                 midseason with good   *needs protection from*
                 repeat   *mildew*
                 p. 395

Sarabande

Plant height:
to 2½ ft.
Blossom width: 2½ in.
Blooms profusely in
midseason with
excellent repeat
p. 396

Slight, spicy fragrance
Winter hardy with
some protection
Disease resistant

Trumpeter

Plant height:
3½–4½ ft.
Blossom width: 3½ in.
Blooms extremely well
in midseason with
excellent repeat
p. 399

Slight fragrance
Winter hardy
Disease resistant

Impatient   Plant height: 3–3½ ft.   Slight fragrance
                             Blossom width: 3 in.   Winter hardy
                             Blooms well in   Disease resistant
                             midseason with fair
                             repeat
                             p. 392

Cathedral   Plant height: 3½–4 ft.   Slight fragrance
                             Blossom width: 4–5 in.   Winter hardy
                             Blooms well in   Disease resistant
                             midseason with good
                             repeat
                             p. 385

Frensham

Plant height: 2½–3 ft.
Blossom width: 3 in.
Blooms extremely well
in midseason with good
repeat
p. 390

Slight fragrance
Winter hardy
Disease resistant

Eye Paint

Plant height: 3–4 ft.
Blossom width: 2½ in.
Blooms in midseason
with good repeat
p. 388

Slight fragrance
Winter hardy
Disease resistant, but
needs protection from
black spot

Europeana Plant height: 2½–3 ft. *Very slight fragrance*
Blossom width: 3 in. *Winter hardy*
Blooms abundantly in *Disease resistant*
midseason with good
repeat
p. 387

Showbiz *Plant height: 2½–3 ft.* *Slight fragrance*
Blossom width: *Winter hardy*
2½–3 in. *Disease resistant*
Blooms well all season
p. 397

Dusky Maiden

Plant height: 2–3 ft.
Blossom width:
3–3½ in.
Blooms abundantly in
midseason with
excellent repeat
p. 386

Fragrant
Winter hardy
Disease resistant

Intrigue

Plant height: to 3 ft.
Blossom width: 3 in.
Blooms well in
midseason with good
repeat
p. 392

Strong fragrance
Not winter hardy
without protection
Disease resistant

Eutin

Plant height: 2½–3 ft.
Blossom width:
1–1½ in.
Blooms in midseason or
later, until first frost
p. 388

Very slight fragrance
Winter hardy
Disease resistant

Apache Tears

Plant height:
2½–3½ ft.
Blossom width: 3½ in.
Good midseason bloom
with excellent repeat
p. 384

Slight fragrance
Winter hardy
Disease resistant

Grandifloras

Gold Medal

Plant height:
4½–5½ ft.
Blossom width: 3½ in.
Blooms well all season
p. 403

Slight, fruity fragrance
Not winter hardy;
needs protection
Disease resistant but
needs protection from
black spot

Prominent

Plant height:
3½–4½ ft.
Blossom width: 3½ in.
Blooms extremely well
all season
p. 404

Slight fragrance
Winter hardy
Disease resistant

Sundowner

Plant height:
4½–5½ ft.
Blossom width: 4 in.
Blooms well all season
p. 406

Very fragrant
Winter hardy
Disease resistant, but
susceptible to mildew in
cool, wet climates

Comanche

Plant height: 4½–5 ft.
Blossom width:
3–3½ in.
Blooms abundantly all
season
p. 402

Slight fragrance
Winter hardy
Disease resistant

Shreveport

Plant height: 4½–5 ft.
Blossom width:
3½–4 in.
Blooms fairly well all
season
p. 405

Slight fragrance
Winter hardy
Disease resistant

Queen Elizabeth

Plant height: 5–7 ft.
Blossom width:
3½–4 in.
Abundant midseason
bloom; excellent repeat
bloom
p. 405

Fragrant
Winter hardy
Disease resistant

Montezuma   Plant height: 4½–5 ft.   Slight fragrance
                 Blossom width: Winter hardy
                 3½–4 in.   Disease resistant
                 Blooms well all season
                 p. 403

Aquarius   Plant height: 4½–5 ft.   Slight fragrance
                 Blossom width: Winter hardy
                 3½–4½ in.   Disease resistant
                 Blooms well all season
                 p. 402

Pink Parfait

Plant height:
3½–4½ ft.
Blossom width:
3½–4 in.
Blooms abundantly at
midseason with good
repeat
p. 404

Slight fragrance
Winter hardy
Disease resistant

Camelot

Plant height: 5–5½ ft.
Blossom width:
3½–4 in.
Good all-season bloom
p. 402

Spicy fragrance
Winter hardy
Disease resistant

Love   *Plant height: 3–3½ ft.*   *Very slight fragrance*
             Blossom width: 3½ in.   *Winter hardy*
             Blooms well all season   *Disease resistant*
             p. 403

White Lightnin'   *Plant height: 4½–5 ft.*   *Very fragrant*
                        Blossom width: *Winter hardy*
                        3½–4 in.   *Disease resistant*
                        Blooms well all season
                        p. 406

Hybrid Teas

Kaiserin Auguste Viktoria

Plant height: 5–7 ft.
Blossom width:
4–4½ in.
Blooms profusely, early to midseason, with fair repeat
p. 421

Strong fragrance
Winter hardy
Disease resistant

Honor

Plant height: 5–5½ ft.
Blossom width: 4–5 in.
Blooms well all season
p. 420

Slight fragrance
Not winter hardy without protection
Disease resistant

White Masterpiece *Plant height: to 3 ft.* *Slight fragrance*
Blossom width: *Not winter hardy*
5–5½ in. *without protection*
Blooms sparsely all *Disease resistant*
season
p. 435

Pascali *Plant height: 3½–4 ft.* *Very slight fragrance*
Blossom width: *Winter hardy*
4–4½ in. *Disease resistant*
Blooms extremely well
all season
p. 429

Pristine

Plant height: 4–4½ ft.
Blossom width:
4½–6 in.
Blooms well all season
p. 431

Slight fragrance
Winter hardy
Disease resistant

Garden Party

Plant height: 5–6 ft.
Blossom width:
5–5½ in.
Blooms profusely in
midseason with good
repeat
p. 418

Fragrant
Winter hardy
Disease resistant, but
susceptible to mildew

La France

Plant height: 4–5 ft.
Blossom width:
4–4½ in.
Blooms profusely, early
to midseason, with good
repeat
p. 423

Very fragrant
Winter hardy
Disease resistant

Peace

Plant height: 5–6 ft.
Blossom width:
5½–6 in.
Blooms well all season
p. 429

Slight fragrance
Winter hardy
Disease resistant

Kordes' Perfecta
Plant height: 4–5 ft.
Blossom width:
4½–5 in.
Blooms well all season
p. 423

Very fragrant
Winter hardy
Disease resistant

Granada
Plant height: 5–6 ft.
Blossom width: 4–5 in.
Blooms abundantly all season
p. 418

Spicy fragrance
Needs winter protection in severe climates
Disease resistant, but needs protection from mildew

| Princesse de Monaco | Plant height: 4–4½ ft. Blossom width: 4½ in. Blooms sparsely in midseason with fair repeat p. 431 | Fragrant Hardiness uncertain Disease resistant |

| Chicago Peace | Plant height: 4½–5½ ft. Blossom width: 5–5½ in. Blooms well all season p. 412 | Slight to moderately strong fragrance Winter hardy Disease resistant |

Duet

Plant height:
4½–5½ ft.
Blossom width: 4 in.
Good midseason bloom
with excellent repeat
p. 415

Fragrant
Winter hardy
Disease resistant

Medallion

Plant height:
4½–5½ ft.
Blossom width:
5–5½ in.
Blooms profusely in
midseason with good
repeat
p. 424

Fruity fragrance
Not reliably winter
hardy without
protection
Disease resistant

Michèle Meilland

Plant height: 3–4 ft.
Blossom width:
3½–4 in.
Blooms extremely well
all season
p. 424

Slight fragrance
Winter hardy
Disease resistant

Helen Traubel

Plant height: 5–5½ ft.
Blossom width:
4½–5 in.
Blooms well all season
p. 419

Moderate fragrance
Winter hardy
Disease resistant

Tiffany

Plant height: 4–4½ ft. *Very fragrant*
Blossom width: 4–5 in. *Winter hardy*
Blooms well all season *Disease resistant*
p. 434

Royal Highness

Plant height: 4½–5 ft. *Very fragrant*
Blossom width: *Not winter hardy*
5–5½ in. *Disease resistant*
Blooms well all season.
p. 432

Charlotte Armstrong

Plant height: 4–5 ft.
Blossom width:
3½–4½ in.
Blooms in early
summer with good
repeat
p. 411

Fragrant
Winter hardy with
some protection
Disease resistant

Dainty Bess

Plant height: 3½–4 ft.
Blossom width: 3½ in.
Blooms well all season
p. 414

Fragrant
Winter hardy
Disease resistant

Lady X

Plant height: 5–7 ft.
Blossom width:
4½–5 in.
Blooms well all season
p. 423

Fragrant
Winter hardy
Disease resistant

Sterling Silver

Plant height: 2½–3 ft.
Blossom width: 3½ in.
Blooms fairly well all
season
p. 432

Strong lemon fragrance
Winter hardy
Disease resistant, but
susceptible to black spot
and mildew

Blue Moon

Plant height: 4–5 ft.
Blossom width: 4½ in.
Blooms well all season
p. 410

Strong lemon fragrance
Not reliably winter
hardy without
protection
Disease resistant

Kölner Karneval

Plant height: 2½–3 ft.
Blossom width: 5½ in.
Blooms well all season
p. 422

Slight fragrance
Winter hardy
Disease resistant

Bewitched

Plant height: 7–9 ft.
Blossom width: 5 in.
Blooms well all season
p. 410

Moderate to strong fragrance
Winter hardy with some protection
Disease resistant, but needs protection from mildew

Perfume Delight

Plant height: 4–4½ ft.
Blossom width: 4–4½ in.
Blooms abundantly in midseason with fair repeat
p. 430

Fragrance varies
Not winter hardy without protection
Disease resistant, but susceptible to black spot and mildew

Sweet Surrender   *Plant height: 3½–5 ft.*   *Strong fragrance*
                      Blossom width: *Not reliably winter*
                      3½–4½ in.   *hardy*
                      Blooms fairly well all
                      season
                      p. 434

Pink Peace   *Plant height:*   *Very fragrant*
                 4½–5½ ft.   *Winter hardy*
                 Blossom width: *Disease resistant*
                 4½–6 in.
                 Blooms well all season
                 p. 430

Friendship

Plant height: 5–6 ft.
Blossom width: 5½ in.
Blooms well all season
p. 418

Very fragrant
Winter hardy
Disease resistant

Double Delight

Plant height: 3½–4 ft.
Blossom width: 5½ in.
Blooms extremely well
all season
p. 415

Spicy fragrance
Winter hardy
Disease resistant, but
susceptible to mildew in
some regions

Color Magic
Plant height: 3½–4 ft.
Blossom width: 5 in.
Blooms continuously all season
p. 413

Slight fragrance
Not winter hardy without protection
Disease resistant

Mon Cheri
Plant height: 2½–3 ft.
Blossom width: 4½ in.
Blooms well all season
p. 426

Moderate fragrance
Winter hardy
Disease resistant

First Prize

Plant height: to 5 ft.
Blossom width:
5–5½ in.
Blooms well in
midseason with good
repeat
p. 416

Fragrant
Not winter hardy
Disease prone; needs
protection from mildew
and black spot

Paradise

Plant height: 4–4½ ft.
Blossom width:
3½–4½ in.
Blooms well all season
p. 428

Fragrant
Winter hardy
Disease resistant, but
susceptible to mildew in
cool, wet climates

Seashell

Plant height: 3½–4 ft.
Blossom width: 4–5 in.
Blooms fairly well all season
p. 432

Fragrant
Winter hardy
Disease resistant

Pink Favorite

Plant height: 4–4½ ft.
Blossom width:
3½–4 in.
Blooms profusely in midseason with good repeat
p. 430

Slight fragrance
Winter hardy
Disease resistant

Electron

*Plant height:
2½–3½ ft.
Blossom width: 5 in.
Blooms abundantly all
season
p. 416*

*Very fragrant
Winter hardy
Disease resistant*

Oklahoma

*Plant height: 5–6 ft.
Blossom width:
4–5½ in.
Blooms abundantly all
season
p. 427*

*Very fragrant
Winter hardy
Disease resistant*

Keepsake

Plant height: 5–6 ft.
Blossom width: 5 in.
Blooms well all season
p. 421

Very fragrant
Winter hardy
Disease resistant

Crimson Glory

Plant height: 3½–4 ft.
Blossom width:
4–4½ in.
Blooms well all season
p. 413

Very fragrant
Winter hardy
Disease resistant

Mirandy

Plant height: 4–5 ft.
Blossom width:
4½–5 in.
Blooms well all season
p. 425

Strong true-rose
fragrance
Winter hardy
Disease resistant

Precious Platinum

Plant height: to 4 ft.
Blossom width: 3½ in.
Blooms abundantly all
season
p. 431

Slight fragrance
Winter hardy
Disease resistant

Mister Lincoln

Plant height:
4½–5½ ft.
Blossom width:
5–5½ in.
Blooms well all season
p. 425

Very fragrant
Winter hardy
Disease resistant

Chrysler Imperial

Plant height: 4–5 ft.
Blossom width:
4½–5 in.
Blooms profusely in
midseason with good
repeat
p. 413

Very fragrant
Winter hardy
Disease resistant, but
susceptible to mildew in
cool, wet climates

Christian Dior

*Plant height: 4–5 ft.
Blossom width:
4–4½ in.
Blooms in midseason
with fair repeat
p. 412*

*Slight fragrance
Not winter hardy
without protection
Disease resistant, but
susceptible to mildew*

Gypsy

*Plant height: 4–5 ft.
Blossom width:
4–4½ in.
Blooms well all season
p. 419*

*Slight fragrance
Winter hardy
Disease resistant*

Dolly Parton

Plant height: 4–5 ft.
Blossom width:
4½–5 in. wide
Blooms well all season
p. 414

Intense fragrance
Hardiness uncertain
Disease resistant

Olympiad

Plant height: 4–5 ft.
Blossom width:
4–4½ in.
Blooms well all season
p. 427

Slight fragrance
Winter hardy
Disease resistant

American Pride *Plant height: 5–5½ ft.* *Little or no fragrance*
Blossom width: *Winter hardy*
4½–5½ in. *Disease resistant*
Blooms best in early
summer and fall
p. 410

Fragrant Cloud *Plant height: 4–5 ft.* *Intense true-rose*
Blossom width: 5 in. *fragrance*
Blooms well all season *Winter hardy*
p. 417 *Disease resistant*

Miss All-American Beauty

Plant height: 4–5 ft.
Blossom width: 5 in.
Blooms abundantly in midseason with good repeat
p. 425

Very fragrant
Winter hardy
Disease resistant

Tropicana

Plant height: 4–5 ft.
Blossom width: 5 in.
Blooms extremely well all season
p. 434

Very strong, fruity fragrance
Winter hardy
Disease resistant

Yankee Doodle
Plant height: 4–4½ ft.
Blossom width: 4 in.
Blooms extremely well
all season
p. 435

Slight fragrance
Winter hardy
Disease resistant

Sutter's Gold
Plant height: 4–4½ ft.
Blossom width: 4–5 in.
Blooms well all season
p. 433

Strong, fruity
fragrance
Moderately winter
hardy
Disease resistant

Mojave

Plant height: 4–5 ft.
Blossom width:
4–4½ in.
Blooms well all season
p. 426

Fragrant
Winter hardy
Disease resistant

Brandy

Plant height: 4–5 ft.
Blossom width:
4–4½ in.
Blooms profusely all
season
p. 411

Moderately strong,
fruity fragrance
Winter hardy with
some protection
Disease resistant, but
susceptible to black spot

Fred Edmunds   *Plant height: 2½–3 ft.*   *Very spicy fragrance*
Blossom width: *Winter hardy*
5–5½ in.   *Disease resistant*
Blooms well all season
p. 417

Eclipse   *Plant height: 3½–4 ft.*   *Slight fragrance*
Blossom width: *Not reliably winter*
3½–4 in.   *hardy without*
Blooms profusely in   *protection*
midseason with fair   *Disease resistant*
repeat
p. 415

King's Ransom   Plant height: 4½–5 ft.   Fragrant
                     Blossom width: 5–6 in.   Not reliably winter
                     Blooms profusely in   hardy in severe climates
                     midseason with good   Disease resistant, but
                     repeat   susceptible to mildew
                     p. 422

Oregold   Plant height: 3½–4 ft.   Slight fragrance
                     Blossom width: Not reliably winter
                     4½–5 in.   hardy without
                     Blooms abundantly in   protection
                     midseason with fair   Disease resistant, but
                     repeat   susceptible to black spot
                     p. 428   and mildew

Irish Gold

Plant height: 4–4½ ft.
Blossom width: 6–7 in.
Blooms well all season
p. 420

Light, sweet fragrance
Not reliably winter
hardy without
protection
Disease resistant

Summer Sunshine

Plant height: 4–5 ft.
Blossom width:
3½–5 in.
Blooms extremely well
all season
p. 433

Slight fragrance
Not entirely winter
hardy
Disease resistant

New Day

Plant height: to 4 ft.
Blossom width: 4–5 in.
Blooms abundantly in
midseason with good
repeat
p. 427

Strong, spicy fragrance
Winter hardy
Disease resistant

John F. Kennedy

Plant height: 3–4 ft.
Blossom width:
5–5½ in.
Blooms well all season
p. 421

Fragrant
Not winter hardy
without protection
Disease resistant

Miniatures

Jet Trail

Plant height:
10–14 in.
Blossom width: 1¼ in.
Blooms in midseason
with good repeat
p. 452

Fragrant
Winter hardy
Disease resistant

Simplex

Plant height:
15–18 in.
Blossom width: 1¼ in.
Blooms in midseason
with excellent repeat
p. 465

Slight fragrance
Winter hardy
Disease resistant

Popcorn

Plant height:
12–14 in.
Blossom width: ¾ in.
Blooms in midseason
with excellent repeat
p. 461

Honey fragrance
Winter hardy
Disease resistant

Baby Betsy McCall

Plant height:
12–18 in.
Blossom width:
1–1½ in.
Blooms in midseason
with good repeat
p. 439

Fragrant
Winter hardy
Disease resistant

Starglo

Plant height:
10–14 in.
Blossom width: 1¾ in.
Blooms in midseason
with good repeat
p. 466

Very fragrant
Winter hardy
Disease resistant

Center Gold

Plant height:
14–18 in.
Blossom width: 1½ in.
Blooms in midseason
with good repeat
p. 442

Little or no fragrance
Winter hardy
Disease resistant

Green Ice

Plant height: 8–16 in.
Blossom width: 1¼ in.
Blooms in midseason
with good repeat
p. 448

Slight fragrance
Winter hardy
Disease resistant

Yellow Doll

Plant height: 8–10 in.
Blossom width: 1½ in.
Blooms in midseason
with good repeat
p. 468

Slight fragrance
Winter hardy
Disease resistant

Jean Kenneally
Plant height:
10–14 in.
Blossom width: 1½ in.
Blooms in midseason
with excellent repeat
p. 452

Slight fragrance
Winter hardy
Disease resistant

Gold Coin
Plant height: 8–12 in.
Blossom width: 1½ in.
Blooms extremely well
in midseason with good
repeat
p. 447

Fragrant
Winter hardy
Disease resistant

Party Girl

Plant height:
12–14 in.
Blossom width: 1¼ in.
Blooms in midseason
with good repeat
p. 458

Sweet, spicy fragrance
Winter hardy
Disease resistant

Summer Butter

Plant height:
10–14 in.
Blossom width: 1½ in.
Blooms in midseason
with good repeat
p. 467

Strong, spicy, sweet
fragrance
Winter hardy
Disease resistant

Rise 'n' Shine

Plant height:
10–14 in.
Blossom width:
1½–1¾ in.
Blooms in midseason
with good repeat
p. 463

Slight fragrance
Winter hardy
Disease resistant

Rainbow's End

Plant height:
10–14 in.
Blossom width: 1½ in.
Blooms in midseason
with good repeat
p. 462

Little or no fragrance
Winter hardy
Disease resistant

Lemon Delight   *Plant height: to 12 in.*   *Slight, sweet fragrance*
                       Blossom width: 1¼ in.   *Winter hardy*
                       Blooms in midseason   *Disease resistant*
                       with good repeat
                       p. 455

Baby Masquerade   *Plant height:*   *Slight, fruity fragrance*
                       10–14 in.   *Winter hardy*
                       Blossom width: 1½ in.   *Disease resistant*
                       Blooms in midseason
                       with good repeat
                       p. 440

Avandel

Plant height: to 12 in.
Blossom width:
1–1½ in.
Blooms extremely well
in midseason with good
repeat
p. 438

Strong, fruity
fragrance
Winter hardy
Disease resistant

Fairlane

Plant height:
10–12 in.
Blossom width: 1½ in.
Blooms in midseason
with good repeat
p. 446

Fragrant
Winter hardy
Disease resistant

Nancy Hall

Plant height:
10–14 in.
Blossom width: 1¼ in.
Blooms in midseason
with good repeat
p. 457

Fragrant
Winter hardy
Disease resistant

Hokey Pokey

Plant height:
12–14 in.
Blossom width: 1½ in.
Blooms in midseason
with good repeat
p. 449

Little or no fragrance
Winter hardy
Disease resistant

Cinderella

Plant height: 8–10 in.
Blossom width: ¾ in.
Blooms very well in
midseason with
excellent repeat
p. 444

Very spicy fragrance
Winter hardy
Disease resistant

Peachy White

Plant height:
10–14 in.
Blossom width: 1½ in.
Blooms in midseason
with good repeat
p. 459

Slight fragrance
Winter hardy
Disease resistant

Pink Petticoat

*Plant height:
14–18 in.
Blossom width: 1½ in.
Blooms in midseason
with good repeat
p. 460*

*Slight fragrance
Winter hardy
Disease resistant*

Seabreeze

*Plant height:
10–14 in.
Blossom width: 1¼ in.
Blooms extremely well
in midseason with
excellent repeat
p. 465*

*Little or no fragrance
Winter hardy
Disease resistant*

Pompon de Paris
Plant height: 8–10 in.
Blossom width: ¾ in.
Blooms in midseason
with good repeat
p. 461

Little or no fragrance
Winter hardy
Disease resistant

Peachy Keen
Plant height: 8–12 in.
Blossom width:
1–1¼ in.
Blooms in midseason
with good repeat
p. 459

Slight fragrance
Winter hardy
Disease resistant

Choo-Choo Centennial

Plant height: 10–18 in.
Blossom width: 1½ in.
Blooms profusely in midseason with good repeat
p. 443

Slight fragrance
Winter hardy
Disease resistant

Helen Boehm

Plant height: 10–12 in.
Blossom width: 1½ in.
Blooms in midseason with good repeat
p. 449

Slight fragrance
Winter hardy
Disease resistant

Rosmarin   *Plant height:*   *Fragrant*
              15–18 in.   *Very winter hardy*
              Blossom width: 1 ½ in. *Disease resistant*
              Blooms in midseason
              with excellent repeat
              p. 464

Baby Cheryl   *Plant height: 8–12 in.*   *Spicy fragrance*
                 Blossom width: 1 ¼ in.   *Winter hardy*
                 Blooms in midseason   *Disease resistant*
                 with good repeat
                 p. 439

Rosa rouletti

Plant height:
15–18 in.
Blossom width:
¾–1 in.
Blooms in midseason
with good repeat
p. 464

Little or no fragrance
Winter hardy
Disease resistant

Heidi

Plant height: to 12 in.
Blossom width: 1¼ in.
Blooms in midseason
with good repeat
p. 448

Very sweet fragrance
Winter hardy
Disease resistant

Lavender Jewel
Plant height:
10–15 in.
Blossom width: 1½ in.
Blooms in midseason
with good repeat
p. 454

Slight fragrance
Winter hardy
Disease resistant

Cupcake
Plant height:
12–14 in.
Blossom width: 1½ in.
Blooms in midseason
with good repeat
p. 445

Little or no fragrance
Winter hardy
Disease resistant

Lavender Lace   *Plant height: 8–12 in.*   *Slight fragrance*
Blossom width: 1½ in.   *Winter hardy*
Blooms in midseason   *Disease resistant*
with good repeat
p. 455

Loveglo   *Plant height:*   *Fragrant*
12–18 in.   *Winter hardy*
Blossom width: 1½ in.   *Disease resistant*
Blooms in midseason
with good repeat
p. 456

Peaches 'n' Cream
Plant height: 15–18 in.
Blossom width: 1½ in.
Blooms in midseason with good repeat
p. 458

Slight fragrance
Winter hardy
Disease resistant

Little Jackie
Plant height: 14–18 in.
Blossom width: 1½ in.
Blooms in midseason with excellent repeat
p. 456

Very fragrant
Winter hardy
Disease resistant

Mary Marshall

Plant height:
10–14 in.
Blossom width: 1½ *in.*
Blooms in midseason
with good repeat
p. 457

Slight fragrance
Winter hardy
Disease resistant

Angel Darling

Plant height:
12–18 in.
Blossom width: 1½ *in.*
Blooms in midseason
with good repeat
p. 438

Slight fragrance
Winter hardy
Disease resistant, but
susceptible to fungus
diseases, black spot, and
mildew

Chipper

*Plant height:
10–14 in.
Blossom width: 1¼ in.
Good midseason bloom
with excellent repeat
p. 443*

*Slight fragrance
Winter hardy
Disease resistant*

Persian Princess

*Plant height:
12–18 in.
Blossom width: 1¾ in.
Blooms in midseason
with excellent repeat
p. 460*

*Slight fragrance
Winter hardy
Disease resistant*

Judy Fischer

*Plant height:
18–24 in.
Blossom width: 1 ½ in.
Blooms in midseason
with excellent repeat
p. 453*

*Moderate fragrance
Winter hardy
Disease resistant*

Petite Folie

*Plant height:
10–14 in.
Blossom width: 1 ¼ in.
Blooms in midseason
with good repeat
p. 460*

*Slight fragrance
Winter hardy
Disease resistant*

Bit O' Magic

Plant height:
12–14 in.
Blossom width: 1½ in.
Blooms extremely well
in midseason with good
repeat
p. 440

Slight fragrance
Winter hardy
Disease resistant

Stars 'n' Stripes

Plant height:
10–14 in.
Blossom width: 1¾ in.
Blooms in midseason
with good repeat
p. 466

Little or no fragrance
Winter hardy
Disease resistant

Toy Clown
Plant height:
10–14 in.
Blossom width: 1½ in.
Blooms in midseason
with good repeat
p. 467

Little or no fragrance
Winter hardy
Disease resistant

Kathy Robinson
Plant height: to 14 in.
Blossom width: 1½ in.
Blooms in midseason
with excellent repeat
p. 454

Very slight fragrance
Winter hardy
Disease resistant

Antique Rose

*Plant height:
14–16 in.
Blossom width: 1¾ in.
Blooms in midseason
with good repeat
p. 438*

*Slight fragrance
Winter hardy
Disease resistant*

Hotline

*Plant height:
15–18 in.
Blossom width: 1½ in.
Blooms in midseason
with good repeat
p. 451*

*Little or no fragrance
Winter hardy
Disease resistant*

Valerie Jeanne
Plant height:
15–18 in.
Blossom width: 1¾ in.
Blooms in midseason
with good repeat
p. 468

Slight fragrance
Winter hardy
Disease resistant

Kara
Plant height: 6–8 in.
Blossom width: 1 in.
Blooms in midseason
with excellent repeat
p. 453

Fragrant
Winter hardy
Disease resistant

Magic Carrousel

Plant height:
15–18 in.
Blossom width:
1¾–2 in.
Blooms in midseason
with good repeat
p. 456

Little or no fragrance
Winter hardy
Disease resistant

Dreamglo

Plant height:
18–24 in.
Blossom width: 1 in.
Blooms extremely well
in midseason with good
repeat
p. 446

Slight fragrance
Winter hardy
Disease resistant

Charmglo   *Plant height:*   *Slight fragrance*
10–14 in.   *Winter hardy*
Blossom width: 1½ in.   *Disease resistant*
Blooms in midseason
with good repeat
p. 442

Over the Rainbow   *Plant height:*   *Little or no fragrance*
12–14 in.   *Winter hardy*
Blossom width: *Disease resistant*
1¼–1½ in.
Blooms in midseason
with excellent repeat
p. 458

Shooting Star

Plant height:
10–12 in.
Blossom width: 1½ in.
Blooms in midseason
with excellent repeat
p. 465

Slight fragrance
Winter hardy
Disease resistant

Julie Ann

Plant height:
10–14 in.
Blossom width: 1½ in.
Blooms in midseason
with good repeat
p. 453

Fragrant
Winter hardy
Disease resistant

Puppy Love

Plant height:
12–15 in.
Blossom width: 1½ in.
Blooms in midseason
with good repeat
p. 462

Little or no fragrance
Winter hardy
Disease resistant

Bonny

Plant height: 6–8 in.
Blossom width: ¾ in.
Blooms in midseason
with excellent repeat
p. 441

Slight fragrance
Winter hardy
Disease resistant

Fire Princess *Plant height:* *Little or no fragrance*
12–14 in. *Winter hardy*
Blossom width: 1½ in. *Disease resistant*
Blooms extremely well
in midseason with good
repeat
p. 447

Chattem Centennial *Plant height: to 10 in.* *Slight, fruity fragrance*
Blossom width: 1½ in. *Winter hardy*
Blooms extremely well *Disease resistant*
in midseason with good
repeat
p. 442

Darling Flame

Plant height:
10–14 in.
Blossom width: 1 ½ in.
Blooms in midseason
with good repeat
p. 445

Fruity fragrance
Winter hardy
Disease resistant, but
susceptible to black spot
and mildew

Cricket

Plant height: to 14 in.
Blossom width: 1 ¼ in.
Blooms in midseason
with good repeat
p. 444

Slight fragrance
Winter hardy
Disease resistant

Holy Toledo
Plant height:
15–18 in.
Blossom width: 1¾ in.
Blooms in midseason
with good repeat
p. 449

Slight fragrance
Winter hardy
Disease resistant

Hot Shot
Plant height: 8–10 in.
Blossom width: 1¾ in.
Blooms in midseason
with excellent repeat
p. 450

Very slight fragrance
Winter hardy
Disease resistant

Humdinger

Plant height: 8–10 in.
Blossom width: 1 in.
Blooms in midseason
with excellent repeat
p. 451

Slight fragrance
Winter hardy
Disease resistant

Hula Girl

Plant height: to 12 in.
Blossom width: 1¼ in.
Blooms in midseason
with good repeat
p. 451

Fruity fragrance
Winter hardy
Disease resistant

Kathy
Plant height: 8–10 in.
Blossom width: 1½ in.
Blooms in midseason
with excellent repeat
p. 454

Fragrant
Winter hardy
Disease resistant

Carol-Jean
Plant height:
10–18 in.
Blossom width: 1 in.
Blooms in midseason
with good repeat
p. 441

Slight fragrance
Winter hardy
Disease resistant

Starina

Plant height:
12–16 in.
Blossom width: 1½ in.
Blooms in midseason
with excellent repeat
p. 466

Little or no fragrance
Winter hardy
Disease resistant

Cuddles

Plant height:
14–16 in.
Blossom width: 1¼ in.
Blooms extremely well
in midseason with good
repeat
p. 444

Slight fragrance
Winter hardy
Disease resistant

Beauty Secret

Plant height:
10–18 in.
Blossom width: 1½ in.
Blooms extremely well
in midseason with
excellent repeat
p. 440

Very fragrant
Winter hardy
Disease resistant

Red Beauty

Plant height:
10–12 in.
Blossom width: 1½ in.
Blooms in midseason
with good repeat
p. 463

Slight fragrance
Winter hardy
Disease resistant

Honest Abe
Plant height: to 12 in.
Blossom width: 1¼ in.
Blooms in midseason
with fair repeat
p. 450

Very sweet fragrance
Winter hardy
Disease resistant

Dwarfking
Plant height: 8–10 in.
Blossom width: 1¼ in.
Blooms in midseason
with good repeat
p. 446

Slight fragrance
Winter hardy
Disease resistant

Red Cascade

Plant height: 2–6 ft.
Blossom width: 1½ in.
Blooms in midseason
with good repeat
p. 463

Little or no fragrance
Winter hardy
Disease resistant, but
susceptible to mildew in
some climates

Poker Chip

Plant height:
15–18 in.
Blossom width: 1½ in.
Blooms in midseason
with good repeat
p. 461

Very sweet fragrance
Winter hardy
Disease resistant

Galaxy

Plant height: to 12 in.
Blossom width: 1½ in.
Blooms in midseason
with good repeat
p. 447

Little or no fragrance
Winter hardy
Disease resistant

Zinger

Plant height:
14–18 in.
Blossom width: 1½ in.
Blooms in midseason
with good repeat
p. 468

Little or no fragrance
Winter hardy
Disease resistant

Species Roses

Natural wild roses—commonly called species roses—grow
throughout the Northern Hemisphere, from North America to
Europe, China, and Japan. They are known to thrive in a very wide
range of habitats and climates, flourishing from the far North down
to the northern reaches of Africa.

A Matter of Debate
What constitutes a species rose is a matter of continuing academic
debate. According to the usual concept, there are about 200 wild
roses, but some authorities claim to be able to distinguish many
times that number. Linnaeus himself commented that those who
had examined just a few species could explain them a great deal
better than those who had examined many.

While the debate rages on among the experts, most gardeners are
satisfied to define a species rose as one that bears a single
(five-petaled) flower that sets self-pollinated hips and produces
seedlings resembling the parent in every particular.

Living History
The group of species roses described in this book is by no means
exhaustive; the roses included here were chosen for their particular
beauty and for the contributions that they have made to the heritage
of the many rose cultivars that exist today. *Rosa spinosissima,* for
example, is the ancestor of many fine horticultural varieties,
including Frühlingsgold and Frühlingsmorgen, which belong to the
shrub rose class. *Rosa multiflora* forms part of the background of the
polyantha roses—shrub roses that bear their flowers in clusters—and,
by extension, of all roses descended from the polyanthas, including
the entire floribunda class. *Rosa wichuraiana* is included in the
parentage of many notable climbers, including Silver Moon and
Albéric Barbier. And the list goes on, making it easy to see why it is
not only interesting but also helpful to have some understanding of
these beautiful roses that grow in the wild.

Even in the wild, species roses are known to hybridize very freely.
This fact accounts, at least in part, for the rather indeterminate
boundaries that exist between some species, and for the extent to
which the exact number of species roses is still in dispute. What is
more, many species roses have, over the centuries, developed strains
that can appear very different. *Rosa multiflora,* for example, has many
very thorny strains, yet also occurs with canes that are almost
thornless.

Abundant Blooms
Species roses are for the most part once-blooming, and most of them
flower early in the season, in May or June. They produce an
enormous crop of blossoms each year. In most instances, the flowers
are followed by brightly colored fruits, known as seed hips, which
prolong the beauty of the plants and provide feed for birds. Rose

hips also make attractive subjects for flower and foliage arrangements.

Wild Roses in Your Garden

Species roses require little care in the garden. Many of these vigorous roses are also extremely hardy, although it is well to remember, if you are considering using species roses in your garden, that some are more naturally cold-tolerant than others. The kind of environment that suits them in the wild will also suit them admirably in your backyard.

If you do decide to plant species roses in your garden, make certain that you have allowed enough room for these vigorous plants. Many of them are extremely bushy and will grow up to eight or nine feet tall and just as wide.

As garden subjects, species roses are delightful and varied. Some—especially the larger varieties—are ideally suited for hedges, while others, such as *Rosa wichuraiana,* are very sprawling in their growth and make a good ground cover. Individual bushes or a row of species roses will make a very fine backdrop for many other plants, including other types of roses.

Any species roses that are sold commercially or that may, with proper permission, be collected in the wild can be used in some way in a garden setting. They offer something of interest at all times of the year, with flowers, hips, foliage, thorns, and canes all contributing in some way, expected or unexpected, to the visual appeal of your garden.

Rosa banksiae lutea, *p. 87*
(J. D. Parks, 1824)

Also called the Yellow Lady Banks Rose, this early bloomer was named for Lady Banks, the wife of the director of Kew Gardens at the time of its introduction. It is not quite as vigorous or fragrant as the white form, *Rosa banksiae albo-plena.*

Flowers
1 in. (2.5 cm) wide. Light to medium yellow. Double; perhaps 45–50 petals. The very early-season blooms are not recurrent. Slight fragrance. The very full, old rose form gives it a rather raggedy look, like a double-flowering cherry.

Foliage
20–30 ft. (6–9 m) tall. Very long canes, very vigorous growth, not winter hardy. Disease resistant. Almost thornless. Leaves small, long, light green.

Rosa carolina, *p. 78*
(1826)

A native American rose, this pink species is sometimes called the Pasture Rose.

Flowers
2 in. (5 cm) wide. Medium pink. Single; 5 petals. Midseason bloom followed by bright red hips. Blooms mostly single, sometimes in clusters. Fragrant.

Foliage
3–6 ft. (1–1.8 m) tall. Upright, spreading by means of suckers. Disease free. Winter hardy except in severe winter climates. Canes fairly smooth, with few thorns. Leaves medium green, glossy.

Rosa chinensis viridiflora, *p. 86*
(Before 1845)

Also known as the Green Rose, this flower is a curiosity. Its petals have been transformed into sepals, giving them a deformed look.

Flowers
1½–2½ in. (4–6 cm) wide. Green. Double. Continuous bloom. No fragrance.

Foliage
3–4 ft. (1–1.2 m) tall. Upright. Can be grown in a pot. Disease resistant. Not winter hardy. Leaves medium to dark green.

Rosa eglanteria, p. 81
(Before 1551)

The Sweetbriar, or Shakespeare's Eglantine, has a sweet, true-rose fragrance; the foliage is strongly apple-scented, especially when it is wet.

Flowers
1–1½ in. (2.5–4 cm) wide. Light to medium pink. Single; 5 petals. Blooms early; not recurrent. Has a light, sweet, true-rose fragrance. Blooms in clusters, with blossoms opening flat to reveal showy yellow stamens. Clusters of bright red oval hips appear later in the season.

Foliage
8–10 ft. (2.4–3 m) tall. Upright, vigorous. Disease free and winter hardy. Canes very thorny. Leaves small, abundant, medium green, and glossy, with a fragrance of apples.

Rosa foetida bicolor, p. 84
(Before 1590)

Also called the Austrian Copper, this sport, or mutation, of *Rosa foetida* shares that rose's heavy aroma.

Flowers
2–2½ in. (5–6 cm) wide. Orange-red with yellow reverse. Single; 5 petals. Early-season bloom, not recurrent. The fragrance has been called heavy but not unpleasant; to some, it is reminiscent of boiled linseed oil.

Foliage
4–5 ft. (1.2–1.5 m) tall. Upright, irregularly branched, and rather gaunt. Prone to black spot. Not reliably winter hardy. Canes moderately thorny with small, dull, medium green, and rather sparse leaves.

Rosa foetida persiana, *p. 85*
(1837)

Also called the Persian Yellow, this rose is
the ancestor of many of our yellow and
bicolor varieties.

Flowers
2½–3 in. (6–7.5 cm) wide. Medium to deep
yellow. Semidouble; 24–30 petals. Early-
season bloom, not recurrent. Loose, cupped
form.

Foliage
4–5 ft. (1.2–1.5 m) tall. Upright. Moderately
vigorous; much more so in very warm
climates. Susceptible to black spot. Leaves
small, ferny, and medium green.

Rosa × highdownensis, *p. 84*
(1796)

This rose is widely distributed in this
country as Geranium, another variety or
possible hybrid of *Rosa moyesii*.

Flowers
1½ in. (4 cm) wide. Medium red, fading to
deep cerise pink. Single; 5 petals. Early-season
bloom is followed by bright orange, vase-
shaped hips. Fragrant. Blossoms open flat,
occurring singly and in clusters.

Foliage
9–12 ft. (2.7–3.5 m) tall. Strong, arching,
moderately thorny canes. Disease free and
winter hardy. Leaves small, blue-green to
dark green.

Rosa hugonis, *p. 86*
(Father Hugh Scanlon, 1899)

This species is also called Father Hugo's
Rose and the Golden Rose of China. It does
best in poor soil.

Flowers
1½–2 in. (4–5 cm) wide. Pale yellow.
Single; 5 petals. Very early bloom, not
recurrent. Little or no fragrance. Opens to
cup shape, with showy golden stamens. The
small maroon hips that develop later are not
conspicuous.

Foliage
Up to 6 ft. (1.8 m) tall and as wide, with
arching canes. Disease free. Winter hardy
except in extreme climates. Leaves small,
light to medium green, and ferny.

Rosa laevigata, *p. 76*
(1759)

Originally from China, *Rosa laevigata* had
become naturalized in the southeastern part
of North America by 1759. It is also known
as the Cherokee Rose.

Flowers
2½–3½ in. (6–8 cm) wide. Single; 5 petals.
Usually white; sometimes (but rarely) pink.
Early-season bloom; does not repeat.
Fragrant. Large, open flowers with yellow
stamens are followed by large, decorative,
bristly red hips.

Foliage
6–20 ft. (1.8–6 m) tall. Upright, arching,
and bushy. Disease resistant. Not winter
hardy. Canes very thorny. Leaves fine, bright
medium green, glossy. Almost evergreen in
very mild climates.

Rosa moyesii, *p. 85*
(Discovered by Hemsley and Wilson;
introduced in 1894, again in 1903)

This extraordinary deep blood-red species
from western China is named for the
Reverend E. J. Moyes, a missionary in that
country. *Rosa moyesii* is grown for its
spectacular hip display as well as for its
flowers.

Flowers
1¾–2½ in. (4.5–6 cm) wide. Deep blood-
red, although lighter shades have occurred in
the wild. Single; 5 petals. Early to midseason
bloom, not recurrent. Little fragrance.
Blooms singly and in small clusters. Long,
vase-shaped hips with retentive sepals;
brilliant red, with some bristles.

Foliage
10 ft. (3 m) tall or taller. Canes somewhat
sparse, upright, treelike. Disease resistant and
winter hardy, with moderately thorny canes.

Leaves small, delicate, ferny; medium to dark green, dull to semiglossy.

Rosa multiflora, p. 77
(Before 1868)

Often sold as a "living fence," this many-flowered rose has become a noxious weed in some regions of the country. Widely used as an understock, *Rosa multiflora* is the ancestor of many popular polyantha and floribunda varieties.

Flowers
½ in. (1.3 cm) wide, in large clusters. White. Single; 5 petals. Honey-scented. Early to midseason bloom, not recurrent. Blossoms appear in large, airy clusters. Tiny, round red hips follow later in the season.

Foliage
7–12 ft. (2.1–3.5 m) tall. Upright, arching canes. Disease free, and winter hardy in all but the most severe winter climates. Many strains are thorny, but there are some thornless *multifloras*. Leaves light to medium green; long, narrow, and glossy.

Rosa palustris, p. 79
(1726)

This sweetly fragrant pink species, also called the Swamp Rose, grows in wet, swampy soil, where it forms dense thickets.

Flowers
2½ in. (6 cm) wide. Medium pink. Single; 5 petals. Late-season bloom, not recurrent. Very sweet fragrance. Blossoms open flat, showing bright golden stamens. Blooms singly and in clusters.

Foliage
6–12 ft. (1.8–3.5 m) tall or taller. Upright, in dense thickets. Disease free and winter hardy. Light green canes very smooth, with few thorns. Soft, dull leaves, pale to medium green.

Rosa pendulina, p. 81
(1683)

Known as the Alpine Rose, this pink species bears conspicuous pear-shaped hips later in the season.

Flowers
2 in. (5 cm) wide. Medium pink to deep pink, sometimes mauve. Single; 5 petals. Light, sweet fragrance. Mid- to late-season bloom. Blossoms open flat, showing bright yellow stamens. Blooms singly and in clusters. Hips bright red, pear shaped.

Foliage
4 ft. (1.2 m) tall. Arching, graceful growth. Disease free and winter hardy. Canes very smooth, almost thornless. Leaves finely divided, medium green, glossy.

Rosa pomifera, p. 82
(1771)

This mauve-pink species is also called the Apple Rose, in reference to the large hips that appear later in the season.

Flowers
2 in. (5 cm) wide. Mauve-pink. Single; 5 petals. Fragrant. Early-season bloom, not recurrent. Large, round reddish hips follow later in the season.

Foliage
5–7 ft. (1.5–2.1 m) tall. Very upright. Disease free, winter hardy. Canes somewhat thorny. Leaves medium-size, blue-green.

Rosa roxburghii, p. 83
(1814)

This rose is also known as the Burr Rose and the Chestnut Rose, and more correctly called *R. roxburghii plena.* It is the double form of the species *roxburghii,* but it was discovered 94 years before the true species (which was named *R. roxburghii normalis*) and given the species name in error.

Flowers
3–3½ in. (7½–9 cm) wide. Light pink. Double; probably 45–55 petals. Early-season

bloom; a long blooming season in the South, where it is essentially a repeat-bloomer. Little or no fragrance. Outer petals open wide to reveal a mass of shorter central petals; all petals have a papery feel.

Foliage
5–6 ft. (1.5–1.8 m) tall. Upright, irregularly branched growth. Not as vigorous as *Rosa roxburghii normalis.* Gray, peeling canes. Disease resistant. Tender. Leaves long and narrow; light to medium green and very evenly spaced, giving a ladderlike effect.

Rosa roxburghii normalis, p. 80
(1908)

This rose is the true *roxburghii* species. It is more vigorous than the double form (*Rosa roxburghii*), which ironically has been known for nearly a century longer.

Flowers
3½–4 in. (9–10 cm) wide. Light pink. Single; 5 petals. Early-season bloom, not recurrent. Light, sweet fragrance. Large, crinkly petals open flat, revealing showy golden stamens. The petals have a papery quality. Bristly hips later in the season.

Foliage
7–9 ft. (2.1–2.7 m) tall. Upright, irregularly branched growth. Gray, peeling canes. Disease free and borderline hardy (cannot survive harsh winters). Leaves long, narrow, and very evenly spaced, giving unusual ladderlike effect; light to medium green.

Rosa rubrifolia, p. 80
(Before 1830)

There are several strains of this species, some producing smaller plants and others growing into very large bushes. Its Latin name refers to the plant's red leaves; *Rosa rubrifolia* is worth growing for its foliage alone.

Flowers
½ in. (1.3 cm) wide. Light pink with a white eye. Single; 5 petals. Early-season bloom, not recurrent. Fragrant. Blossoms open flat and occur in small clusters. Small, dark red, shiny hips appear in fall.

Foliage
4–8 ft. (1.2–2.4 m) tall. Upright, open,
arching canes. Disease free. Winter hardy in
all but severe winter climates. Canes red,
very smooth, and almost thornless. Leaves
are an unusual dark maroon.

Rosa rugosa, *p. 83*
(1845)

Originally discovered in northeastern Asia,
this species has become naturalized in the
northeastern United States, and it is found
along beaches in New England. It can lend
architectural quality to a garden, and it
makes a good hedge. Its large hips look like
cherry tomatoes; edible, they are an excellent
source of vitamin C.

Flowers
2½–3½ in. (6–9 cm) wide. Medium
mauve-pink. Single; 5–12 petals (variable).
Continuously in bloom during the entire
growing season. Intensely fragrant. Blossom
opens its wide, crinkly, cupped petals to
reveal golden stamens. Continues to bloom
even after its large red hips form.

Foliage
3–5 ft. (1–1½ m) tall. Upright, vigorous,
and spreading, forming a dense bush. Disease
free and winter hardy. Canes very thorny.
Dark green, leathery leaves, deeply etched
(rugose) and glossy.

Rosa rugosa alba, *p. 76*
(1845)

This white rose is a sport of *Rosa rugosa,*
which it resembles in everything but color.

Flowers
2½–3½ in. (6–9 cm) wide. White. Single;
5–12 petals (variable). Continuously in
bloom. Intense clove fragrance. Large, bright
orange-red hips, resembling cherry tomatoes,
appear later in the season.

Foliage
3–5 ft. (1–1.5 m) tall. Upright, vigorous,
and spreading, forming a dense bush. Disease
free and winter hardy. Dark green leathery
leaves, deeply etched (rugose) and glossy.

Rosa rugosa rubra, *p. 82*
(1845)

This is a color sport, or mutation, of *Rosa rugosa.* Its pink flowers, present all season long, are intensely fragrant.

Flowers
2½–3½ in. (6–9 cm) wide. Deep mauve-pink. Single; 5 to 12 petals (variable). Continuously in bloom. Intensely fragrant. Bright red hips form later in the season.

Foliage
3–5 ft. (1–1.5 m) tall. Upright, vigorous, spreading, and dense. Disease free and winter hardy, with very thorny canes. The glossy, leathery leaves are dark green and deeply etched (rugose).

Rosa soulieana, *p. 77*
(1896)

This species from western China is very thorny. It often grows in a climbing or trailing fashion.

Flowers
1½ in. (4 cm) wide. White. Single; 5 petals. Early- to mid-season bloom, not recurrent. Little or no fragrance. Blooms occur in large clusters. Tiny orange-red hips appear later in the season.

Foliage
12 ft. (3.5 m) tall. Upright, arching growth. Disease free. Not reliably winter hardy. Canes very thorny. Leaves gray-green.

Rosa spinosissima, *p. 79*
(Cultivated prior to 1600)

Also known as the Scotch Rose or Burnet Rose, this species is sometimes referred to as *Rosa pimpinellifolia.* It is the ancestor of several cultivated forms.

Flowers
1¼–2 in. (3–5 cm) wide. Cream, white, or light yellow; pink and purple forms have also been found in the wild. Single; 5 petals. Slight fragrance. Very early bloom; does not recur. Small, round hips, purple or black.

Foliage
3-4 ft. (1-1.2 m) tall. Bushy, spreading.
Disease resistant and winter hardy. Canes
very thorny. Small, ferny leaves are a dull
medium green.

Rosa spinosissima altaica, *p. 87*
(1820)

Originating in western Asia, this variety of
Rosa spinosissima was introduced into
cultivation in 1820. It closely resembles
Rosa spinosissima, but is considerably more
vigorous.

Flowers
1½-2½ in. (4-6 cm) wide. Single; 5 petals.
Pale yellow to white. Very early bloom; not
recurrent. Blossoms open wide, with petals
that do not overlap, to reveal thick bright
stamens. Slight fragrance. Globular hips are
maroon to purple.

Foliage
6 ft. (1.8 m) tall and as wide. Upright,
bushy. Disease resistant and winter hardy,
with thorny canes. Leaves small, dull,
gray-green.

Rosa wichuraiana, *p. 78*
(1891)

Also known as the Memorial Rose, this
species is the parent of many climbing roses.
It makes a good ground cover.

Flowers
1½-2 in. (4-5 cm) wide. White. Single;
5 petals. Late-season bloom, not recurrent.
Fragrant. Blooms occur in clusters. Small,
red, oval hips appear later in season.

Foliage
10-20 ft. (3-6 m) tall. Procumbent, but can
be trained to grow upward. Disease free.
Hardy in all but very severe winter climates.
Canes moderately thorny. Leaves medium-
size, dark green, and very glossy.

Climbers

Left to grow on their own, climbing roses do not actually climb at all—they lack the tendrils that other climbing plants, such as vines, use to attach themselves to structures. There are several different kinds of climbing roses, some of them actually sports, or chance mutations, of bush roses. But all climbing roses have long, supple or sturdy canes that support the growth of blossoms along their lengths.

Climbing roses must be tied to a support, such as a trellis or a wall. There they serve a variety of purposes, covering ugly structures or forming beautiful arbors.

Here we recognize seven different groups of climbing roses: hybrid bracteata, hybrid gigantea, climbing hybrid teas, kordesii climbers, large-flowered climbers, hybrid wichuraiana climbers, and ramblers.

Hybrid Bracteatas

There are only a very few hybrid bracteata climbers in commerce today—perhaps because they require a lot of space. Mermaid is a popular one. It will cover a large trellis, the roof of a low building, or a rough bank.

Cerise Bouquet, another commercially available variety, forms an upright small tree in just three or four years. For both of these roses, plenty of space must be allocated, for there is no hope of pruning them to a smaller area.

Hybrid Giganteas

The hybrid gigantea climbers are very tender, and may be grown only in regions with mild winters, where they are almost evergreen. They have very large blooms, sweetly perfumed. With a long season of bloom, they are perfect for arbors and trellises. The variety found most often in this country, notably in California, is Belle of Portugal.

Climbing Hybrid Teas

Mostly sports of the bush varieties, climbing hybrid tea roses are usually classed along with the bush forms. There are, however, a few climbing hybrid teas for which there is no bush form. They resemble other hybrid teas in every way, being medium-size, upright, rather stiffly caned plants.

Kordesii Climbers

Every once in a while, the rose helps the hybridizer out by spontaneously changing something in its genetic makeup; this is what happened for Wilhelm Kordes, a well-known 20th-century rose specialist. A new species, called *Rosa kordesii* in his honor, came into being, and Kordes used this species to develop many new varieties. The kordesii roses are medium-size climbers. They come in an assortment of colors, in intense hues, with well-shaped blooms and dark, hollylike foliage. Kordesii climbers make wonderful pillar roses,

and they are perfect for planting along a fence. They tend to be quite winter hardy.

Large-flowered Climbers
A catch-all class of climbing roses, the large-flowered climbers do not belong in any other group. These roses have medium-size to large blooms, usually in small clusters. Some large-flowered climbers are repeat bloomers, but others are not. Some of them, on the basis of their parentage, might well be considered climbing hybrid teas for which there is no bush form. Others are of mixed or even unknown parentage.

Hybrid Wichuraiana Climbers
Derived from the Memorial Rose, *Rosa wichuraiana,* the hybrid wichuraiana climbers are large, strong climbers, with canes reaching as long as 20 feet or more. Foliage is shining, dark green, and disease proof. The sweetly scented blooms are large and well shaped, in shades of white and pink. Wichuraiana climbers are once-blooming, and some varieties have a pleasing hip display later in the fall.

Ramblers
The last of the climbers to come into bloom are the rambler roses. Without exception, they are once-blooming, but they extend the rose season with very bright colors of pink, red, and purple. Many of them are derived from *Rosa multiflora,* although some ramblers are based on other species.

Ramblers have long, pliable canes that can easily be trained to a trellis or fence. They are not the best choices for walls, being very susceptible to mildew. (There is one shining exception, the variety Chevy Chase.) Good air circulation is a must.

The best rambler blooms are made up of tiny flowers in huge clusters. These usually come on second-year canes, so it is a good idea to prune away the oldest canes each year. It is generally recommended that this pruning be done after flowering, but unless you are a very experienced pruner, it is best to wait for the late winter or early spring, when the plants are just coming out of dormancy and there is no foliage to hide the canes.

Albéric Barbier, *p. 90*
(Barbier, 1900)

This is a wichuraiana climber—therefore, it
is extremely vigorous, with large flowers that
occur in small clusters.

Flowers
3–3½ in. (7.5–9 cm) wide. Light yellow,
fading to white at edges. Double; perhaps
45–55 petals. A long period of bloom occurs
late in the season; not recurrent. Fragrance
reminiscent of green apples. Blossoms
cupped, in clusters.

Foliage
20 ft. (6 m) tall. Vigorous, spreading.
Disease free and winter hardy. Canes
moderately thorny. Dark green, glossy leaves.

Aloha, *p. 100*
(Boerner, 1949)

This fragrant pink rose is a climbing hybrid
tea for which there is no bush form. It is a
good pillar rose, and also does well on a
small to medium-size trellis.

Flowers
3½ in. (9 cm) wide. Medium pink with
lavender-pink reverse. Double; 55–60 petals.
Good all-season bloom. Very fragrant. Buds
are short and appear malformed when first
opening, but become somewhat cupped and
globular.

Foliage
8–10 ft. (2.4–3 m) tall. Upright, vigorous.
Disease resistant, but slightly prone to
mildew unless planted where there is good
air circulation. Winter hardy. Leaves dark
green, leathery.

America, *p. 103*
(Warriner, 1976)

An All-America Rose Selection for 1976.
This fragrant rose is one of the very few
climbers to receive this distinction.

Flowers
3½–4½ in. (9–11.5 cm) wide. Coral salmon.
Double; 40–45 petals. Good midseason

bloom, followed by fair repeat bloom.
Fragrant. Very full, evenly petaled, high-
centered bloom, becoming cupped.

Foliage
9–12 ft. (2.7–3.5 m) tall. Upright, vigorous,
and bushy. Disease resistant and winter
hardy. Leaves medium green, semiglossy.

American Pillar, *p. 97*
(Van Fleet, 1902)

Like its wild ancestors, *Rosa wichuraiana* and
Rosa setigera, American Pillar is vigorous and
disease free.

Flowers
2–3 in. (5–7.5 cm) wide. Deep pink with
white eye. Single; 5 petals. Very abundant,
long, late-season bloom with little or no
fragrance. Blossoms occur in immense
clusters, and red hips appear later in the fall.

Foliage
15–20 ft. (4.5–6 m) tall. Upright, vigorous
growth. Disease resistant, but subject to
mildew in the South. Winter hardy. Canes
moderately thorny. Leaves medium green,
leathery, glossy.

Baltimore Belle, *p. 98*
(Feast, 1843)

This large-flowered climber is descended
from *Rosa setigera,* a vigorous native
American species.

Flowers
2–2½ in. (5–6 cm) wide. Light pink, fading
to white. Double; 45–55 petals. Late-season
bloom, not recurrent, with little or no
fragrance. The very full blossom sometimes
has a button center. Blooms in clusters.

Foliage
8–10 ft. (2.4–3 m) tall. Upright, sturdy, and
pliable. Disease resistant and winter hardy.
Canes moderately thorny, with dark green,
leathery, semiglossy leaves.

Blaze, *p. 105*
(Kallay, 1932)

Perhaps the most floriferous of the short climbers, Blaze remains in bloom for most or all of the growing season. It is reported to be descended from Paul's Scarlet Climber crossed with Grüss an Teplitz.

Flowers
2½–3 in. (6–7.5 cm) wide. Medium red. Semidouble; perhaps 18–24 petals. Good midseason bloom and excellent repeat. Slight fragrance. Cupped blossoms, in clusters.

Foliage
7–9 ft. (2.1–2.7 cm) tall. Upright, vigorous. Disease resistant and winter hardy. Leaves medium green, semiglossy.

Blossomtime, *p. 96*
(O'Neal, 1951)

This very fragrant large-flowered climber makes a good pillar or trellis rose.

Flowers
3½–4 in. (9–10 cm) wide. Medium pink with deeper pink reverse. Double; 35–40 petals. Very fragrant. Good midseason bloom with sparse repeat bloom. The high-centered, classic blossoms occur in clusters.

Foliage
7–9 ft. (2.1–2.7 m) tall. Upright, vigorous, bushy. Disease resistant and winter hardy. Canes thorny, with medium green, semiglossy leaves.

City of York, *p. 91*
(Tantau, 1945)

This very fragrant white climber won the American Rose Society National Gold Medal Certificate in 1950.

Flowers
3–3½ in. (7.5–9 cm) wide. White. Semidouble; 15 petals. Long midseason bloom, not recurrent. Very fragrant. Flower opens to become saucer shaped, revealing bright golden stamens. The blossoms have several central petaloids.

Foliage
20 ft. (6 m) tall. Upright, very vigorous.
Disease free. Winter hardy. Canes moderately
thorny, with light to medium green, glossy
leaves.

Clair Matin, *p. 99*
(Meilland, 1963)

This profusely blooming pink climber was
awarded the Bagatelle Gold Medal in 1960.

Flowers
2½–3 in. (6–7.5 cm) wide. Medium pink.
Semidouble; 12–18 petals. Profuse, long
midseason bloom, not recurrent. Fragrant.
Blooms in clusters, with cupped to flat
blossoms.

Foliage
10–12 ft. (3–3.5 cm) tall. Upright, vigorous,
and bushy. Disease resistant and winter
hardy. Canes moderately thorny. Leaves dark
green, leathery.

Coral Dawn, *p. 101*
(Boerner, 1952)

The deep pink flowers of Coral Dawn look
especially attractive when this rose is grown
on a pillar or trellis.

Flowers
4½–5 in. (11.5–12.5 cm) wide. Deep
coral-pink. Double; 30–35 petals. Good
midseason bloom followed by a fair repeat
bloom. Fragrant. High-centered blossoms
become cupped, occurring in clusters.

Foliage
8–12 ft. (2.4–3.5 m) tall. Upright, vigorous.
Disease resistant. Winter hardy. Canes
moderately thorny, with medium green,
leathery leaves.

Don Juan, *p. 103*
(Malandrone, 1958)

This deep red climber makes an excellent
pillar or trellis rose, particularly in areas with
mild winter climates.

Flowers
4½–5 in. (11.5–12.5 cm) wide. Dark red.
Double; 35 petals. Profuse midseason bloom
with good repeat bloom. Very fragrant. The
blossoms have a classic, high-centered form.

Foliage
8–10 ft. (2.4–3 m) tall. Upright, vigorous.
Disease resistant, but not dependably winter
hardy. Leaves dark green, leathery, and
glossy.

Dorothy Perkins, *p. 101*
(Jackson & Perkins, 1901)

This popular rambler was once one of the
most overplanted roses in America, and in
some areas it continues to flourish despite
conditions of neglect.

Flowers
¾ in. (2 cm) wide. Medium pink. Double;
perhaps 35–40 petals. Late-season bloom, not
recurrent, with little or no fragrance. Blooms
occur in large clusters.

Foliage
10–12 ft. (3–3.5 m) tall. Very vigorous, but
susceptible to mildew. Winter hardy. Canes
moderately thorny. Leaves small, dark green,
glossy.

Dortmund, *p. 105*
(Kordes, 1955)

This kordesii climber makes a wonderful
pillar rose, and its brilliant red, white-
centered blossom is spectacular.

Flowers
3–3½ in. (7.5–9 cm) wide. Medium red
with white eye at center. Single; 5 petals.
Profuse midseason bloom followed by good
repeat bloom. Fragrant. Blossoms, which
occur in large clusters, open flat to reveal
showy stamens. Large bright red hips appear
later in the fall.

Foliage
10–12 ft. (3–3.5 m) tall. Upright, vigorous.
Disease free and winter hardy, with dark
green, glossy leaves.

Dr. Huey, *p. 102*
(Thomas, 1914)

Dr. Huey was awarded the American Rose Society's Gertrude M. Hubbard Gold Medal in 1924. It is widely used as an understock, and may persist long after the death of the rose that was originally budded onto it.

Flowers
3–3½ in. (7.5–9 cm) wide. Dark, deep maroon. Semidouble; 15 petals. Long midseason bloom, not recurrent. Fragrant. Blossoms open to become saucer-shaped, contrasting with bright golden stamens. Blooms in clusters.

Foliage
12–18 ft. (3.5–5.4 m) tall. Upright, vigorous, arching. Disease resistant and winter hardy, with moderately thorny canes. Leaves dark green, semiglossy.

Dr. J. H. Nicolas, *p. 99*
(Nicolas, 1940)

This excellent pillar rose is also suitable for a trellis of low to medium height.

Flowers
4½–5 in. (11.5–12.5 cm) wide. Medium pink. Double; 50 petals. Profuse midseason bloom followed by good repeat bloom. Very fragrant. Blossoms have a classic, high-centered form.

Foliage
8–10 ft. (2.4–3 m) tall. Upright, vigorous. Disease resistant and winter hardy, with dark green, leathery leaves.

Dublin Bay, *p. 104*
(McGredy, 1975)

This large-flowered climber puts out profuse, fragrant red blooms at midseason, and usually follows up with a good repeat bloom.

Flowers
4½ in. (11.5 cm) wide. Medium red. Double; 25 petals. Profuse midseason bloom; good repeat. Blossoms fragrant and cupped.

Foliage
8–14 ft. (2.4–6 m) tall. Upright, vigorous,
and well branched. Disease resistant. Winter
hardy. Canes moderately thorny, with
medium to dark green, leathery leaves.

Elegance, *p. 90*
(Brownell, 1937)

The abundant yellow flowers of this
handsome climber make an attractive accent
for a wall or large trellis.

Flowers
4½–5½ in. (11.5–14 cm) wide. Medium
yellow. Double; 45–50 petals. Abundant
midseason bloom, not recurrent. Fragrant
blossoms have a cupped form.

Foliage
12–15 ft. (3.5–4.5 m) tall. Upright, very
vigorous. Disease resistant and winter hardy,
with medium green, semiglossy leaves.

Excelsa, *p. 102*
(Walsh, 1909)

Also known as the Red Dorothy Perkins,
this rambler won the American Rose
Society's Gertrude M. Hubbard Gold Medal
in 1914.

Flowers
¾ in. (2 cm) wide. Medium red. Double;
perhaps 35–40 petals. Late-season bloom, not
recurrent. With little or no fragrance.
Cupped blossoms occur in large clusters.

Foliage
12–18 ft. (3.5–5.4 m) tall. Very vigorous and
winter hardy, although susceptible to
mildew. Canes moderately thorny. Leaves
small, medium green, glossy.

Golden Showers, *p. 94*
(Lammerts, 1956)

An All-America Rose Selection for 1957 and
winner of the Portland Gold Medal in 1957,
Golden Showers is the most floriferous of
the shorter climbers within its color range.

Flowers
3½–4 in. (9–10 cm) wide. Medium yellow.
Double; 20–35 petals. Blooms abundantly
throughout the growing season. Fragrant,
cupped blossoms.

Foliage
8–10 ft. (2.4–3 m) tall. Upright, vigorous,
and bushy. Disease resistant. Winter hardy
except in severe winter climates. Canes
moderately thorny, with dark green, glossy
leaves.

Handel, *p. 95*
(McGredy, 1965)

Excellent for a wall or large trellis, Handel
produces abundant cream-colored blossoms
with a bright pink edge.

Flowers
3½ in. (9 cm) wide. Cream, edged in pink.
Double; 22 petals. Good midseason bloom
followed by good repeat bloom. Slight
fragrance. Blossoms have a high-centered to
cupped form.

Foliage
12–15 ft. (3.5–4.5 m) tall. Upright, vigorous.
Disease resistant. Winter hardy. Canes
moderately thorny. Leaves medium green,
glossy.

High Noon, *p. 93*
(Lammerts, 1948)

An All-America Rose Selection for 1948,
High Noon is a climbing hybrid tea for
which there is no bush form. It is suitable
for a pillar or small to medium-size trellis.

Flowers
3–4 in. (7.5–10 cm) wide. Light yellow
petals have red edges. Double; 25–30 petals.
Good all-season bloom with a spicy
fragrance. Blossoms have a loosely cupped
form.

Foliage
8–10 ft. (2.4–3 m) tall. Upright, vigorous.
Disease resistant and winter hardy. Leaves
medium green, leathery, glossy.

Joseph's Coat, *p. 94*
(Armstrong & Swim, 1964)

This kaleidoscopic climber was the winner of
the Bagatelle Gold Medal in 1964. A
"changing-colors" rose in a climber.

Flowers
3–4 in. (7.5–10 cm) wide. Double; 24–30
petals. Blossoms are yellow, gradually
turning red. Good midseason bloom
followed by fair repeat bloom. Slight
fragrance. Blossoms have open, cupped form;
occur in clusters.

Foliage
8–10 ft. (2.4–3 m) tall. Upright, vigorous.
Disease resistant. Not dependably winter
hardy. Leaves dark green, glossy.

Lawrence Johnston, *p. 95*
(Pernet-Ducher; date uncertain)

Also called Hidcote Yellow, Lawrence
Johnston is a vigorous climber that requires
plenty of space.

Flowers
3–3½ in. (7.5–9 cm) wide. Medium yellow.
Semidouble; 18–24 petals. Early to midseason
bloom, not recurrent. Fragrant. Cupped
blossoms occur in clusters.

Foliage
20 ft. (6 m) tall. Upright, very vigorous.
Disease resistant in some areas; highly prone
to black spot in the South. Winter hardy.
Thorny canes and medium green, glossy
leaves.

Leverkusen, *p. 92*
(Kordes, 1954)

This pale yellow kordesii climber is an
excellent rose for a pillar or trellis.

Flowers
3–3½ in. (7.5–9 cm) wide. Light yellow.
Double; 24–30 petals. Good midseason
bloom is followed by a good repeat bloom.
Slight fragrance. The high-centered,
hybrid–tea type forms occur in clusters.

Foliage
8–10 ft. (2.4–3 m) tall. Upright and
vigorous. Disease free, winter hardy, with
dark green, glossy leaves.

May Queen, *p. 98*
(Manda, 1898)

May Queen is a little less vigorous and
spreading than many other wichuraianas and
can be used in a variety of situations.

Flowers
3–3½ in. (7.5–9 cm) wide. Medium pink.
Double; 45–55 petals. Long midseason
bloom, not recurrent. Fragrant scent, like
that of green apples. Full blooms, slightly
cupped, quartered, with a button center.

Foliage
15 ft. (4.5 m) tall. Upright, vigorous.
Disease free and winter hardy. Moderately
thorny canes bear glossy leaves.

Mermaid, *p. 93*
(Paul, 1918)

Mermaid was the winner of the Royal
National Rose Society Gold Medal in 1917.
This hybrid bracteata climber or trailer
should not be pruned any more than is
absolutely necessary. It will form a ground
cover and can be used to cover an arbor.

Flowers
4½–5½ in. (11.5–14 cm) wide. Medium
yellow, fading to light yellow. Single; 5
petals. Fragrant. Very long midseason bloom.
Blossoms open to become cupped.

Foliage
20 ft. (6 m) plus. Vigorous and very lax,
but can be trained up. Disease resistant.
Tender, not winter hardy. Canes are rather
brittle. Leaves dark green, glossy.

New Dawn, *p. 97*
(Dreer, 1930)

This rose was the world's first patented
plant. An everblooming sport of Dr. W.

Van Fleet, New Dawn's flower form is not quite as fine, and some find it less vigorous than its relative.

Flowers
3–3½ in. (7.5–9 cm) wide. Light pink. Semidouble; 18–24 petals. Good midseason bloom with good repeat bloom. Fragrant. Cupped blooms show bright yellow stamens.

Foliage
12–15 ft. (3.5–4.5 m) tall. Upright, vigorous, and bushy. Disease free and winter hardy, with moderately thorny canes and medium green, glossy leaves.

Paul's Lemon Pillar, *p. 91*
(Paul, 1915)

A climbing hybrid tea, Paul's Lemon Pillar won the Royal National Rose Society Gold Medal in 1915. The word "Lemon" refers to the rose's fragrance, not to its color.

Flowers·
3½–4 in. (9–10 cm) wide. White. Double; 35–45 petals. Good all-season bloom. Very fragrant lemon scent. Blossoms have the classic hybrid tea form.

Foliage
10–12 ft. (3–3.5 m) tall. Upright, vigorous. Disease resistant, but tender. Abundant dark green, glossy leaves.

Paul's Scarlet Climber, *p. 104*
(Paul, 1916)

This popular large-flowered climber won the National Rose Society Gold Medal in 1915 and the Bagatelle Gold Medal in 1918.

Flowers
3–3½ in. (7.5–9 cm) wide. Medium red. Double; 24–30 petals. Profuse midseason bloom, not recurrent. Slight fragrance. Cupped blossoms occur in clusters.

Foliage
12–15 ft. (3.5–4.5 cm) tall. Upright, vigorous. Disease resistant and winter hardy, with moderately thorny canes and dark green, semiglossy leaves.

Silver Moon, *p. 92*
(Van Fleet, 1910)

Descended in part from *Rosa wichuraiana,*
Silver Moon is a magnificent rose requiring
plenty of space.

Flowers
3½–4½ in. (9–11.5 cm) wide. White.
Semidouble; 12–20 petals. Long midseason
bloom, not recurrent. Fragrant. Cupped
blossoms open to saucer shape.

Foliage
20 ft. (6 m) tall. Upright, vigorous, arching.
Disease free and winter hardy. Moderately
thorny canes bear dark green, glossy leaves.

Veilchenblau, *p. 96*
(Schmidt, 1909)

This rose can sometimes be found as a
surviving understock in old gardens.

Flowers
1¼ in. (3 cm) wide. Violet with a white
center. Semidouble; perhaps 18–24 petals.
Mid- to late-season bloom, not recurrent.
Fragrance like that of green apples. Petals
open flat. Blossoms occur in clusters.

Foliage
12 ft. (3.5 m) tall. Upright, vigorous.
Disease resistant and winter hardy. Canes
smooth, almost thornless. Leaves long and
pointed, medium green.

Viking Queen, *p. 100*
(Phillips, 1963)

Bred for winter hardiness, this large-flowered
climber is suitable for a wall or large trellis.

Flowers
3–4 in. (7.5–10 cm) wide. Medium to deep
pink. Double; 60 petals. Midseason bloom
followed by good repeat bloom. Very
fragrant. Full, globular blossoms in clusters.

Foliage
12–15 ft. (3.5–4.5 m) tall. Upright, vigorous.
Disease resistant and winter hardy, with dark
green, leathery, glossy leaves.

Shrub Roses

Like many terms used in horticulture, the word shrub is open to several different interpretations. For the purposes of this discussion, the shrub roses—also called modern shrub roses—include several subclasses: the hybrid eglantines, hybrid musks, hybrid rugosas, hybrid spinosissimas (in part), polyanthas, and shrub roses. This last group is a catch-all class whose members fit the category of modern shrub roses—having come into cultivation after the mid-19th century—but do not fall into any of the other five categories named above.

Hybrid Eglantines
The hybrid eglantines, descended from *Rosa eglanteria,* were developed by Lord Penzance in the late 1800s and are usually classified with the shrub roses.

These hybrids are upright, treelike shrubs, with flowers a little larger than those produced by the species. The improvement, however, is only slight when you consider that the foliage is not usually as fragrant; what is more, because the cross was made with *R. foetida,* a proclivity for black spot was bred in. Nonetheless, these hybrids offer a range of colors, and there are undoubtedly good uses for them in the garden. Hebe's Lip, a later development by William Paul, may be the most refined of the group.

Hybrid Musk Roses
A 20th-century development, the hybrid musk roses are really like big, blowsy, overgrown floribundas. They are so far removed from the influence of the Musk Rose (*Rosa moschata*) that they really should be called hybrid multifloras, for their immediate background is *Rosa multiflora.*

Hybrid musks can be used as big, freestanding bushes or hedges, or trained as low climbers. The blooms are mostly delicate shades that quickly fade to white and give a white effect in the garden even before the color fades. There are a few in deeper tones. As a class these roses are fragrant, and a few of them have the sweet-pea fragrance of *Rosa moschata.*

Hybrid musks have an exceptionally good repeat bloom if they are planted in full sun; when planted in partial shade, they will usually repeat sparingly in the fall. A few varieties have attractive fall hips.

Hybrid Rugosas
Another 20th-century group, the hybrid rugosas are a varied lot. Some have the deeply etched foliage typical of the wild roses, while others do not. Some produce good repeat blooms while others have neither repeat blooms nor good hip displays. None of them has the quality of the species *Rosa rugosa,* from which they are derived; but some are nonetheless outstanding in their own right. Some of the most unusual varieties in the group are borderline winter hardy, which is a great disappointment to those gardeners who live in

severe winter climates and are accustomed to depending on this class when all else fails.

Hybrid Spinosissimas

There are two categories of hybrid spinosissimas. The first includes ancient varieties (notably Stanwell Perpetual) and is grouped with the old garden roses. The second includes the modern shrub hybrid spinosissimas, particularly the Frühlings series developed by Wilhelm Kordes.

These hybrid spinosissimas are upright, arching bushes, rather open and gaunt in habit, with very early blooms. The very large, sweetly fragrant flowers are mostly single, but some varieties are fully double.

The ancient spinosissimas grow in low mounds of ferny foliage, but the modern ones form arching hoops of seven to nine feet, making a tremendous display in early spring.

Polyantha Roses

The early polyantha roses were derived from *Rosa multiflora* and various forms of *Rosa chinensis*. The polyanthas (from the Greek for "many-flowered") started out as everblooming dwarf forms of once-blooming climbing and rambling roses. They are very hardy, and though they are among the last of the rose varieties to come into bloom, they then continue to flower until frost. Polyanthas are neat little shrubs, and they come in many colors of white, pink, red, coral, and orange. They make a bright accent in the garden and can always be depended upon. Some of them are borderline hardy in really severe winter climates, but many of them are rock hardy. Eventually, the polyanthas came to be crossed with various hybrid teas. The resulting roses—the floribundas—soon surpassed the polyanthas in popularity, and the latter tended to be neglected. Because of the explosion of popularity of the miniature roses, polyanthas continue to be neglected today. Fortunately, however, a great many polyanthas have been preserved, and—luckily—they do still have their champions among discriminating gardeners.

Agnes, *p. 129*
(Saunders, 1900)

Agnes is a cross of *Rosa rugosa* with *Rosa foetida persiana* (Persian Yellow), an attempt to breed the yellow color into the rugosa hybrids. This strong bush may repeat bloom when very well established.

Flowers
3-3½ in. (7.5-9 cm) wide. Light yellow. Double; 24-30 petals. Very fragrant. Early to midseason bloom, sometimes recurrent. Cupped form.

Foliage
5 ft. (1.5 m) tall. Upright, vigorous, bushy. Disease resistant and winter hardy. Canes very thorny; leaves dull, dark green.

Alchymist, *p. 127*
(Kordes, 1956)

The apricot-colored Alchymist can be used as a climber, as it is an excellent pillar rose and also does well on a trellis.

Flowers
3½-4 in. (9-10 cm) wide. Apricot blend. Very double; 65-75 petals. Early to midseason bloom, not recurrent. Fragrant. Blossoms have an old garden rose form; sometimes quartered.

Foliage
8-12 ft. (2.4-3.5 m) tall. Upright, vigorous, and arching. Disease resistant, winter hardy. Very thorny canes bear large, dark green, glossy leaves.

Baby Faurax, *p. 120*
(Lille, 1924)

This polyantha variety is good for edgings and accents in the garden, where its deep violet color makes an attractive accent.

Flowers
2 in. (5 cm) wide. Mauve. Double; 18-24 petals. Blooms first at midseason or later, continuous bloom thereafter until frost. Little or no fragrance. Blossoms cupped, in clusters.

Foliage
8–12 in. (20–30 cm) tall. A bushy, dense
dwarf plant. Disease resistant and winter
hardy with dark green, glossy leaves.

Ballerina, *p. 112*
(Bentall, 1937)

With its arching growth, this hybrid musk
makes a good "weeping" standard. The
shape of the plant is reminiscent of a
ballerina's skirt—hence the name.

Flowers
2 in. (5 cm) wide. Pink with a deeper pink
edge and a white center. Yellow stamens
turn dark rather quickly. Single; 5 petals.
Midseason bloom with good repeat bloom.
Slight musky fragrance, like sweet peas.
Blooms in clusters.

Foliage
3–4 ft. (1–1.2 m) tall. Arching growth,
about as wide as high. Disease resistant and
winter hardy. Canes smooth, with few
thorns. Leaves light green, semiglossy.

Belinda, *p. 119*
(Bentall, 1936)

The vigorous Belinda grows dense and
bushy, and it makes a good hedge rose.

Flowers
¾ in. (2 cm) wide. Medium pink.
Semidouble; 12–15 petals. Midseason bloom
with good repeat bloom. Light fragrance.
Blooms in clusters.

Foliage
4–6 ft. (1.2–1.8 m) tall. Upright, vigorous,
bushy, and dense. Disease resistant; winter
hardy. Fairly smooth canes with few thorns
bear light green, semiglossy leaves.

Belle Poitevine, *p. 121*
(Bruant, 1894)

Belle Poitevine is a big, billowing shrub.
Almost always in bloom, it is intensely
fragrant, with an aroma of cloves.

Flowers
3½–4 in. (9–10 cm) wide. Medium pink
with a mauve tint. Semidouble; 18–24 petals.
Profuse early-season bloom followed by good
repeat bloom. Very fragrant; clove-scented.
Blossoms have a cupped form.

Foliage
7–9 ft. (2.1–2.7 m) tall and as wide.
Upright, vigorous, spreading. Disease free
and winter hardy. Very thorny canes bear
medium green, leathery, deeply etched
(rugose) leaves.

Birdie Blye, *p. 120*
(Van Fleet, 1904)

This pink shrub rose has an interesting
parentage; it is the product of tea and
multiflora ancestors.

Flowers
3½–4 in. (9–10 cm) wide. Medium pink.
Double; 24–30 petals. Midseason bloom with
fair repeat bloom. Slight fragrance. Blossoms
cupped, in clusters.

Foliage
4–5 ft. (1.2–1.5 m) tall. Upright, vigorous,
arching. Disease resistant and winter hardy,
with light green, glossy leaves.

Blanc Double de Coubert, *p. 108*
(Cochet-Cochet, 1892)

One of the most popular of the shrub roses.
Deadheading will encourage more blooms,
and removing only the spent petals will
make it possible to enjoy the hips.

Flowers
2½–3 in. (6–7.5 cm) wide. White.
Semidouble; 18–24 petals. Good early to
midseason bloom, followed by fair repeat
bloom. Very fragrant. Rather raggedy spent
blooms hang on, looking limp and dirty.
Good hips later in season.

Foliage
4–6 ft. (1.2–1.8 m) tall. Upright, moderately
vigorous. Disease free and very winter hardy.
Leaves light green and leathery, turning
bright yellow in the fall.

Buff Beauty, *p. 128*
(Pemberton, 1922)

There is very little influence of *Rosa moschata*
in the hybrid musk roses, and they might
better be called hybrid multifloras. Like any
rose, Buff Beauty will grow nicely in partial
shade, but it will bloom well only when
provided with a half-day's sunlight.

Flowers
3 in. (7.5 cm) wide. Apricot, blended with
deep yellow and gold. Double; perhaps
30–40 petals. Midseason bloom with good
repeat bloom. Fragrant. Fully double blooms
reflex into balls.

Foliage
6 ft. (1.8 m) tall. Vigorous, bushy. Disease
resistant. Winter hardy. Canes moderately
thorny. Leaves light to medium green,
semiglossy.

Cécile Brunner, *p. 114*
(Ducher, 1881)

Cécile Brunner is famous as a buttonhole
rose. An exceptionally fine climbing form is
available.

Flowers
1½ in. (4 cm) wide. Light pink. Double.
Profuse late-season bloom with excellent
repeat bloom. Slight fragrance. Blossoms
have a classic hybrid tea form in miniature;
borne in clusters.

Foliage
2½–3 ft. (75–90 cm) tall. Upright, bushy,
spreading. Disease resistant. Not dependably
winter hardy in severe winter climates. Canes
very smooth with few thorns. Abundant,
dark green leaves are small and semiglossy.

China Doll, *p. 117*
(Lammerts, 1946)

Blooming late in the season, this pink
polyantha makes a good low edging.

Flowers
1–2 in. (2.5–5 cm) wide. Medium pink.
Double; 20–26 petals. Blooms first late in

the season, with continuous blooms until
frost. Slight fragrance. Blossoms cupped, in
clusters.

Foliage
1½ ft. (45 cm) tall. Bushy, spreading,
compact. Disease resistant and winter hardy.
Leaves medium green, leathery.

Conrad Ferdinand Meyer, *p. 113*
(Müller, 1899)

The fragrance of this rose is intense and
carrying—it will perfume your whole garden.
The plant requires careful placement, but is a
wonderful rose when it can be grown.

Flowers
3½–4½ in. (9–11.5 cm) wide. Light to
medium pink. Very double; 65–75 petals.
Long, early to midseason bloom, not
recurrent. Intensely fragrant damask, or true-
rose, scent. Full blossoms are globular,
sometimes quartered.

Foliage
9–12 ft. (2.7–3.5 m) tall. Upright and very
vigorous, with rather gaunt canes. Disease
free but not dependably winter hardy. Very
thorny canes with rather sparse, gray-green
leaves.

Constance Spry, *p. 116*
(Austin, 1961)

Named for the English author, floral
designer, and collector of old garden roses,
Constance Spry is a modern shrub rose with
the true old garden rose form and
fragrance.

Flowers
4½–5 in. (11.5–12.5 cm) wide. Light to
medium pink. Double; 45–55 petals. Long
midseason bloom, not recurrent. Very
fragrant scent, like myrrh. Blossoms full,
globular.

Foliage
5–6 ft. (1.5–1.8 m) tall. Upright, vigorous,
arching. Disease resistant and winter hardy.
Moderately thorny canes with dark green,
semiglossy leaves.

Cornelia, *p. 112*
(Pemberton, 1925)

It appears that the rose originally introduced by Pemberton under this name is not the same as the rose sold today. Unless further research turns up the modern rose's true name, experts and novices alike must be content to live with this ambiguity.

Flowers
1 in. (2.5 cm) wide. Medium pink with mauve and yellow tints. Double; 20–30 petals. Midseason bloom with good repeat bloom. Fragrant. Rosette form, in clusters.

Foliage
6–8 ft. (1.8–2.4 m) tall. Vigorous and arching, with a somewhat loose growth habit. Disease resistant and winter hardy. Canes moderately thorny. Leaves medium to dark green, leathery, semiglossy.

Delicata, *p. 121*
(Cooling, 1898)

This clove-scented, mauve-pink hybrid rugosa is a smaller version of Belle Poitevine.

Flowers
3–3½ in. (7.5–9 cm) wide. Mauve-pink. Semidouble; 18–24 petals. Abundant early to midseason bloom, followed by good repeat bloom. Very fragrant, clove scent. Blossom has cupped form.

Foliage
3½–4½ ft. (105–135 cm) tall. Upright, vigorous, well branched, and compact. Disease free and winter hardy. Very thorny canes bear light green, leathery, deeply etched (rugose) leaves.

Elmshorn, *p. 124*
(Kordes, 1951)

Many hardy roses have come from the Kordes firm, which has made this quality a special consideration in the roses they develop.

Flowers
1½ in. (4 cm) wide. Medium red. Double;

20 petals. Midseason bloom with good repeat bloom. Slight fragrance. Blossoms cupped, occurring in clusters.

Foliage
5–6 ft. (1.5–1.8 m) tall. Upright, vigorous, bushy. Disease resistant and winter hardy. Moderately thorny canes with long, medium green, semiglossy leaves.

Erfurt, *p. 119*
(Kordes, 1939)

Erfurt gives somewhat the same garden effect as a single rose, without being a true single. The hybrid musks are arching rather than upright, a characteristic that contributes to the abundance of their blossoms.

Flowers
3½ in. (9 cm) wide. Wide pink edge, lemon-white in center, with yellow stamens. Semidouble; 10–15 petals. Good continuous bloom throughout the season. Intensely fragrant. Bloom opens to become saucer-shaped. Blossoms occur in clusters.

Foliage
5–6 ft. (1.5–1.8 m) tall. Very vigorous, bushy. Disease resistant and winter hardy, with moderately thorny canes. Abundant dark green leaves are large, leathery, and wrinkled.

F. J. Grootendorst, *p. 124*
(de Goey, 1918)

Like carnations and pinks, this rose has petals with serrated edges. F. J. Grootendorst has several color sports.

Flowers
1½ in. (4 cm) wide. Medium red. Double; perhaps 35–45 petals. Profuse midseason bloom followed by good repeat bloom. No fragrance. Petals have serrated edges. Blossoms occur in large clusters.

Foliage
6–8 ft. (1.8–2.4 m) tall. Upright, vigorous, bushy. Disease resistant and winter hardy. Moderately thorny canes bear small, wrinkled, leathery, dark green leaves.

Frau Dagmar Hastrup, *p. 110*
(Unknown, c. 1914)

Also called Frau Dagmar Hartopp, this pink
favorite has an architectural value in the
garden landscape, as it makes an excellent
low hedge. It is beloved of bees.

Flowers
3–3½ in. (7.5–9 cm) wide. Light pink.
Single; 5 petals. Early to midseason bloom
followed by good repeat bloom. Very
fragrant clove scent. Blooms open to become
saucer-shaped with bright golden stamens.
Large, bright red hips appear later in the
season.

Foliage
2½–3 ft. (75–90 cm) tall. Upright, vigorous,
dense, and spreading. Disease free, winter
hardy, with very thorny canes. Leaves
medium green, deeply etched (rugose).

Fred Loads, *p. 127*
(Holmes, 1968)

Winner of the Royal National Rose Society
Gold Medal in 1967, this big, husky bush is
almost always in bloom and is excellent for
garden display.

Flowers
3–3½ in. (7.5–9 cm) wide. Orange.
Semidouble; 12–18 petals. Good all-season
bloom. Little or no fragrance. Blossoms
cupped to saucer-shaped, in clusters.

Foliage
4½–5 ft. (1.3–1.5 m) tall. Upright, vigorous,
well branched. Disease resistant. Winter
hardy. Moderately thorny canes bear dark
green, glossy leaves.

Frühlingsgold, *p. 131*
(Kordes, 1937)

This rose and Frühlingsmorgen are part of a
series developed by Kordes, who used *Rosa
spinosissima,* the Scotch Rose, as a parent.

Flowers
3–3½ in. (7.5–9 cm) wide. Light yellow.
Single; 5 petals. Early-season bloom, not

326

recurrent. Fragrant. Blossom opens to saucer shape with showy golden stamens.

Foliage
5–7 ft. (1.5–2.1 m) tall. Upright, arching, vigorous. Disease free, winter hardy, with moderately thorny canes. Leaves soft, dull, light green.

Frühlingsmorgen, *p. 111*
(Kordes, 1942)

The name of this hybrid spinosissima means "spring morning." This rose is very similar to Frühlingsgold except in the color of the bloom.

Flowers
3–3½ in. (7.5–9 cm) wide. Pink with light yellow at base. Single; 5–7 petals. Profuse early-season bloom, not recurrent. Fragrant. Blossom opens to become saucer-shaped with unusual maroon stamens.

Foliage
5–7 ft. (1.5–2.1 m) tall. Upright, arching, vigorous. Disease free. Winter hardy. Canes moderately thorny; leaves soft, dull, dark green.

Gartendirektor Otto Linne, *p. 122*
(Lambert, 1934)

This bushy variety makes an excellent hedge, and its deep pink blossoms provide a bright touch of color.

Flowers
1½–2 in. (4–5 cm) wide. Deep pink. Double; 25–35 petals. Midseason bloom followed by good repeat bloom. Little or no fragrance. Blossom form cupped, in clusters.

Foliage
3½–4½ ft. (105–135 cm) tall. Upright, bushy, spreading. Disease resistant. Winter hardy. Canes smooth, nearly thornless. Leaves light to medium green, semiglossy.

Goldbusch, *p. 129*
(Kordes, 1954)

Supposedly a hybrid eglanteria, Goldbusch actually has little affinity with that group and is here classed as a shrub.

Flowers
2½–3 in. (6–7.5 cm) wide. Medium yellow, becoming paler on edges. Double; 24–30 petals. Mid- to late-season bloom, with good repeat bloom. Fragrant. Open, cupped form. Blossoms occur in clusters.

Foliage
5 ft. (1.5 m) tall. Upright, vigorous, bushy. Disease resistant. Winter hardy. Moderately thorny canes bear light green, semiglossy leaves.

Golden Wings, *p. 130*
(Shepherd, 1956)

Winner of the American Rose Society National Gold Medal Certificate in 1958, Golden Wings is almost the earliest rose to bloom and remains in flower longest of all roses. A favorite of bees, it is also popular with people, and is considered the most valuable of landscape roses.

Flowers
4–5 in. (10–12.5 cm) wide. Light yellow. Single; 5 petals. Excellent all-season bloom. Slight fragrance. Blooms open to become saucer-shaped, revealing golden stamens.

Foliage
4½–5½ ft. (1.4–1.7 m) tall. Upright, vigorous, well branched. Disease resistant. Winter hardy except in very severe winter climates. Canes moderately thorny. Leaves dull, light green.

Hansa, *p. 122*
(Schaum & Van Tol, 1905)

Growing in a bushy, dense fashion, this hybrid rugosa is popular because of its architectural value in the garden.

Flowers
3–3½ in. (7.5–9 cm) wide. Red-violet.

Double; perhaps 35–45 petals. Early to
midseason bloom with good repeat bloom.
Fragrant; clove-scented. Bloom form rather
loose, cupped. Large red hips appear later in
the season.

Foliage
5 ft. (1.5 m) tall. Upright, vigorous, bushy,
dense. Disease resistant and winter hardy.
Canes very thorny. Leaves dark green, deeply
etched (rugose).

Happy, *p. 125*
(De Ruiter, 1954)

Named Alberich in Europe, this polyantha is
a good repeat bloomer.

Flowers
1½–2 in. (4.5–5 cm) wide. Medium red.
Double; 24–30 petals. Midseason bloom with
good repeat. Little or no fragrance. Cupped
blossoms occur in clusters.

Foliage
1½–2 ft. (45–60 cm) tall. Upright, well
branched, and compact. Disease resistant and
winter hardy. Leaves dark green, glossy.

Harison's Yellow, *p. 131*
(Harison, 1830)

This popular shrub rose has bright yellow
flowers that hold their color. After the
flowers have bloomed, the ferny foliage
remains healthy and attractive.

Flowers
2–2½ in. (5–6 cm) wide. Deep yellow.
Double; 20–24 petals. Very early-season
bloom, not recurrent. Blooms cupped with
showy golden stamens. Blossoms occur along
arching canes.

Foliage
5–7 ft. (1.5–2.1 m) tall. Upright, spreading,
arching habit. Disease resistant. Winter
hardy. Canes dark mahogany-brown, very
thorny. Leaves small, abundant, light to
medium green, ferny.

Hebe's Lip, *p. 110*
(Paul, 1912)

Also called Reine Blanche and Rubrotincta,
this hybrid eglanteria probably has a damask
rose in its ancestry. A smaller plant than is
typical for its class.

Flowers
3 in. (7.5 cm) wide. Creamy white,
margined with red. Semidouble; 12–15
petals. Early, profuse bloom does not repeat.
Moderate rose fragrance. Fat, pointed buds
are tipped with red, opening to flat, white
blooms, tipped in red on outer petals. Showy
golden stamens.

Foliage
4 ft. (1.2 m) tall. Upright, bushy, and
moderately vigorous. Disease free and winter
hardy. Canes moderately thorny. Leaves dull,
dark green, with a fragrance of apples.

La Marne, *p. 116*
(Barbier, 1915)

An example of the wide diversity to be
found among the polyanthas. In the South,
La Marne has good color only in the spring
and fall.

Flowers
1½–2 in. (4–5 cm) wide. White, edged with
pink. Single; 5 petals. Midseason to late-
season bloom, with good repeat bloom.
Little or no fragrance. Blooms in large, loose
clusters.

Foliage
1½–2 ft. (45–60 cm) tall. Bushy, compact.
Disease resistant. Winter hardy. Leaves
medium green, glossy.

Lavender Lassie, *p. 123*
(Kordes, 1960)

Very often the name of a rose expresses what
the breeder was trying to achieve, rather
than the reality of the rose itself. Reports
from many sections of the country confirm
that Lavender Lassie is really a pure, even,
medium pink.

Flowers
3 in. (7.5 cm) wide. Medium pink; said to
have lilac shadings in some regions.
Semidouble; 20–30 petals. Midseason bloom
with good repeat bloom. Very fragrant.
Cup-shaped blossoms, in clusters.

Foliage
5–7 ft. (1.5–2.1 m) tall. Upright, vigorous,
bushy. Disease resistant. Winter hardy. Canes
smooth with few thorns. Leaves abundant,
large, medium green.

Maigold, *p. 130*
(Kordes, 1953)

This bushy, deep yellow rose is excellent for
a shrub border.

Flowers
4 in. (10 cm) wide. Deep yellow.
Semidouble; 14 petals. Early to midseason
bloom, not recurrent. Very fragrant. Cupped
form.

Foliage
5 ft. (1.5 m) tall. Upright, vigorous, bushy.
Disease resistant and winter hardy. Leaves
medium green, glossy.

Margo Koster, *p. 126*
(Koster, 1931)

Perhaps the most popular of the dwarf
polyantha roses, Margo Koster has sported
many times, and is itself a sport of Dick
Koster. A climbing form is available.

Flowers
1–1½ in. (2.5–4 cm) wide. Coral. Almost
single; 7–12 petals. Late-season bloom with
excellent repeat bloom. Slight fragrance.
Blossoms cup-shaped, in clusters.

Foliage
1 ft. (30 cm) tall. Bushy, compact. Disease
resistant. Winter hardy. Canes very smooth
with few thorns. Leaves medium gray-green,
semiglossy.

Marguerite Hilling, *p. 118*
(Hilling, 1959)

A pink sport of Nevada. Marguerite Hilling's
red canes will enliven the gray landscape of
winter in your garden.

Flowers
4 in. (10 cm) wide. Light to deep pink.
Single; 5 petals. Midseason bloom with
excellent repeat bloom. Little or no
fragrance. Form open, saucer-shaped.

Foliage
6–8 ft. (1.8–2.4 m) tall. Upright, arching,
bushy. Disease resistant. Winter hardy. Canes
red, with few thorns. Leaves small, gray-
green, semiglossy.

Nevada, *p. 111*
(Dot, 1927)

This beautiful shrub rose is reportedly a
moyesii hybrid, but many authorities have
questioned this attribution. Nevada is
supposedly sterile, but interested gardeners
may want to try to germinate seeds from the
occasional orange hips.

Flowers
3½–4 in. (9–10 cm) wide. White. Single;
5 petals. Midseason bloom with excellent
repeat bloom. Little or no fragrance. Bloom
form open, saucer-shaped, with yellow
stamens. Blossoms may be tinged with pink
in the fall.

Foliage
6–8 ft. (1.8–2.4 m) tall. Upright, arching,
bushy. Disease resistant and winter hardy.
Canes are red, with few thorns. Leaves small,
gray-green, semiglossy.

Nymphenburg, *p. 117*
(Kordes, 1954)

This is one of the most beautiful and
fragrant roses in its class. Unfortunately, it
cannot be counted on for hardiness.

Flowers
4 in. (10 cm) wide. Salmon with yellow at
base, brushed with pink at petal edges.

Semidouble; 18–24 petals. Very fragrant.
Midseason bloom with good repeat bloom.
Cupped blossoms occur in clusters.

Foliage
8 ft. (2.4 m) tall. Upright, vigorous, well
branched. Disease resistant. Not reliably
winter hardy in severe winter climates. Canes
very smooth, with few thorns. Leaves large,
medium green, glossy.

Orange Triumph, *p. 125*
(Kordes, 1937)

This polyantha claimed the Royal National
Rose Society Gold Medal in 1937. Actually a
medium red, Orange Triumph illustrates the
tendency of breeders to name a rose variety
for their hopes rather than reality.

Flowers
1–1½ in. (2.5–4 cm) wide. Medium red.
Semidouble; 18–24 petals. Late-season bloom
followed by good repeat bloom. Little or no
fragrance. Blossoms cupped, in clusters.

Foliage
1½–2 ft. (45–60 cm) tall. Upright, vigorous,
compact. Disease resistant. Winter hardy.
Moderately thorny canes bear dark green,
glossy leaves.

Penelope, *p. 108*
(Pemberton, 1924)

Penelope makes an excellent hedge, and the
very pale coral-pink blossoms give a white
effect. The hips are quite unusual—not
spectacular, but pleasing.

Flowers
3 in. (7.5 cm) wide. Pale coral-pink, fading
to blush. Semidouble; 18–24 petals.
Midseason bloom with good repeat,
particularly in fall. Very fragrant. Blossoms,
in clusters, become cup-shaped. Hips
appear in fall; green, turning coral-pink.

Foliage
5–7 ft. (1.5–2.1 m) tall. Upright, bushy,
dense. Disease resistant and winter hardy.
Moderately thorny canes support medium
green, dense, semiglossy leaves.

Pink Grootendorst, *p. 115*
(Grootendorst, 1923)

This is a color sport of the red variety, F. J. Grootendorst.

Flowers
1½ in. (4 cm) wide. Medium pink. Double; perhaps 35–45 petals. Profuse midseason bloom followed by good repeat bloom. No fragrance. Petals have serrated edges, like carnations. Blooms in large clusters.

Foliage
5–6 ft. (1.5–1.8 m) tall. Upright, vigorous, bushy. Disease resistant. Winter hardy. Moderately thorny canes with small, wrinkled, leathery, dark green leaves.

Robin Hood, *p. 118*
(Pemberton, 1927)

Robin Hood is widely used as a hedge rose—a purpose to which it, like many other hybrid musk roses, is well suited.

Flowers
¾ in. (2 cm) wide. Light red. Semidouble; 18–24 petals. Midseason bloom with excellent repeat bloom. Moderate fragrance. Blooms in large clusters.

Foliage
5–7 ft. (1.5–2.1 m) tall. Upright, vigorous, bushy, dense. Disease resistant and winter hardy. Canes moderately thorny. Leaves medium green, semiglossy.

Roseraie de l'Haÿ, *p. 123*
(Cochet-Cochet, 1901)

This large, fragrant hybrid rugosa is named for a famous French rose garden.

Flowers
4–4½ in. (10–11.5 cm) wide. Dark reddish purple. Semidouble; perhaps 18–24 petals. Blooms very early in season, with occasional repeats. Very fragrant. Blossoms loosely cupped.

Foliage
7–9 ft. (2.1–2.7 m) tall. Upright, sturdy,

treelike. Disease free and winter hardy. Canes thorny with gray bark. Leaves large, dark green, deeply etched (rugose).

Sarah Van Fleet, *p. 113*
(Van Fleet, 1926)

This is a very fragrant hybrid rugosa that will form quite a good hedge.

Flowers
3–3½ in. (7.5–9 cm) wide. Medium pink. Semidouble; 18–24 petals. Early to midseason bloom, followed by good repeat bloom. Very fragrant. Blossoms cupped, with showy yellow stamens.

Foliage
6–8 ft. (1.8–2.4 m) tall. Upright, vigorous, bushy. Disease resistant and winter hardy. Canes thorny, with dark green, leathery, deeply etched (rugose) leaves.

Schneezwerg, *p. 109*
(Lambert, 1912)

Also called Snowdwarf, Schneezwerg makes an excellent hedge. Its orange-red hips are smaller than those of most other hybrid rugosas.

Flowers
3–3½ in. (7.5–9 cm) wide. White. Semidouble; 18–24 petals. Abundant early to midseason bloom followed by good repeat bloom. Slight fragrance. Bloom opens flat, showing light yellow stamens. Orange-red hips.

Foliage
5 ft. (1.5 m) tall and as wide. Vigorous, spreading, bushy. Disease free and winter hardy, with very thorny canes. Leaves light to medium green, deeply etched (rugose).

Sea Foam, *p. 109*
(Schwartz, 1964)

Sea Foam captured the Rome Gold Medal in 1963 and the American Rose Society David Fuerstenberg Prize in 1968. It makes an excellent ground cover, perfect for rough areas and for trailing down embankments.

Flowers
2–2½ in. (5–6 cm) wide. Light pink, fading to white. Double. Midseason bloom with excellent repeat bloom. Slight fragrance. Blossoms cupped, in clusters.

Foliage
8–12 ft. (2.4–3.5 m) long. Vigorous trailer; can be trained upright. Disease resistant and winter hardy. Moderately thorny canes with abundant, small, leathery, glossy leaves.

Sparrieshoop, *p. 114*
(Kordes, 1953)

A beautiful and popular rose, Sparrieshoop has fragrant, single blooms.

Flowers
4 in. (10 cm) wide. Light pink. Single; 5 petals. Good midseason bloom with fair repeat bloom. Very fragrant. Blossoms open to saucer shape, with golden stamens. Blooms in clusters.

Foliage
5 ft. (1.5 m) tall. Upright, very vigorous, bushy. Disease resistant and winter hardy. Leaves medium green, leathery.

The Fairy, *p. 115*
(Bentall, 1932)

Roses—even individual cultivars—are to a degree variable, although some rose specialists feel that this variability may reflect a lack of precision in the labelling of certain plants. The Fairy is sometimes encountered as a ground-hugging trailer, and in other instances as an upright hedge.

Flowers
1–1½ in. (2.5–4 cm) wide. Medium pink. Double; 24–30 petals. Late-season bloom, followed by excellent repeat bloom. Little or no fragrance. Blossoms cupped, in clusters.

Foliage
1½–2 ft. (45–60 cm) tall. Upright, bushy, compact. Disease resistant and winter hardy.

Moderately thorny canes bear tiny, abundant
leaves that are light to medium green and
glossy.

Westerland, *p. 128*
(Kordes, 1969)

Growing upright and well branched, this
shrub rose makes an excellent pillar,
colorfully enhanced by the bright apricot
blooms.

Flowers
3 in. (7.5 cm) wide. Apricot blend. Double;
20 petals. Long midseason bloom. Very
fragrant. Blossoms somewhat like those of
hybrid teas, but not high-centered.

Foliage
5–6 ft. (1.5–1.8 m) tall. Upright, vigorous,
well branched. Disease resistant and winter
hardy, with moderately thorny canes. Leaves
dark green, semiglossy.

Will Scarlet, *p. 126*
(Hilling, 1948)

A lighter colored sport, or mutation, of the
cultivar Skyrocket, Will Scarlet has attractive
hips.

Flowers
3 in. (7.5 cm) wide. Light red. Semidouble;
24–30 petals. Midseason bloom with good
repeat bloom. Moderate fragrance. Blossoms
open to become cup-shaped, in clusters.

Foliage
6 ft. (1.8 m) tall. Upright, vigorous, bushy.
Disease resistant and winter hardy, with
moderately thorny canes and medium to
dark green leaves.

Old Garden

Forming a very large class, the old garden roses have been in cultivation since before the development of the modern kinds. Many of these roses are still available today, and they are regaining the popularity that they had begun to lose to the hybrid perpetuals in the 19th century.

The question of which subgroups to include under the old garden rose heading has been much debated by rose authorities. Some feel the old European garden roses, those in cultivation before the advent of the China and tea roses, should remain in a class by themselves. This arrangement would exclude the Bourbon roses and the hybrid perpetuals, but not the Portland roses. Other experts point out that the China and tea roses were themselves among the most ancient of garden roses, and believe they should be included within the old garden rose designation, along with the roses that developed from combining European and Chinese roses.

Here we recognize the following subclasses of old garden roses, distinguished chiefly by their parentage: alba, Bourbon, centifolia, China, damask, gallica, hybrid perpetual, hybrid spinosissima, moss, Noisette, Portland, and tea roses.

It is possible to assign categories based on ancestry, and when ancestry is very mixed, on flower and plant habit, but it is not possible to assign a date before which every rose was "old-fashioned," and after which "modern." We do it for convenience, but it can only be arbitrary. The American Rose Society has settled on the date of 1867—the introduction date of La France, one of the early hybrid teas—as the dividing line. All roses belonging to a class established before that date are designated as old garden roses; all roses belonging to a class established after that date are considered modern roses.

For purposes of exhibition, the American Rose Society recognizes only those varieties of old garden roses that were in existence prior to 1867, making many individual varieties introduced after 1867 ineligible for the higher prizes and awards—even though they may be pure to their type.

Alba Roses

Producing white and pale pink blooms, the alba roses include forms and descendants of *Rosa alba,* which is itself believed to be a natural hybrid of *R. gallica* and *R. canina.* However, this genealogy is just guesswork. Until science can analyze genetic material in such a way as to determine ancestry, that of the albas is lost in the mists of time. Alba roses are very tall and upright. The foliage is soft and downy, and the canes are rather thorny. Like all old garden roses, albas are extremely fragrant. In every case they are once-blooming.

Bourbon Roses

A natural hybrid, *Rosa borboniana* was discovered on the Isle of Bourbon (now Reunion Island), where farmers hedged their fields

Roses

with China and damask roses—its parents. Seeds and plants of the new rose were sent back to France, where new varieties were soon developed and Bourbon roses became popular garden flowers. Taller and more vigorous than either parent, and with a much larger bloom, the moderately hardy Bourbons are much more shapely than the China and more recurrent than the damasks.

Centifolia Roses

Believed to have been developed in Holland during the 17th and 18th centuries, and found also in the Provence region of France, the centifolia (*Rosa centifolia*) is considered to be the youngest of the true old garden roses. The varieties and hybrids were popular garden roses in the late 18th and early 19th centuries.

Centifolia roses have very full-petaled double flowers; they are once-blooming. The large outer petals enclose many tightly packed inner petals, often with a button center, often quartered. The perfume is intense.

The very thorny, long, sparsely foliaged canes spring up in all directions; very few centifolia varieties grow into a full, dense bush.

China and Tea Roses

European explorers of the late 1700s and early 1800s collected some very important China roses and tea-scented China roses. Unlike European roses, Chinas and teas were capable of dependable repeat flowering.

The original China roses were mostly dwarf bushes. The blooms, which are rather loosely cup-shaped, tend to darken in the sun instead of fading, and they shatter cleanly when fully expanded and aged. (Thus the early Chinas came to be known as the aristocrats of the roses, because they knew how to die gracefully.)

Chinas bloom almost continually during the growing season, and bear very smooth stems and leaves. They are not very winter hardy, but being fairly small plants may be grown in pots indoors in the winter.

The tea roses, whether dwarf bushes or rampant climbers, have loosely cupped blooms in delicate shades and blends of white, pink, and pale yellow. They are very smooth, with glossy leaves and few real thorns. Like Chinas, they bloom nearly all season long.

The teas are the roses that, crossed with the hybrid perpetuals, gave us our reliably repeat-flowering hybrid teas.

Damask Roses

Hybrids of *Rosa damascena,* the damask roses—along with the gallicas—are among the most ancient of garden roses. Known to the Romans, the damasks were pruned and grown in heated houses so that they would bloom out of season. Grown throughout the Roman Empire, they would have died out in medieval times had it not been for the hundreds of monasteries across Europe, where roses

Old Garden Roses

and many other flowers were grown for medicinal purposes and thus preserved.

Damasks require careful cultivation. They are mostly very thorny shrubs, with blooms in clusters of three or five; some varieties are repeat bloomers. The cup-shaped, intensely fragrant flowers sometimes cannot open fully because of the tight clusters.

Gallica Roses

Like the damasks, the gallica roses were cultivated by the Romans, who took them to the farthest reaches of their empire. After the fall of Rome, gallica roses became established wherever they had been planted—a process that continues today.

Rosa gallica crossbred readily and also sported prolifically. Varieties appeared in deep shades of pink, sometimes striped or mottled with lighter pink, sometimes shading into lavender and violet; some of the deepest of purples are also found among the gallicas. All these shades of rich color are enhanced by showy yellow or golden-yellow stamens.

Tidy, neat, upright roses that hold their flowers poised aloft, gallicas are fragrant—remarkably more so when the petals are dried. Gallicas are once-blooming and produce attractive hips later in the season.

Hybrid Perpetuals

The forerunners of our modern hybrid teas, the hybrid perpetuals are of mixed ancestry, descended mainly from teas, Bourbons, and Portlands. They were the popular garden rose from 1840 to 1880, but were cultivated before that time and continued to be developed long afterwards; many varieties continued to be widely grown into the 1920s.

The hybrid perpetuals can be divided into three groups. The first and earliest varieties strongly resemble the old garden rose form, with tightly packed central petals surrounded by larger outer guard petals, sometimes quartered, with a button center. The second stage gave rise to roses with very full, globular blooms; some of the largest blooms ever developed belong to this group. In the third stage of development, some hybrid perpetuals began to take on the characteristics of the modern hybrid tea, and while usually fuller than today's typical hybrid tea, resemble it in every other way, having the long central petals that give it its distinctive form.

Hybrid Spinosissimas

Also known as Scotch, burnet, and pimpinellifolia roses, the hybrid spinosissimas are varieties of *R. spinosissima*. Most roses of this lineage are shrub roses, but some of the older varieties are ancient and thus classed as old garden roses.

The Scotch roses were ferny, low-growing shrubs, with surprisingly well-formed blooms. The most notable variety, and the only one that currently produces a good repeat bloom, is Stanwell Perpetual, which was introduced into commerce in 1838 by Lee. This rose produces a large, full, beautifully formed bloom on a ferny mound of foliage. No long straight stems here, but a delightful fragrance.

Moss Roses

These roses are a single group derived from two sources: those that sported from the centifolias and those that sported from the damask perpetuals. It is easy to tell the difference between the roses in these two categories, because the former have heavy green moss on calyx and stems, while the latter have rather sparse, brownish moss, and bloom a second time in the fall.

Moss roses were very popular during Victorian times. The mossy buds yield a pine scent when touched, further enhancing the pleasure of the intensely fragrant, fully double bloom with its tightly packed petals. The mossy side buds, with their long, fringed sepals, make a finished picture surrounding the open bloom.

Noisette Roses

Early in the 1800s, a wealthy American planter and gardening enthusiast by the name of Champneys developed a repeat-blooming climber from a cross between China and musk roses. This was Champneys' Pink Cluster. Champneys' friend, a nurseryman named Noisette, sent it to his brother in France, who developed many more varieties; these became known as Noisette roses. Most Noisettes were developed in the first half of the 19th century. They flourished in warm climates but lacked winter hardiness, so they never became popular except in those areas best suited to them.

Portland Roses

Sometimes called damask perpetuals, the Portland roses are descended from the autumn damask, gallica, and China roses. They represent the direction nurserymen were taking in the early 19th century to develop repeat-blooming roses. This effort was abandoned when Chinas and tea-scented Chinas, dependable repeat bloomers, became widely available.

The Portland roses reached their peak of popularity in the third quarter of the 19th century. Today, the varieties are few, but those Portlands that have survived show very good repeat blooming characteristics. They are neat, rounded bushes, with the smooth stems and foliage granted by their China ancestry. The fully double blooms have short stems, so that they nestle among their leaves. They are very fragrant and when fully expanded the outer petals curl in on themselves, creating fluffy balls.

Alfred de Dalmas, *p. 143*
(Portemer, 1855)

Like other perpetual damask mosses, Alfred de Dalmas has a repeat bloom in the fall.

Flowers
2½–3 in. (6–7.5 cm) wide. Light blush pink, fading to white. Double; 55–65 petals. Midseason bloom with fair repeat bloom. Fragrant. Cupped blossom form. Sparse, brownish moss on calyx and stems. Blooms in clusters.

Foliage
2½–3 ft. (75–90 cm) tall. Upright, bushy, spreading. Disease resistant and winter hardy. Canes very bristly, with rough, gray-green leaves.

American Beauty, *p. 167*
(Ledechaux, 1875)

This famous greenhouse rose is named Madame Ferdinand Jamain in Europe. A later, or third-stage, example of hybrid perpetual development, it is identical in many important characteristics to the hybrid teas of today.

Flowers
5–6 in. (12.5–15 cm) wide. Deep pink. Double; 50 petals. Midseason bloom with fair repeat bloom in the fall. Very fragrant. Bloom form full, globular, tending toward the classic high center of the hybrid teas.

Foliage
5–6 ft. (1.5–1.8 m) tall. Vigorous, upright. Disease resistant and winter hardy. Canes fairly smooth, with few thorns. Leaves medium to dark green, semiglossy.

Archduke Charles, *p. 158*
(Laffay, 1840)

As with China roses, the color of Archduke Charles intensifies, rather than fades, in sunlight.

Flowers
2½–3 in. (6–7.5 cm) wide. Pink blended with white, becoming medium red. Double;

perhaps 35–40 petals. Good all-season bloom. Blossoms rather loose, informally shaped.

Foliage
2–3 ft. (60–90 cm) tall. Moderately vigorous, bushy. Disease resistant, but tender. Smooth, reddish canes bear a few large red thorns. Leaves smooth, red when young; rather sparse and glossy.

Baron Girod de l'Ain, *p. 173*
(Reverchon, 1897)

At some seasons the white deckle edging of Baron Girod de l'Ain is hardly noticeable; at others it is quite marked. A distinctly beautiful rose either way, it is a sport of Eugène Fürst.

Flowers
4 in. (10 cm) wide. Medium red, tipped white. Double; 35–40 petals. Good midseason bloom with fair repeat bloom in the fall. Fragrant. Blossom form cupped; when fully expanded, outer row of petals assumes a saucer shape, while central petals remain cupped.

Foliage
4–5 ft. (1.2–1.5 m) tall. Upright, vigorous, well branched. Disease resistant and winter hardy. Canes moderately thorny. Leaves medium to dark green, semiglossy.

Baronne Prévost, *p. 165*
(Despres, 1842)

This pink rose is an early hybrid perpetual of the old garden rose type, representing the first stage of development of the class. The larger outer petals enclose many tightly packed, shorter central petals.

Flowers
3½–4 in. (9–10 cm) wide. Medium pink. Fully double; perhaps 100 petals. Good midseason bloom with good repeat bloom in the fall. Fragrant. Old garden rose bloom form, full and quartered.

Foliage
4–6 ft. (1.2–1.8 m) tall. Upright, vigorous, bushy. Disease resistant and winter hardy.

Canes very thorny, with rough, dark green
leaves.

Baroness Rothschild, *p. 155*
(Pernet Père, 1868)

Also known as Baronne Adolphe de
Rothschild, this rose is a sport of Souvenir
de la Reine d'Angleterre.

Flowers
5½–6 in. (13.8–15 cm) wide. Light pink.
Double; 40 petals. Profuse midseason bloom
with fair repeat bloom in fall. Very fragrant.
Bloom form very full, globular.

Foliage
4–6 ft. (1.2–1.8 m) tall. Upright, vigorous,
well branched. Disease resistant and winter
hardy. Canes quite smooth with few thorns.
Leaves light to medium green, semiglossy.

Belle Amour, *p. 148*
(Ancient)

Said to have been discovered at a convent at
Elboeuf in Germany, Belle Amour is
believed to be a cross between an alba and a
damask rose.

Flowers
3½ in. (9 cm) wide. Light pink.
Semidouble; 20–30 petals. Profuse early-
season bloom. Intensely fragrant; spicy scent
mixed with a faint bitterness, said to
resemble myrrh. Very symmetrical,
camellialike form, opening to show bright
yellow stamens. Round red hips appear later
in the season.

Foliage
5–6 ft. (1.5–1.8 m) tall. Upright, vigorous,
bushy. Disease free and winter hardy. Canes
moderately thorny. Leaves rough, dull,
blue-green.

Belle de Crècy, *p. 171*
(Unknown; 1848)

Named for Madame de Pompadour, this rose
is said to have been grown in her garden at

her estate at Crècy. The violet tones develop very quickly, so blooms of pink and shades of mauve occur in fresh condition on the bush at the same time.

Flowers
2½–3 in. (6-7.5 cm) wide. Pink, turning mauve. Very double; perhaps 200 petals. Long midseason bloom, not recurrent. Very fragrant. Very full, evenly petaled bloom with green pip at center; reflexes into a ball on full expansion.

Foliage
3½–4½ ft. (105-135 cm) tall. Upright, vigorous, rounded, and compact. Disease resistant and winter hardy. Canes bristly but not thorny, with rough, dull, medium to dark green leaves.

Belle Isis, *p. 149*
(Parmentier, 1845)

All the gallica roses developed in the 19th century must be considered late or "modern" developments in a class that goes back to Roman times and beyond—undoubtedly into prehistory.

Flowers
2½–3 in. (6-7.5 cm) wide. Light pink. Double; perhaps 45-55 petals. Midseason bloom, not recurrent. Fragrant. Blossom cupped, well filled with tightly packed petals.

Foliage
2½–3 ft. (75-105 cm) tall. Compact, rounded, bushy. Disease resistant and winter hardy. Canes bristly but not thorny, with small, gray-green leaves.

Blush Noisette, *p. 141*
(Noisette, 1817)

This tall, pale Noisette is a blush to white seedling of Champneys' Pink Cluster.

Flowers
2 in. (5 cm) wide. Blush white. Double; 24 petals. Midseason bloom with excellent repeat bloom. Very fragrant. Cupped form, blooming in clusters.

Foliage
8–12 ft. (2.4–3.5 m) tall. Upright, vigorous,
arching. Disease resistant, but tender. Canes
very smooth with few thorns. Leaves light
green, glossy.

Boule de Neige, *p. 139*
(Lacharme, 1867)

This Bourbon rose is aptly named—"boule
de neige" is French for "snowball." When
the bloom is fully expanded, the outer petals
curl in, giving the impression of a great
white ball.

Flowers
2½–3½ in. (6–9 cm) wide. Pink buds open
to creamy white blooms. Double; perhaps
100 petals. Long midseason bloom with
good repeat bloom. Fragrant. Fully expanded
blooms reflex into a ball.

Foliage
4–5 ft. (1.2–1.5 m) tall. Upright, slender
growth. Disease resistant and winter hardy,
with moderately thorny canes and dark
green, leathery leaves.

Camaieux, *p. 179*
(Unknown; 1830)

The foliage of Camaieux, like that of other
gallicas, is susceptible to mildew in some
areas, especially in the South. In other
regions, however, the problem is minimal or
even absent.

Flowers
3–3½ in. (7.5–9 cm) wide. Blush with even,
deep pink stripes; fading to white and
mauve. Double; perhaps 65 petals. Fragrant.
Blooms early to midseason; no repeat. Very
evenly petaled, full, cupped, camellialike
blossoms. Hips appear later in season.

Foliage
3–3½ ft. (90–105 cm) tall. Upright,
rounded, compact. Disease resistant, but
prone to mildew in South. Winter hardy.
Bristly canes, with few thorns, bear medium
green leaves.

Cardinal de Richelieu, *p. 169*
(Laffay, 1840)

The blooms of this rose are deepest in color of all gallica roses. On an overcast day, very deep midnight blue tones are prevalent; on sunny days the flower is a rich purple. Some authorities point to a possible China rose influence in this variety.

Flowers
2½–3 in. (6–7.5 cm) wide. Purple with white at base. Double; perhaps 35–45 petals. Midseason bloom, not recurrent. Fragrant. Loosely cupped form.

Foliage
2½–3 ft. (75–105 cm) tall. Upright, compact. Disease resistant and winter hardy. Canes moderately thorny with small, dark green, semiglossy leaves.

Celestial, *p. 153*
(Ancient)

Also called Celeste. Like other albas, the pale blossoms of this rose have an intense, sweet fragrance.

Flowers
3½ in. (9 cm) wide. Light blush pink. Semidouble; 20–25 petals. Early blooming, not recurrent. Very sweetly fragrant. Evenly petaled, camellialike, cupped form, showing yellow stamens.

Foliage
4½–5 ft. (1.4–1.5 m) tall and as wide. Upright, vigorous, bushy. Disease free and winter hardy. Canes quite smooth for an alba, with few thorns. Leaves rough, dull, grayish blue-green.

Celine Forestier, *p. 135*
(Trouillard, 1842)

This cultivar was a later development of the Noisette roses, bringing yellow into the class.

Flowers
2–2½ in. (5–6 cm) wide. Light yellow. Double; 24 petals. Midseason bloom with

excellent repeat bloom. Very fragrant.
Cupped blossoms occur in clusters.

Foliage
10–15 ft. (3–4.5 m) tall. Upright, vigorous,
arching. Disease resistant but tender. Canes
fairly smooth with few thorns. Leaves
medium green, semiglossy.

Celsiana, *p. 154*
(Before 1750)

A neat, upright damask, Celsiana is perfect
for the beginner. Some people consider it
ideal for small gardens as well, although
others contend that it is too vigorous for a
limited space.

Flowers
3½–4 in. (9–10 cm) wide. Light pink.
Semidouble; 12–18 petals. Long midseason
bloom, not recurrent. Intensely fragrant.
Bloom opens to wide cupped form, showing
golden stamens. A few long, tubular red hips
later in the season.

Foliage
3½–4 ft. (105–120 cm) tall. Upright,
vigorous, forming an open clump. Disease
free and winter hardy. Moderately thorny
canes bear soft, dull, light green leaves.

Champneys' Pink Cluster, *p. 140*
(Champneys; date uncertain)

The forerunner of the Noisette class,
Champneys' Pink Cluster was an American
invention, the result of crossing China and
musk roses.

Flowers
2 in. (5 cm) wide. Medium pink. Double;
24 petals. Midseason bloom with excellent
repeat bloom. Very fragrant. Cupped form,
blooming in clusters.

Foliage
8–12 ft. (2.4–3.5 m) tall. Upright, vigorous,
arching. Disease resistant; tender. Canes very
smooth with few thorns. Leaves light green,
glossy.

Charles de Mills, *p. 177*
(Unknown; probably 19th century)

By reputation a magenta rose, Charles de Mills has been known to occur in shades of maroon, crimson, purple, wine, and violet. Although no date of origin has been turned up, experts believe that this is a 19th-century gallica.

Flowers
3–3½ in. (7.5–9 cm) wide. Magenta. Very double; perhaps 200 petals. Midseason bloom, not recurrent. Fragrant. Very full, very evenly petaled bloom with swirled petals; flat-topped before expansion, as if sliced off.

Foliage
4½–5 ft. (1.4–1.5 m) tall. Upright, vigorous, bushy, compact. Disease resistant and winter hardy. Moderately bristly canes have few thorns. Leaves rough, medium green.

Chloris, *p. 146*
(Ancient)

As with all albas, the size of the blossoms of this rose will increase with judicious pruning and enriched soil. But the abundance of flowers will not decrease with neglect.

Flowers
3½ in. (9 cm) wide. Soft light pink. Very double; perhaps more than 200 petals. Early blooming, not recurrent. Intense, sweet fragrance. Very full blossom with button center.

Foliage
5–6 ft. (1.5–1.8 m) tall. Upright, vigorous, about two-thirds as wide as tall. Disease free and winter hardy. Canes very smooth with few thorns. Leaves soft, medium green, with a less pronounced bluish tint than is usual with albas.

Commandant Beaurepaire, *p. 179*
(Moreau-Robert, 1874)

This spectacular striped rose is unusual because its white, blush, light pink, and

scarlet stripes and splashes appear against a
deep pink ground.

Flowers
3–3½ in. (7.5–9 cm) wide. Pink striped
with red and white. Double; perhaps 35–45
petals. Blooms in midseason with sparse
repeat bloom. Fragrant.

Foliage
4–5 ft. (1.2–1.5 m) tall. Upright, vigorous.
Disease resistant and winter hardy. Canes
very smooth with few thorns; leaves long,
smooth, light green.

Common Moss, *p. 154*
(Unknown; 1696)

This famous centifolia moss is also known as
Communis, *Rosa centifolia muscosa,* and Old
Pink Moss.

Flowers
3 in. (7.5 cm) wide. Light to medium pink.
Double; perhaps 200 petals. Midseason
bloom, not recurrent. Very fragrant. Very
full bloom with tightly packed petals; usually
quartered, with a button center. Heavy moss
on calyx, stem, and long, fringed sepals. The
green moss is sticky and pine scented.

Foliage
5–7 ft. (1.5–2.1 m) tall. Upright, vigorous,
arching, open growth. Disease resistant and
winter hardy. Canes very bristly and thorny.
Leaves rough, dark green, rather sparse.

Complicata, *p. 167*
(Unknown)

A gallica hybrid of uncertain antecedents,
Complicata may be the progeny of *Rosa
canina* or *R. macrantha.*

Flowers
4–4½ in. (10–11.5 cm) wide. Medium pink
with white at base. Single; 5 petals.
Midseason bloom, not recurrent. Fragrant.
Bloom opens flat, showing golden stamens.

Foliage
5 ft. (1.5 m) tall and as wide. Dense,
vigorous, arching. Disease resistant and

winter hardy. Canes fairly smooth with few thorns. Leaves large, soft, medium green.

Comte de Chambord, *p. 157*
(Moreau-Robert, 1860)

Comte de Chambord is a Portland, or damask perpetual, rose. It has very full mauve-tinted blossoms.

Flowers
3 in. (7.5 cm) wide. Medium pink with mauve tints. Very double; perhaps 200 petals. Midseason bloom followed by good repeat bloom. Very fragrant. Full outer petals enclose many central petals; blcom sometimes quartered, reflexing when fully expanded.

Foliage
3½–4 ft. (105–120 cm) high. Upright, rounded, compact. Disease resistant and winter hardy. Canes moderately thorny. Leaves medium green, semiglossy.

Crested Moss, *p. 163*
(Vibert, 1827)

Also known as Chapeau de Napoléon and *Rosa centifolia cristata,* this fringed bloom is not a true moss rose, but rather a parallel centifolia sport. It is not really mossy; rather, a fringe occurs just on the edges of the sepals, giving the buds the appearance of a three-cornered hat.

Flowers
3–3½ in. (7.5–9 cm) wide. Medium pink. Very double; perhaps 200 petals. Midseason bloom, not recurrent. Very fragrant. Blossoms very full and globular.

Foliage
5–7 ft. (1.5–2.1 m) tall. Upright, vigorous, arching canes, very open plant habit. Disease resistant and winter hardy. Canes very bristly and thorny. Leaves rough, dull, medium green.

Duchesse de Brabant, *p. 150*
(Bernède, 1857)

This tea rose once achieved an interesting distinction—it was well known as Teddy Roosevelt's favorite rose.

Flowers
4–5 in. (10–12.5 cm) wide. Blend of light pink through deep pink. Double; 45 petals. Early to midseason bloom with excellent repeat bloom. Very fragrant. Cupped blossom, well filled with petals.

Foliage
3–5 ft. (1–1.5 m) tall. Upright, vigorous, bushy. Disease resistant. Tender, but closer to borderline hardy than most other tea roses. Canes moderately thorny. Leaves medium to dark green, glossy.

Duchesse de Montebello, *p. 144*
(Laffay, before 1829)

The lax growth of this rose is unusual in a gallica, and it suggests that Duchesse de Montebello may be a hybrid with another species. In addition, it has longer canes than most other varieties. Careful placement in the garden is suggested.

Flowers
2½–3 in. (6–7.5 cm) wide. Light blush pink. Double; perhaps 65 petals. Mid- to late-season bloom, not recurrent. Fragrant. Blossoms, full and globular, occur in loose clusters.

Foliage
5 ft. (1.5 m) tall. Spreading and rather lax; can be trained upright or grown in with other shrubs. Disease resistant and winter hardy. Canes have few thorns. Leaves rough, gray-green.

Empress Josephine, *p. 159*
(Before 1583)

Also known as the Frankfort Rose, Empress Josephine is believed to be a cross between *Rosa cinnamomea* and *R. gallica*. It goes well with other gallica roses in the garden.

Flowers
3–3½ in. (7.5–9 cm) wide. Light to medium pink. Semidouble; perhaps 24–30 petals. Midseason bloom, not recurrent. Slight fragrance. Rather loose form; flowers have a papery quality. Hips, shaped like a top or inverted cone, appear later.

Foliage
3–4 ft. (1–1.2 m) tall. Upright, compact. Disease resistant and winter hardy. Smooth, almost thornless canes bear narrow, gray-green leaves.

Fantin-Latour, *p. 156*
(Hybridizer and date unknown)

It is obvious even to the beginning student of the old roses that this beautiful rose does not really fit into the centifolia class, to which it has been assigned. Research will one day discover its correct identity.

Flowers
3–3½ in. (7.5–9 cm) wide. Pale blush. Double; perhaps 200 petals. Profuse midseason bloom, not recurrent. Very fragrant. The full, rather flat bloom has a good button center.

Foliage
5–6 ft. (1.5–1.8 m) tall. Upright, vigorous, well branched. Disease resistant and winter hardy. Canes have few thorns. Leaves smooth, medium green, semiglossy.

Félicité et Perpétue, *p. 141*
(Jacques, 1827)

This hybrid sempervirens climber is best suited to mild climates, where it is almost evergreen.

Flowers
1½ in. (4 cm) wide. White. Double; perhaps 65 petals. Long late-season bloom, not recurrent. Fragrant. Full, globular blooms in large clusters.

Foliage
20 ft. (6 m) tall. Very vigorous and almost evergreen. Disease free; tender. Leaves small, abundant, medium green, glossy.

Ferdinand Pichard, *p. 178*
(Tanne, 1921)

This hybrid perpetual shows great similarity to the Bourbon rose Commandant Beaurepaire, although there is no record of parentage linking the earlier rose to this one.

Flowers
3–3⅓ in. (7.5–8.3 cm) wide. Red and white striped. Double; 25 petals. Good midseason bloom followed by fair repeat bloom. Fragrant. Blossom form cupped.

Foliage
4–5 ft. (1.2–1.5 m) tall. Upright, moderately vigorous, compact. Disease resistant and winter hardy. Canes fairly smooth, with few thorns. Long leaves, light to medium green, and soft.

Frau Karl Druschki, *p. 137*
(Lambert, 1901)

This white hybrid perpetual is also called Reine des Neiges, Snow Queen, and White American Beauty. Representative of the third, or final, stage of development in the class, it is identical in many ways to hybrid teas.

Flowers
4–4½ in. (10–11.5 cm) wide. White. Double; 35 petals. Midseason bloom with good repeat in the fall. Little or no fragrance. Blossoms have classic hybrid tea shape.

Foliage
5–7 ft. (1.5–2.1 m) tall. Upright, vigorous, well branched. Disease resistant and winter hardy. Canes fairly smooth with few thorns. Leaves soft, medium green.

Général Kléber, *p. 144*
(Robert, 1856)

This centifolia moss rose has a praiseworthy clear pink bloom. Its dense, pleasing habit of growth is unusual—most moss roses, and most centifolias, have rangy, sparse, gaunt canes.

Flowers
2½–3 in. (6–7.5 cm) wide. Medium pink.
Double; perhaps 100 petals. Blooms at
midseason or later; does not recur. Very
fragrant. Blossom form full, quartered, with
a button center. Buds mossy.

Foliage
5 ft. (1.5 m) tall. Upright, vigorous, bushy.
Disease resistant and winter hardy. Canes
thorny. Leaves rough, dull, light to medium
green.

Georg Arends, *p. 151*
(Hinner, 1910)

A later, or third-stage, hybrid perpetual rose,
Georg Arends comes very close to fitting in
the hybrid tea class.

Flowers
4–4½ in. (10–11.5 cm) wide. Light to
medium pink. Double; 25 petals. Midseason
bloom with good repeat bloom in the fall.
Very fragrant. Classic hybrid tea form, with
petals unfurling evenly from a high center.

Foliage
4–5 ft. (1.2–1.5 m) tall. Upright, vigorous,
well branched. Disease resistant and winter
hardy. Fairly smooth canes, with few thorns,
bear medium green, semiglossy leaves.

Gloire de Dijon, *p. 135*
(Jocotot, 1853)

A good pillar rose, Gloire de Dijon needs
the protection of a wall in borderline
climates. The canes become leggy at base, a
fault you can obscure by other plantings.

Flowers
4 in. (10 cm) wide. Yellow with orange at
center, sometimes shaded with pink. Double;
45–55 petals. Early-season bloom with good
repeat bloom. Fragrant. Very full hybrid
tea–type bloom with occasional quartering.

Foliage
10–12 ft. (3–3.5 m) tall. Upright, vigorous,
arching. Disease resistant; tender. Canes
moderately thorny, with medium green,
glossy leaves.

Gloire de France, *p. 152*
(1819)

Gallica roses are well suited to the small garden, offering a wide variety of colors and shapes and blooming over a six-week period at the beginning of summer.

Flowers
2½–3 in. (6–7.5 cm) wide. Medium pink. Double; perhaps 200 petals. Midseason bloom, not recurrent. Fragrant. Blossom pompon shaped; reflexes into a ball upon full expansion.

Foliage
2–2½ ft. (60–75 cm) tall. Upright, bushy, spreading. Disease resistant and winter hardy. Canes bristly but not thorny, with rough, gray-green leaves.

Gloire de Guilan, *p. 146*
(Hilling, 1949)

This exotic rose was first discovered by Miss Nancy Lindsay in the Caspian provinces of Persia.

Flowers
3 in. (7.5 cm) wide. Light pink. Double; perhaps 45–55 petals. Profuse early to midseason bloom, not recurrent. Intensely fragrant. Bloom form full, globular, with quartered center.

Foliage
3–5 ft. (1–1.5 m) tall. Vigorous, sprawling. Disease free and winter hardy. Canes moderately thorny, with soft, dull, light green leaves.

Gloire des Mousseuses, *p. 147*
(Laffay, 1852)

This centifolia moss has very large blooms for its class. Its name is alternately spelled Mousseaux and Mousseux.

Flowers
3 in. (7.5 cm) wide. Light to medium pink with a faint lavender tint. Very double; perhaps 200 petals. Midseason bloom, not recurrent. Very fragrant. Bloom form very

full, quartered, with a button center. Buds and stems very mossy.

Foliage
2½–3 ft. (75–90 cm) tall. Upright, moderately vigorous, compact. Disease resistant and winter hardy. Canes very thorny; leaves soft, dull, light green.

Gloire des Rosomanes, *p. 174*
(Vibert, 1825)

Also called Ragged Robin, this red China rose is sometimes used as an understock.

Flowers
3 in. (7.5 cm) wide. Medium red. Double; perhaps 25–30 petals. Good all-season bloom. Little or no fragrance. Blossom form rather loose, cupped.

Foliage
3½–4½ ft. (1.1–1.4 m) tall. Upright, vigorous, bushy. Disease resistant; moderately hardy. Fairly smooth canes, with few thorns, bear medium to dark green, semiglossy leaves.

Gruss an Teplitz, *p. 175*
(Geschwind, 1897)

Of mixed parentage, this rose has been classed several ways. But its growth habit and style of bloom place it appropriately with the Bourbons.

Flowers
3–3½ in. (7.5–9 cm) wide. Medium red. Double; 34–40 petals. Profuse midseason bloom followed by good repeat bloom. Strong, spicy fragrance. Blossom cupped, well filled with petals.

Foliage
5–6 ft. (1.5–1.8 m) tall. Upright, vigorous, bushy. Disease resistant; winter hardy, except in very severe winter climates. Leaves dark green, semiglossy.

Henri Martin, *p. 176*
(Laffay, 1863)

Like the other moss roses that have sported from centifolias, Henri Martin is not a repeat bloomer, and it has heavy green moss on the calyx and sepals.

Flowers
2½ in. (6 cm) wide. Dark red. Double; perhaps 65–75 petals. Mid- to late-season bloom, not recurrent. Fragrant. Blossom globular, well filled with petals. Very well mossed.

Foliage
5 ft. (1.5 m) tall. Upright, vigorous, bushy. Disease resistant and winter hardy. Canes thorny. Leaves medium to dark green, rough, abundant.

Henry Nevard, *p. 175*
(Cant, 1924)

Henry Nevard represents the third stage of hybrid perpetual development; it is very close in many ways to the hybrid tea class.

Flowers
4–4½ in. (10–11.5 cm) wide. Dark red. Double; 30 petals. Good midseason bloom with good repeat bloom in the fall. Very fragrant. Blossom cupped, well filled with petals.

Foliage
4–5 ft. (1.2–1.5 m) tall. Upright, vigorous, bushy. Disease resistant and winter hardy. Very thorny canes bear dark green, semiglossy leaves.

Hermosa, *p. 160*
(Marcheseau, 1840)

Widely planted at one time, Hermosa is a China rose that was formerly classed with the Bourbons.

Flowers
3 in. (7.5 cm) wide. Light pink. Double; 35 petals. Good all-season bloom. Fragrant. Form high centered, rather globular.

Foliage
3–4 ft. (1–1.2 m) tall. Upright, moderately
vigorous, and bushy. Disease resistant, but
not winter hardy. Canes very smooth, with
few thorns. Leaves blue-green to medium
green, semiglossy.

Ispahan, *p. 148*
(Before 1832)

Also named Pompon des Princes. Ispahan is
classed as a damask, although some experts
feel that it may have other parentage in its
background as well.

Flowers
2½–3 in. (6–7.5 cm) wide. Medium pink.
Double; perhaps 24–30 petals. Long
midseason bloom, not recurrent. Very
fragrant. Bloom form loosely cupped.

Foliage
3–4 ft. (1–1.2 m) tall. Upright, moderately
vigorous, bushy. Disease free and winter
hardy. Canes thorny. Leaves small, medium
green, semiglossy.

John Hopper, *p. 176*
(Ward, 1862)

This hybrid perpetual is one of the rare
examples of the early development of that
class.

Flowers
4 in. (10 cm) wide. Medium pink with
deeper center and lavender edges. Very
double; 70 petals. Good midseason bloom
with occasional repeat bloom in the fall.
Very fragrant. Larger outer petals enclosing
many tightly packed central petals; center
usually muddled.

Foliage
5–7 ft. (1.5–2.1 m) tall. Upright, vigorous,
bushy. Disease resistant and winter hardy.
Canes very thorny; leaves medium green,
semiglossy.

Königin von Dänemark, *p. 160*
(1826)

A distinctive alba rose. Most blooms have a quartered appearance, with 3, 4, or 5 divisions, and show a good button center.

Flowers
3½ in. (9 cm) wide. Light pink, with a deeper pink center. Very double; perhaps 200 petals. Early bloom, not recurrent. Intense, sweet fragrance. Quartered blossom has button center. Upon full expansion, outer petals reflex and fade to nearly white.

Foliage
6 ft. (1.8 m) tall. Upright, treelike habit, more slender and open than more typical albas. Disease free and winter hardy. Canes very thorny, with rough, dull, blue-green leaves, darker than those of most albas.

La Noblesse, *p. 162*
(1856)

A typical centifolia, or Provence, rose, La Noblesse has gaunt, thorny canes that are often a problem to manage. Using a low trellis, pegging down, or close planting (treating 3 plants as 1) may solve the problem in some garden situations.

Flowers
3–3½ in. (7.5–9 cm) wide. Light pink. Very double; perhaps 200 petals. Profuse mid- to late-season growth, not recurrent. Extremely fragrant. The very full bloom, usually muddled or quartered, has large outer petals surrounding many shorter petals.

Foliage
5 ft. (1.5 m) tall. Upright, arching, loose habit. Disease free and winter hardy. Canes very thorny. Leaves rough, dull, medium to dark green.

La Reine Victoria, *p. 161*
(Schwartz, 1872)

This profuse bloomer has overlapping shell-shaped petals. It makes a nice garden grouping with Madame Pierre Oger and Louise Odier.

Flowers
3–3½ in. (7.5–9 cm) wide. Medium pink.
Double; perhaps 35 petals. Abundant
midseason bloom with good repeat bloom in
the fall. Very fragrant. Bloom cup-shaped.

Foliage
4½–5½ ft. (135–165 cm) tall. Upright,
slender growth. Disease resistant and winter
hardy. Canes quite smooth, with few thorns.
Leaves soft, dull, medium green.

La Ville de Bruxelles, *p. 157*
(Vibert, 1849)

The weight of this rose's large, heavy blooms
makes them nod down into the foliage.
Otherwise, this is a fine variety.

Flowers
3½–4 in. (9–10 cm) wide. Medium to deep
pink. Double; perhaps 45–55 petals.
Abundant midseason bloom, not recurrent.
Very fragrant. Very full, quartered bloom
with button center.

Foliage
5 ft. (1.5 m) tall. Upright, vigorous, bushy.
Disease free and winter hardy. Canes
moderately thorny. Leaves abundant, light
green, semiglossy.

Lady Hillingdon, *p. 134*
(Lowe & Shawyer, 1910)

The bush form of Lady Hillingdon is not
very vigorous, but the climbing form is an
excellent rose for pillar or trellis.

Flowers
3½ in. (9 cm) wide. Apricot-yellow.
Semidouble; 18–24 petals. Early-season bloom
with good repeat bloom. Fragrant. Blossom
form rather loose, but classic hybrid tea
shape.

Foliage
2½–3 ft. (75–90 cm) tall. Upright, bushy,
not very vigorous; the vigorous climbing
form reaches 15 ft. Disease resistant but not
winter hardy. Canes very smooth with few
thorns. Leaves dark green, glossy.

Leda, *p. 181*
(Before 1827)

Also called the Painted Damask, Leda is
difficult to manage because of its lax habit.
It is nonetheless worth the effort of training
to a low trellis or other support.

Flowers
2½–3 in. (6–7.5 cm) wide. White with red
edge. Double; perhaps 200 petals. Midseason
bloom, not recurrent. Fragrant. Fat red buds
open to very full white blooms with button
centers.

Foliage
2½–3 ft. (75–90 cm) tall if trained upright.
Lax, trailing. Disease free and winter hardy.
Thorny canes bear dark gray-green leaves.

Little Gem, *p. 163*
(Paul, 1880)

A pretty little pompon rose, Little Gem has
been alternately described as being heavily or
sparsely mossed. Most reports, however,
indicate that the moss is not abundant.

Flowers
2 in. (5 cm) wide. Medium red. Double;
perhaps 55–65 petals. Midseason bloom; no
repeat. Fragrant. Bloom has pompon form.

Foliage
4 ft. (1.2 m) tall. Upright, compact. Disease
resistant and winter hardy. Canes thorny.
Leaves small, abundant, medium green.

Louis Gimard, *p. 151*
(Pernet Père, 1877)

Like other centifolia mosses, Louis Gimard
has abundant green, pine-scented moss on its
calyx and sepals.

Flowers
3–3½ in. (7.5–9 cm) wide. Mauve pink.
Double; 65–75 petals. Midseason bloom, not
recurrent. Very fragrant. Bloom very full
with muddled center. Buds well mossed.

Foliage
4–5 ft. (1.2–1.5 m) tall. Upright, vigorous,

bushy. Disease resistant and winter hardy. Canes very thorny. Leaves rough, medium green.

Louise Odier, *p. 158*
(Margottin, 1851)

Considering its petal count, Louise Odier has very full blossoms, but the rather slender, upright bush is not typical of the big, blowsy Bourbons. It makes a good trio with La Reine Victoria and Madame Pierre Oger.

Flowers
3½ in. (9 cm) wide. Medium pink. Double; 35–45 petals. Abundant midseason bloom followed by good repeat bloom. Very fragrant. Classic old rose form, sometimes quartered.

Foliage
4½–5½ ft. (135–165 cm) tall. Upright, slender. Disease resistant and winter hardy. Canes smooth with few thorns. Leaves light to medium green.

Mabel Morrison, *p. 140*
(Broughton, 1878)

This hybrid perpetual has been compared to the Portlands because the bloom is closely surrounded with foliage.

Flowers
3½–4 in. (9–10 cm) wide. White. Double; 30 petals. Good midseason bloom with good repeat in the fall. Fragrant. Blossom cupped. Fall blooms sometimes splashed with pink.

Foliage
4–4½ ft. (120–135 cm) tall. Upright, vigorous, well branched. Disease resistant and winter hardy. Canes moderately thorny. Leaves medium to dark green, semiglossy.

Madame Alfred Carrière, *p. 136*
(Schwartz, 1879)

A wall may offer enough protection to enable this beauty to be grown in borderline winter conditions.

Flowers
2½–3 in. (6–7.5 cm) wide. White. Double;
35 petals. Midseason bloom with excellent
repeat bloom. Fragrant. Evenly petaled,
gardenia-shaped blossoms, in clusters.

Foliage
10–15 ft. (3–4.5 m) tall. Upright, vigorous,
arching. Disease resistant. Borderline hardy.
Moderately thorny canes bear medium green,
semiglossy leaves.

Madame de la Roche-Lambert, *p. 164*
(Robert, 1851)

This centifolia moss has large outer petals
enclosing many tightly packed smaller petals.

Flowers
3 in. (7.5 cm) wide. Medium pink with
purple shadings. Double; 65–75 petals.
Midseason bloom, not recurrent. Very
fragrant. Very full bloom form, usually with
a button center. Buds well mossed.

Foliage
4–5 ft. (120–150 cm) tall. Upright, arching
growth. Disease resistant and winter hardy.
Canes very thorny. Leaves rough, dull, light
to medium green.

Madame Hardy, *p. 138*
(Hardy, 1832)

Considered to represent the very finest
development of its particular style of floral
art, Madame Hardy is perhaps the most
popular white rose of its type.

Flowers
3–3½ in. (7.5–9 cm) wide. White. Very
double; perhaps 200 petals. Midseason
bloom, not recurrent. Fragrant. Very full,
evenly petaled blossoms with a green pip in
the center.

Foliage
5–5½ ft. (150–165 cm) tall. Upright,
vigorous, bushy. Disease free and winter
hardy. Canes moderately thorny. Leaves
gray-green, rough, abundant.

Madame Isaac Pereire, *p. 164*
(Garçon, 1881)

This is a typical Bourbon rose, big and billowy. It is famous for its intense fragrance. It has a lighter pink sport, Madame Ernst Calvat.

Flowers
3½–4 in. (9–10 cm) wide. Deep pink. Double; perhaps 45–55 petals. Profuse midseason bloom followed by fair repeat bloom. Intensely fragrant. Large, full, globular blossoms usually quartered, sometimes muddled.

Foliage
5–6 ft. (1.5–1.8 m) tall. Upright and well-branched; vigorous, bushy, and spreading. Disease resistant and winter hardy, with moderately thorny canes. Leaves dark green, semiglossy.

Madame Lauriol de Barny, *p. 162*
(Trouillard, 1868)

Madame Lauriol de Barny is considered by some authorities to be one of the finest of the Bourbon roses.

Flowers
3½–4 in. (9–10 cm) wide. Light pink. Very double; 45–55 petals. Fruity fragrance. Abundant midseason bloom; followed occasionally by repeat bloom. Flower form full, globular, sometimes quartered.

Foliage
5–6 ft. (1.5–1.8 m) tall. Upright, vigorous, bushy. Disease resistant and winter hardy. Moderately thorny canes bear large, dull, medium green leaves.

Madame Legras de St. Germain, *p. 136*
(1846)

Thought to be an alba crossed with a damask, Madame Legras de St. Germain has delicate blooms. It is tougher than it looks, however, and not easily spoiled by rain.

Flowers
3½ in. (9 cm) wide. White with lemon

yellow center. Very double; perhaps 200 petals. Early blooming, not recurrent. Very sweet fragrance. Upon full expansion, tightly packed petals reflex into a ball.

Foliage
6–7 ft. (1.8–2.1 m) tall. Upright, treelike habit. Disease free and winter hardy. Canes very smooth, almost thornless. Leaves light to medium green.

Madame Louis Lévêque, *p. 153*
(Lévêque, 1898)

Monsieur Louis Lévêque must have loved his wife very much, for he named three roses for her: a tea rose, a hybrid perpetual, and this one, a perpetual damask moss.

Flowers
3–3½ in. (7.5–9 cm) wide. Light pink. Double; perhaps 100 petals. Midseason bloom; well-established plants will repeat bloom in the fall. Very fragrant. Very full, globular form. Sparsely mossed.

Foliage
4–5 ft. (1.2–1.5 m) tall. Upright, arching. Disease resistant and winter hardy. Canes very thorny. Leaves dull, rough, medium green.

Madame Pierre Oger, *p. 150*
(Oger, 1878)

A color sport of La Reine Victoria, to which it is similar in every other way. Blooms are very pale at first, particularly in overcast weather, but the color deepens wherever touched by sunlight.

Flowers
3–3½ in. (7.5–9 cm) wide. Pale blush, deepening in the sun. Double; perhaps 35 petals. Abundant midseason bloom, good repeat bloom in the fall. Very fragrant. Bloom cupped.

Foliage
4½–5½ ft. (135–165 cm) tall. Upright, slender growth. Disease resistant. Winter hardy. Canes very smooth with few thorns. Leaves soft, dull, medium green.

Madame Plantier, *p. 139*
(Plantier, 1835)

Thought to be a hybrid between the albas and the musks, Madame. Plantier will grow upward and then billow out, especially if given some training. It can be trained onto a trellis or into a small tree, where its canes will grow longer.

Flowers
2½–3 in. (6–7.5 cm) wide. White. Very double; perhaps over 200 petals. Profuse midseason bloom, not recurrent. Very fragrant. Very full blooms in clusters. Good button eye. Fully expanded bloom reflexes into a ball.

Foliage
5–6 ft. (1.5–1.8 m) tall. Upright, vigorous, dense, bushy. Disease free and winter hardy. Very smooth canes have few thorns. Leaves smooth, long, medium green.

Maiden's Blush, *p. 145*
(Before 1600)

Perhaps this rose's long history accounts for the many names it has been given: Great Maiden's Blush, La Virginale, La Séduisante, Incarnata, and Cuisse de Nymphe; when deeper color develops, the rose is sometimes called Cuisse de Nymphe Emué. There is also a Small Maiden's Blush, which is exactly the same except for the size of the bush.

Flowers
2½–3 in. (6–7.5 cm) wide. Light blush pink. Very double; perhaps over 200 petals. Extremely profuse early to midseason bloom, not recurrent. Very fragrant. Very full blooms have muddled centers, but occasionally blooms develop a good button center under good cultivation.

Foliage
5–6 ft. (1.5–1.8 m) tall. Upright; treelike at first, then arching out. Disease free and winter hardy. Canes bristly and thorny. Leaves rough, dull, blue-green.

Maman Cochet, *p. 159*
(Cochet, 1893)

One of the most popular of the tea roses,
this pink and yellow rose has a climbing
form and a white sport, White Maman
Cochet.

Flowers
3½–4 in. (9–10 cm) wide. Light pink with
deeper center; base of petals yellow. Double;
35–45 petals. Midseason bloom with
excellent repeat bloom. Fragrant. Classic
hybrid tea form with petals unfurling evenly
from a high center.

Foliage
3–3½ ft. (90–105 cm) tall. Upright,
vigorous, bushy. Disease resistant. Not
winter hardy. Fairly smooth canes have few
thorns. Leaves medium to dark green, glossy.

Marchioness of Londonderry, *p. 147*
(Dickson, 1893)

This hybrid perpetual, with its full, globular
blossoms, represents the middle stage of
development in this class more than it does
the third stage.

Flowers
4½–5 in. (11.5–12.5 cm) wide. Very light
pink. Double; 50 petals. Profuse midseason
bloom, with occasional repeat in the fall.
Very fragrant. Blossoms full, globular.

Foliage
5–7 ft. (1.5–2.1 m) tall. Upright, vigorous,
arching. Disease resistant and winter hardy.
Canes fairly smooth, with few thorns. Leaves
medium green, semiglossy.

Maréchal Davoust, *p. 161*
(Robert, 1853)

In spite of the influx of hybrid perpetuals
during the Victorian era, moss roses such as
this one retained their popularity.

Flowers
3 in. (7.5 cm) wide. Deep pink with lighter
pink reverse. Double; perhaps 100 petals.
Midseason bloom, not recurrent. Very

fragrant. Very full form, sometimes quartered, with button eye and green pip in center. Sparsely mossed.

Foliage
5 ft. (1.5 m) tall. Upright, vigorous, bushy. Disease resistant and winter hardy. Thorny canes bear soft, dull, medium green leaves.

Mary Washington, *p. 142*
(Ross, 1891)

Mary Washington is currently believed to be a Noisette, although it has sometimes been classed with the hybrid musks.

Flowers
2½ in. (6 cm) wide. White tinged with pink, fading to white. Double; 24 petals. Midseason bloom with good repeat. Fragrant. Cupped blossoms occur in clusters.

Foliage
8–12 ft. (2.4–3.5 m) tall. Very vigorous, upright, and well branched. Disease resistant. Not winter hardy without protection. Canes very smooth with few thorns. Leaves medium green, semiglossy.

Maxima, *p. 137*
(Ancient)

This fragrant rose is also known as the Great Double White and the Jacobite Rose. It has been in cultivation for so long that its date of introduction is unknown.

Flowers
2½–3 in. (6–7.5 cm) wide. White. Very double; perhaps over 200 petals. Profuse early to midseason bloom, not recurrent. Very fragrant. Very full blossoms have muddled centers.

Foliage
6–8 ft. (1.8–2.4 m) tall. Upright, treelike. Disease free and winter hardy. Canes moderately thorny; leaves rough, dull, blue-green.

Nuits de Young, *p. 173*
(Laffay, 1845)

This rose was named for the 18th-century English poet Edward Young. His 9-volume poem, *The Complaint; or, Night-Thoughts on Life, Death, and Immortality*—commonly referred to as *Night Thoughts*—gave rise to the "graveyard school" of poetry.

Flowers
2½ in. (6 cm) wide. Maroon with purple. Double; perhaps 50 petals. Midseason bloom, not recurrent. Very fragrant. Blossom not very full for a moss rose, but well packed with petals and a few golden stamens in the center. Sparsely mossed.

Foliage
5 ft. (1.5 m) tall. Arching, somewhat open. Disease resistant and winter hardy. Canes very thorny. Leaves small, dark green, sparse.

Old Blush, *p. 155*
(1752)

This tender pink rose is believed to be the same as Parsons' Pink China Rose.

Flowers
3 in. (7.5 cm) wide. Medium pink. Double; perhaps 24–30 petals. Good all-season bloom. Little or no fragrance. Bloom form loose, cupped.

Foliage
3–4 ft. (90–120 cm) tall. Upright, moderately vigorous, bushy. Disease resistant. Not winter hardy. Canes smooth, with few thorns. Leaves smooth, medium green, glossy.

Paul Neyron, *p. 168*
(Levet, 1869)

Paul Neyron is a middle-stage hybrid perpetual. Its size is often exaggerated, but a fully expanded bloom can reach 6 or 7 inches on occasion.

Flowers
4½–5½ in. (11.5–14 cm) wide. Medium to lavender-pink or deep pink. Very double;

65-75 petals. Midseason bloom with fair repeat in the fall. Fragrant. Blossom globular to cupped, well filled with tightly packed petals; sometimes quartered but usually layered in rows; muddled when fully expanded.

Foliage
5-6 ft. (1.5-1.8 m) tall. Upright, vigorous, arching. Disease resistant and winter hardy. Canes fairly smooth, few thorns. Leaves medium green, semiglossy.

Petite de Hollande, *p. 156*
(Hybridizer and date uncertain)

This small centifolia is considered to be the best of the Provence roses for smaller gardens.

Flowers
2-2½ in. (5-6 cm) wide. Medium pink. Double; perhaps 45-55 petals. Long midseason bloom, not recurrent. Very fragrant. Very full, globular blossoms.

Foliage
3½-4 ft. (105-120 cm) tall. Upright, vigorous, bushy. Disease resistant and winter hardy. Canes very thorny. Leaves small, medium green.

Reine des Violettes, *p. 169*
(Millet-Malet, 1860)

The Queen of the Violets. This hybrid perpetual has been likened to the Bourbons. The color is a changing blend of lavender, sometimes very much on the blue side of the mauve tones. The foliage is reported to have a pepperlike fragrance, but this is usually difficult to detect.

Flowers
3 in. (7.5 cm) wide. Mauve. Very double; 75 petals. Profuse midseason bloom with occasional sparse repeat bloom in the fall. Very fragrant. Bloom form cupped, muddled.

Foliage
5-6 ft. (1.5-1.8 m) tall and as wide. Upright, vigorous, bushy, and rounded. Disease resistant and winter hardy. Canes

very smooth, with few thorns. Leaves abundant, soft, medium green.

Roger Lambelin, *p. 172*
(Schwartz, 1890)

A sport of Fisher Holmes, Roger Lambelin requires good cultivation and frequent repropagation. At one time there was a sport called Striped Roger Lambelin; interested gardeners may want to watch for its reappearance.

Flowers
2½–3 in. (6–7.5 cm) wide. Maroon, edged in white. Double; 30 petals. Midseason bloom with fair repeat bloom in the fall. Blossom irregular, raggedy looking.

Foliage
2–2½ ft. (60–75 cm) tall. Upright; not vigorous. Disease resistant and winter hardy. Canes moderately thorny. Leaves rough, dark green.

Rosa centifolia variegata, p. 180
(1845)

This garden variety should not have been given a species name. The common names for it, however—Cottage Maid and Village Maid—have also been used for other varieties, which makes for much confusion. In a few remote references it is called Striped Centifolia, which is the only common name that is appropriate.

Flowers
3–3½ in. (7.5–9 cm) wide. White with very delicate pink striping or pencilling. Double; perhaps 200 petals. Abundant midseason bloom, not recurrent. Very fragrant. Large, very full outer petals enclose many tightly packed shorter petals. Often muddled, sometimes quartered, with a button center.

Foliage
5 ft. (1.5 m) tall and as wide. Upright and vigorous; dense and bushy, unlike most in its class. Disease resistant and winter hardy. Canes very thorny. Leaves dull, medium to dark green.

Rosa gallica officinalis, *p. 166*
(Ancient)

This is probably the most famous rose of all time. Known also as the Apothecary Rose, it was tremendously popular for several centuries as the mainstay of a flourishing industry. In dried and candied form, it was fashioned into preserves and syrups as well as powders, and it was believed to cure many and diverse ailments.

Flowers
3–3½ in. (7.5–9 cm) wide. Medium to deep pink. Semidouble; 12–18 petals. Midseason bloom, not recurrent. Fragrant (much more so when petals are dried). Cupped blossoms open to reveal golden stamens. Attractive round, red hips later in season.

Foliage
3–3½ ft. (90–105 cm) tall. Upright, rounded, compact. Disease resistant and winter hardy. Canes have bristles but few thorns. Leaves medium-size, rough, medium green.

Rosa Mundi, *p. 178*
(Before 1581)

The striped sport of *Rosa gallica officinalis,* sometimes called *R. gallica versicolor,* this is the earliest striped rose and the most striking of them all. No two blooms that open on the bush are striped and splashed in exactly the same way.

Flowers
3–3½ in. (7.5–9 cm) wide. Medium to deep pink, striped with blush or white. Semidouble; 18–24 petals. Midseason bloom, not recurrent. Fragrant. Cupped bloom opens to show golden stamens. Round red hips appear later in season.

Foliage
3–3½ ft. (90–105 cm) tall. Upright, rounded, compact. Disease resistant and winter hardy. Canes have bristles but few thorns. Medium-size, rough, medium green leaves.

Rose de Rescht, *p. 174*
(Hybridizer and date uncertain)

This rose was reportedly brought from Persia by Miss Nancy Lindsay, who is also credited with the discovery of Gloire de Guilan. Rose de Rescht is very much like Rose du Roi, except in color.

Flowers
2–2½ in. (5–6 cm) wide. Deep pink with mauve shadings. Double; perhaps 100 petals. Midseason bloom and good repeat bloom. Very fragrant. Blossoms very full, rather raggedy-looking.

Foliage
2½–3½ ft. (75–105 cm) tall. Upright, vigorous, compact. Disease resistant and winter hardy. Canes moderately thorny. Leaves medium green, semiglossy.

Rose des Peintres, *p. 149*
(1596)

Given a species name, *Rosa centifolia,* in error, Rose des Peintres has infertile flowers. Many of the varieties associated with it are sports. Also called the Provence Rose.

Flowers
3–3½ in. (7.5–9 cm) wide. Medium pink. Double; perhaps 200 petals. Profuse midseason bloom, not recurrent. Very fragrant. Very full blooms typically have large outer petals enclosing many shorter petals, often with a button center.

Foliage
5–6 ft. (1.5–1.8 m) tall. Upright and vigorous, with arching, open growth. Disease free and winter hardy. Canes very thorny. Leaves rough, medium to dark green.

Rose du Roi, *p. 170*
(Lelieur, 1815)

This red and purple rose was a sensation in its day. The deepest shadings occur on the outer petals and the top surface.

Flowers
2½ in. (6 cm) wide. Medium red with

purple shadings. Double; perhaps 100 petals.
Midseason bloom with good repeat bloom.
Very fragrant. Large outer petals with shorter
central petals.

Foliage
3–4 ft. (90–120 cm) tall. Upright, vigorous,
compact. Disease resistant and winter hardy.
Canes moderately thorny. Leaves medium
green, semiglossy.

Rosette Delizy, *p. 134*
(Nabonnand, 1922)

A little larger and more vigorous than most
tea roses, Rosette Delizy may be borderline
winter hardy in protected positions. It was
one of the last teas to be introduced.

Flowers
3½–4 in. (9–10 cm) wide. Yellow with
apricot reverse; outer petals deep pink.
Double; 45–55 petals. Midseason bloom with
good repeat. Spicy fragrance. Full, classic
hybrid tea form.

Foliage
3½–4 ft. (105–120 cm) tall. Upright,
vigorous, bushy. Disease resistant. Not
winter hardy. Canes smooth, with few
thorns. Leaves dark green, glossy.

Salet, *p. 152*
(Lacharme, 1854)

Like other perpetual damask mosses, Salet is
sparsely mossed on its calyx and sepals.

Flowers
2½–3 in. (6–7.5 cm) wide. Medium pink.
Double; perhaps 55–65 petals. Midseason
bloom with fair repeat bloom in the fall
when well established; repeats reliably in the
South. Fragrant. Full, globular form.

Foliage
4–5 ft. (1.2–1.5 m) tall. Upright, vigorous,
arching. Disease resistant and winter hardy.
Canes very thorny. Leaves rough, dull,
medium green.

Sombreuil, *p. 138*
(Robert, 1850)

A climbing tea rose, Sombreuil is worth trying in protected positions in northern gardens.

Flowers
3½–4 in. (9–10 cm) wide. Creamy white. Very double; perhaps 100 petals. Early to midseason bloom with good repeat. Fragrant. Blossom cupped, full, often quartered.

Foliage
12–15 ft. (3.5–4.5 m) tall. Upright, vigorous. Disease resistant. Borderline winter hardy. Canes moderately thorny. Leaves medium green, leathery, semiglossy.

Souvenir de la Malmaison, *p. 143*
(Beluse, 1843)

The Empress Josephine, first wife of Napoleon Bonaparte, maintained a fabulous rose garden at Malmaison, her residence just outside of Paris. Named in honor of the garden, this is an unforgettable rose, but unfortunately a very sparse bloomer. A climbing form is available.

Flowers
4½–5 in. (11.5–12.5 cm) wide. Light pink. Very double; perhaps 65–75 petals. Sparse bloom, midseason or late season, with sparse repeat in the fall. Strong spicy fragrance. Large, full blooms are usually well quartered.

Foliage
2 ft. (60 cm) tall; climbing form reaches 6–8 ft. (1.8–2.4 m). Compact. Vigorous, but bush form is a small plant. Climbing form suitable for a low trellis or pillar. Canes moderately thorny; leaves medium green, semiglossy.

Stanwell Perpetual, *p. 142*
(Leė, 1838)

Believed to be a cross between *Rosa damascena semperflorens* and *Rosa spinosissima*, this is the only spinosissima hybrid that is a reliable repeat bloomer. However, to repeat, the plant must be well established in the

garden. The plant is an attractive, ferny
bush.

Flowers
3–3½ in. (7.5–9 cm) wide. Light pink,
fading to white. Double; perhaps 45–55
petals. Fragrant. Early to midseason bloom,
with reliable repeat. Loose, muddled form
gives an even appearance. Blooms appear
singly on very short stems.

Foliage
3–5 ft. (1–1.5 m) tall and as wide. Vigorous,
spreading. Disease resistant and winter hardy.
Canes very thorny. Leaves small, dull,
blue-green to deep green.

Striped Moss, *p. 180*
(Verdier, 1888)

Also called Oeillet Panachée. This variety
shows greater relationship to the perpetual
damask mosses than to the centifolias,
although it does not repeat bloom in the
fall.

Flowers
1½–2 in. (4–5 cm) wide. Red-and-white-
striped in cool, overcast weather, pink-and-
white-striped in full sunlight. Double;
perhaps 45–65 petals. Fragrant. Midseason
bloom, not recurrent. Cupped form with
tightly packed petals. Not very mossy.

Foliage
5–6 ft. (1.5–1.8 m) tall. Upright, vigorous,
bushy. Disease resistant and winter hardy.
Canes very thorny. Leaves small, rough, dark
green.

The Bishop, *p. 170*
(Hybridizer and date uncertain)

The slender habit of The Bishop is not
typical of centifolias. At one time, members
of this class were the most popular garden
roses, which may explain why some roses
that might fit better elsewhere were given
this classification.

Flowers
2½–3 in. (6–7.5 cm) wide. Cerise-magenta,
quickly fading to slate-blue. Very double;

perhaps 200 petals. Early to midseason bloom, not recurrent. Fragrant. Full, rosette form.

Foliage
4–5 ft. (1.2–1.5 m) tall. Upright, slender growth. Moderately vigorous. Disease resistant and winter hardy. Canes moderately thorny. Neat, medium-size leaves are medium green and semiglossy.

Tour de Malakoff, *p. 168*
(Soupert & Notting, 1856)

As this bloom ages, the blue and violet tones take predominance over the pink tones.

Flowers
3–3½ in. (7.5–9 cm) wide. Mauve. Double; perhaps 45–55 petals. Midseason bloom, not recurrent. Very fragrant. Full, rather loose and raggedy bloom form.

Foliage
6–7 ft. (1.8–2.1 m) tall. Upright, vigorous, sprawling. Disease free and winter hardy. Very thorny canes bear large, rough, medium to dark green leaves.

Tuscany, *p. 172*
(1596)

Tuscany is also known as the Old Velvet Rose, for the color and texture of its purple-petaled blossoms.

Flowers
3–3½ in. (7.5–9 cm) wide. Purple. Semidouble; 18–24 petals. Midseason bloom, not recurrent. Very fragrant. Rather loose, cupped bloom form, showing bright golden stamens.

Foliage
3–4 ft. (90–120 cm) tall. Upright, rounded, compact. Disease resistant and winter hardy. Canes have bristles but few thorns. Leaves rough, medium to dark green.

Tuscany Superb, *p. 171*
(Hybridizer and date uncertain)

This is a slightly larger bloom than Tuscany, but its more numerous petals partly obscure the contrasting yellow stamens.

Flowers
3½–4 in. (9–10 cm) wide. Purple. Double; 24–30 petals. Midseason bloom, not recurrent. Very fragrant. Bloom cupped, well filled with petals.

Foliage
3–4 ft. (1–1.2 m) tall. Upright, rounded, compact. Disease resistant and winter hardy. Canes have bristles, few thorns. Leaves rough, medium to dark green.

Ulrich Brunner Fils, *p. 165*
(Levet, 1881)

Also known simply as Ulrich Brunner. This rose has been widely distributed under another name, so rose enthusiasts might look carefully at the plants in their gardens to see if Ulrich Brunner Fils is among them.

Flowers
3½–4 in. (9–10 cm) wide. Deep pink or medium red. Double; 30 petals. Midseason bloom with occasional repeat bloom in the fall. Very fragrant. Classic hybrid tea form, but not particularly high centered.

Foliage
5–7 ft. (1.5–2.1 m) tall. Upright, vigorous, bushy. Disease resistant and winter hardy. Fairly smooth canes with few thorns. Leaves soft, light to medium green.

Variegata di Bologna, *p. 181*
(Bonfiglioli, 1909)

In some climates, this Bourbon is reported to have wine-red or even purple stripes.

Flowers
3½–4 in. (9–10 cm) wide. Red-and-white-striped. Double; perhaps 45–55 petals. Midseason bloom, not recurrent. Fragrant. Very evenly petaled bloom, almost ball-shaped when fully expanded.

Foliage
5–7 ft. (1.5–2.1 m) tall. Upright, slender
growth, suitable for trellis or pillar. Disease
resistant and winter hardy. Canes very
smooth, with few thorns. Leaves light green,
semiglossy.

William Lobb, *p. 177*
(Laffay, 1855)

A centifolia moss. The very mossy buds have
a strong pine scent when touched.

Flowers
3 in. (7.5 cm) wide. Deep mauve. Double;
65–75 petals. Midseason bloom, not
recurrent. Very fragrant. Full blossoms,
usually muddled (rarely quartered); larger
outer petals enclose many shorter central
petals.

Foliage
4–5 ft. (1.2–1.5 cm) tall. Vigorous, upright,
arching, open. Disease resistant and winter
hardy. Canes bristly and thorny. Leaves soft,
medium green.

York and Lancaster, *p. 145*
(1551)

Also called *Rosa damascena versicolor*. This
festive rose has some pink petals and some
white ones mixed irregularly in blooms that
may be all pink or all white, or roughly
half-and-half. York and Lancaster is named
for the rival houses of 15th-century England;
the emblem of York was a white rose, that
of Lancaster a red rose. The periodic battles
of these rivals for the English throne came
to be known as the Wars of the Roses.

Flowers
2½–3 in. (6–7.5 cm) wide. Parti-colored
pink and white. Double; 24–30 petals.
Midseason bloom, not recurrent. Fragrant.
Loosely cup-shaped.

Foliage
3–4 ft. (90–120 cm) tall. Bushy but not very
vigorous. Needs good cultivation and
frequent repropagation to keep it going.
Disease free and winter hardy. Canes very
bristly and thorny. Leaves rough, gray-green.

Zéphirine Drouhin, *p. 166*
(Bizot, 1868)

An excellent low to medium climber, this pink Bourbon is recommended for areas near walkways because of its fragrance and because it is almost thornless.

Flowers
3½–4 in. (9–10 cm) wide. Medium pink. Semidouble; perhaps 20–24 petals. Good all-season bloom. Very fragrant. Loose, cupped form.

Foliage
8–12 ft. (2.4–3.5 m) tall. Upright, vigorous, well branched. Disease resistant and winter hardy. Canes very smooth, almost thornless. Leaves medium green, semiglossy.

Floribundas

Early in the 20th century, in an attempt to bring larger flowers and repeat flowering to winter-hardy roses, the polyantha roses were crossed with the hybrid teas. Working in Denmark in the 1920s, D. T. Poulsen was the first to breed floribundas intentionally, although some experts, reaching back to find the "first" floribunda, have settled on Gruss an Achen (1909) as the earliest example of the class.

A Hardy New Breed
Whatever their strict origins, the roses that resulted from this experimentation were hardy plants with open, cupped or saucer-shaped flowers. Known at the time as hybrid polyanthas, they made wonderful additions to any garden, almost continually in bloom with gay, colorful, outreaching clusters of flowers.

Development Within the Class
By the 1940s, it had become evident that the term "hybrid polyantha" was not suitable. By this time in their development, through continual successful breeding, floribundas had become established as larger, shrubbier plants than the dwarf polyanthas. So the name floribunda was adopted; the term captures the most exciting feature of the class—the prolific blooms that these roses put forth, year after year.

One early and very interesting variety in the class is Betty Prior, which has abundant clusters of single (five-petaled) blossoms. When in bloom, it has the look of a flowering dogwood tree.

The Trend Toward High-Centered Blooms
Toward the second half of this century, breeders began experimenting to develop a floribunda with a formal, high-centered bloom, like that of a hybrid tea. In the 1950s, Gene Boerner developed two varieties, Fashion and Vogue, which are highly acclaimed floribundas with a high-centered, hybrid tea–type bloom.

Prizes and Awards
In addition to Fashion and Vogue, there are many other floribundas that have claimed top awards in the rose world. Frensham, introduced in 1946, Little Darling (1956), and Angel Face (1969), a modern development, have all won prizes through the years. But the most popular floribunda of all time is the dark crimson Europeana, which remains a favorite in its color range and class.

Floribundas Today
Today, floribundas come in an enormously wide range of colors; most varieties bear well-formed flowers in small to large clusters. Floribundas are slightly more hardy and disease resistant than the hybrid teas.

Exceptional Landscape Value

Adaptable to numerous garden settings, floribundas thrive in combination with other roses. Because they come in such a wide array of colors, they are very popular for use as borders. Floribundas will also make fine hedges, planted fairly close in two staggered rows.

Culture

Because most floribundas are quite hardy, they can be grown in a range of locales. Most varieties in this class are resistant to disease, although a few require protection from mildew in cool, wet environments. In the garden, you can treat them as you would hybrid teas, although they require a little less attention throughout the growing season. You should, of course, be careful to maintain them neatly, pruning when necessary and removing spent blooms and twigs.

The Future of Floribundas

The experimentation begun earlier in this century still goes on today; the hybrid tea and floribunda classes are merging, and the creation of the grandiflora class is only one indication of this trend. The firm of Jackson & Perkins has established the so-called flora-tea rose; some of the roses introduced under this heading are sold as floribundas in the United States and as hybrid teas abroad. Inspired by the problems that this merger entails, the World Federation of Rose Societies is attempting to provide a new classification system, which would create new classes based on the distinction between large-flowered and cluster-flowered roses.

Angel Face, *p. 191*
(Swim & Weeks, 1969)

The mauve Angel Face was an All-America
Rose Selection in 1969 and winner of the
American Rose Society John Cook Medal in
1971. There is a climbing form.

Flowers
3½–4 in. (9–11.5 cm) wide. Deep mauve.
Double; 35–40 petals. Midseason bloom
followed by good repeat bloom. Very
fragrant. Formal, high-centered blossom
opens to become cupped; petals ruffled;
showy yellow stamens. Blooms singly and in
small clusters.

Foliage
2½–3 ft. (75–90 cm) tall. Bushy, spreading,
vigorous. Disease resistant and winter hardy.
Dark green, leathery, semiglossy leaves borne
on moderately thorny canes.

Apache Tears, *p. 203*
(Pikiewicz, 1971)

This floribunda variety combines the best
features of two classes: the flower form of
the hybrid tea and the abundant blooms of
the polyanthas.

Flowers
3½ in. (9 cm) wide. Cream, edged with red.
Double; 35 petals. Good midseason bloom
with excellent repeat bloom. Slight
fragrance. Bloom form classic hybrid
tea-type, with petals unfurling evenly from
a high center.

Foliage
2½–3½ ft. (75–90 cm) tall. Upright, bushy,
well branched. Disease resistant and winter
hardy. Canes moderately thorny. Leaves large,
light green, semiglossy.

Apricot Nectar, *p. 184*
(Boerner, 1966)

An All-America Rose Selection for 1966. The
crowded, tight clusters of flowers fail to
present the best aspect of Apricot Nectar; it
is best grown disbudded, like hybrid teas are
for exhibition.

Flowers
4–4½ in. (10–11.5 cm) wide. Apricot-pink,
yellow at base. Abundant midseason bloom
with good repeat bloom. Double; 35 petals.
Fruity fragrance. Hybrid tea–type form.
Blooms singly and in clusters.

Foliage
4–5 ft. (1.2–1.5 m) tall. Upright, vigorous,
slender habit. Disease resistant and very
winter hardy. Canes very smooth, few
thorns. Leaves medium green, semiglossy.

Betty Prior, *p. 194*
(Prior, 1935)

The abundant single flowers of Betty Prior
have an overall effect that has been likened
to that of flowering dogwood.

Flowers
3–3½ in. (7.5–9 cm) wide. Medium to deep
pink. Single; 5 petals. Abundant midseason
bloom with excellent repeat. Fragrant.
Blossom cupped, opening to become saucer
shaped. Blooms in clusters.

Foliage
5–7 ft. (1.5–2.1 m) tall. Upright, vigorous,
bushy. Disease resistant and winter hardy.
Canes moderately thorny. Leaves medium
green, semiglossy.

Cathedral, *p. 199*
(McGredy, 1975)

Also called Coventry Cathedral, this rose was
an All-America Rose Selection in 1976. Its
high-centered blooms resemble those of
hybrid teas.

Flowers
4–5 in. (10–12.5 cm) wide. Apricot blend.
Double; 18–24 petals. Good midseason
bloom with good repeat bloom. Slight
fragrance. Petals open evenly from a high
center.

Foliage
3⅓–4 ft. (100–120 cm) tall. Upright, bushy,
well branched. Disease resistant and winter
hardy. Canes moderately thorny. Leaves dark
green, glossy.

Charisma, *p. 196*
(E. G. Hill Co., 1977)

This red-and-yellow-blend was an
All-America Rose Selection in 1978.

Flowers
2½–3 in. (6–7.5 cm) wide. Red-and-yellow
blend. Double; 35–45 petals. Good
midseason bloom with good repeat bloom.
Slight fragrance. Blossoms have petals
unfurling evenly from a high center. Blooms
singly and in clusters.

Foliage
3–3½ ft. (90–105 cm) tall. Upright, well
branched, spreading. Disease resistant and
winter hardy. Canes moderately thorny.
Leaves medium green, leathery, glossy.

Circus, *p. 195*
(Swim, 1956)

An All-America Rose Selection for 1956,
Circus is one of the multicolored roses that
develop their changing colors on exposure to
sunlight. There is a climbing form.

Flowers
3 in. (7.5 cm) wide. Yellow, changing to
coral, pink, and red in sunlight. Double;
45–58 petals. Midseason bloom with good
repeat bloom. Spicy fragrance. High-centered
form becomes cupped, with gold stamens.

Foliage
2½–3 ft. (75–90 cm) tall. Bushy, spreading.
Disease resistant, but needs protection from
black spot. Winter hardy. Canes moderately
thorny. Leaves medium green, leathery,
semiglossy.

Dusky Maiden, *p. 202*
(LeGrice, 1947)

Royal National Rose Society Gold Medal
winner in 1948. This extremely floriferous
rose is one of the outstanding "Maid" series
of floribundas created by E. B. LeGrice.

Flowers
3–3½ in. (7.5–9 cm) wide. Deep crimson.
Single; 5–7 petals. Abundant midseason

bloom with excellent repeat bloom. Fragrant. Blooms open to become saucer shaped, with bright golden stamens. Blooms in small clusters.

Foliage
2–3 ft. (60–90 cm) tall. Upright, well branched, vigorous. Disease resistant and winter hardy. Canes fairly smooth, with few thorns. Leaves dark green, large, glossy.

Escapade, *p. 190*
(Harkness, 1967)

This prolific bloomer is not a true single—its blossoms have 12 petals—but it has much the same garden effect as a single rose.

Flowers
3 in. (7.5 cm) wide. Pink with a white center. Semidouble; 12 petals. Good midseason bloom with excellent repeat bloom. Fragrant. Blossoms open to become saucer shaped. Blooms in clusters.

Foliage
2½–3 ft. (75–90 cm) tall. Upright, well-branched, spreading. Disease resistant and winter hardy. Canes moderately thorny. Leaves light to medium green, glossy.

Europeana, *p. 201*
(DeRuiter, 1968)

This dark crimson floribunda was an All-America Rose Selection for 1968 and winner of The Hague Gold Medal in 1962. It remains the most popular exhibition rose of its type and color range.

Flowers
3 in. (7.5 cm) wide. Dark crimson. Semidouble; 15–20 petals. Abundant midseason bloom, good repeat bloom. Cupped form blooming in large clusters. Very slight fragrance.

Foliage
2½–3 ft. (75–90 cm) tall. Upright and vigorous; bushy and spreading. Disease resistant. Winter hardy. Canes moderately thorny. Young leaves red, maturing to dark green; leathery, glossy.

Eutin, *p. 203*
(Kordes, 1940)

Many floribundas are, like Eutin, ideal for
hedges because they are spreading,
floriferous, and winter hardy.

Flowers
1–1½ in. (2.5–4 cm) wide. Deep red.
Double; 30 petals. Mid- to late-season bloom,
then continuous bloom until frost. Very
slight fragrance. Cupped blossoms occur in
large clusters.

Foliage
2½–3 ft. (75–90 cm) tall. Upright, vigorous,
bushy, spreading. Disease resistant and
winter hardy. Canes moderately thorny.
Leaves small, abundant, dark green, leathery,
glossy.

Evening Star, *p. 188*
(Warriner, 1974)

Sold as a hybrid tea in Europe, this pure
white rose is one of the "flora-tea" series
introduced by Jackson & Perkins.

Flowers
4–4½ in. (10–11.5 cm) wide. Pure white.
Double; 35 petals. Midseason bloom with
fair repeat bloom. Slightly fragrant. Formal,
high-centered, hybrid tea–type bloom.
Blooms singly and in small clusters.

Foliage
3–3½ ft. (90–105 cm) tall. Upright,
vigorous, bushy. Disease resistant. Very
tender. Leaves dark green, large, leathery.

Eye Paint, *p. 200*
(McGredy, 1975)

The multicolored Eye Paint, with its bushy
habit of growth, performs like a shrub rose
and makes a good hedge.

Flowers
2½ in. (5 cm) wide. Red with white center
and golden stamens. Single; 5–7 petals.
Midseason bloom with good repeat bloom.
Slightly fragrant. Blossom form open, flat; in
clusters.

Foliage
3–4 ft. (90–120 cm) tall. Upright, vigorous, bushy, spreading. Disease resistant, but needs protection from black spot. Winter hardy. Canes rather thorny, with small, abundant, dark green leaves.

Fashion, *p. 195*
(Boerner, 1950)

Fashion is a highly acclaimed floribunda. In addition to being an All-America Rose Selection for 1950, it claimed the Royal National Rose Society Gold Medal in 1948, the Bagatelle Gold Medal in 1949, the Portland Gold Medal in 1949, and the American Rose Society Gold Medal in 1954.

Flowers
3–3½ in. (7.5–9 cm) wide. Coral pink. Double; 21–24 petals. Midseason bloom with excellent repeat. Slight fragrance. Hybrid tea–type form. Blooms singly and in small clusters.

Foliage
3½–4½ ft. (105–145 cm) tall. Upright, vigorous, bushy. Disease resistant and winter hardy. Canes moderately thorny, with medium green, semiglossy leaves.

First Edition, *p. 194*
(Delbard, 1977)

This bright floribunda was an All-America Rose Selection for the year of its introduction.

Flowers
2½–3 in. (6–7.5 cm) wide. Coral-orange. Double; 28 petals. Good midseason bloom with fair repeat bloom. Slight fragrance. Hybrid tea–type form. Blooms singly and in clusters.

Foliage
3½–4 ft. (105–120 cm) tall. Upright, vigorous, well branched. Disease resistant. Not winter hardy without protection. Canes moderately thorny. Leaves large, light green, glossy.

French Lace, *p. 186*
(Warriner, 1980)

An All-America Rose Selection in 1982, French Lace is a hybrid tea–type floribunda variety.

Flowers
3½–4 in. (9–10 cm) wide. White. Double; 35 petals. Good midseason bloom with good repeat bloom. Moderate fragrance. Bloom form classic hybrid tea–type, with petals unfurling evenly from a high center.

Foliage
3–3½ ft. (90–105 cm) tall. Upright, bushy, well branched. Disease resistant and winter hardy. Canes moderately thorny. Leaves medium green, semiglossy.

Frensham, *p. 200*
(Norman, 1946)

Winner of the Royal National Gold Medal in 1943, and the American Rose Society Gold Medal in 1955, Frensham is a classic floribunda variety.

Flowers
3 in. (7.5 cm) wide. Dark red. Semidouble; 15 petals. Excellent midseason bloom with good repeat bloom. Slight fragrance. Bloom form cupped to saucer shaped, in clusters.

Foliage
2½–3 ft. (75–90 cm) tall. Vigorous, bushy, spreading. Disease resistant and winter hardy. Canes moderately thorny. Leaves dark green, semiglossy.

Gene Boerner, *p. 191*
(Boerner, 1969)

An All-America Rose Selection for 1969. This flower's namesake is the hybridizer who has done more than any other in this country toward the development of the floribunda rose.

Flowers
3–3½ in. (7.5–9 cm) wide. Even, medium pink. Double; 35 petals. Good midseason bloom followed by excellent repeat bloom.

Little or no fragrance. Hybrid tea-type form.
Blooms singly and in clusters.

Foliage
4-5 ft. (1.2-1.5 m) tall. Upright, vigorous,
slender habit. Disease resistant and winter
hardy. Canes moderately thorny. Leaves
medium green, semiglossy.

Goldilocks, *p. 184*
(Boerner, 1945)

Goldilocks claimed the American Rose
Society John Cook Medal in 1947. It is a
classic floribunda that has held its place on
the market and in gardens over the years.

Flowers
3½ in. (9 cm) wide. Deep yellow, fading to
cream. Double; 45 petals. Abundant
midseason bloom with good repeat. Little or
no fragrance. Flower form cupped, ruffled;
blooms in clusters.

Foliage
3½-4 ft. (105-120 cm) tall. Vigorous,
bushy, spreading. Disease resistant, but needs
winter protection. Moderately thorny canes
bear medium green, leathery, glossy leaves.

Gruss an Aachen, *p. 188*
(Geduldig, 1909)

Although the floribunda class was established
some 30 years after this rose's introduction,
Grüss an Aachen has been classed with the
floribundas because many experts believe it
expresses the qualities of this group. It was
bred, however, from a Bengal (China) and a
Bourbon, according to the introducer and
hybridizer.

Flowers
3-3½ in. (7.5-9 cm) wide. Flesh pink
fading to cream. Very double; perhaps 200
petals. Early to midseason bloom followed by
good repeat bloom. Fragrant. Old rose form;
when fully expanded, reflexes into a ball of
tightly packed petals.

Foliage
2-2½ ft. (60-75 cm) tall. Vigorous, bushy.
Disease resistant and winter hardy. Canes

very smooth, with few thorns. Leaves small, abundant, medium green, glossy.

Iceberg, *p. 186*
(Kordes, 1958)

This pure white rose is known as Schneewittchen in Germany and Fée de Neiges in France. A Royal National Rose Society Gold Medal winner in 1958, it makes an excellent hedge.

Flowers
3 in. (7.5 cm) wide. Pure white. Double; 30 petals. Early to midseason bloom followed by reliable repeat bloom all season. Fragrant. Hybrid tea form, opening to cupped form, blooming in clusters.

Foliage
4 ft. (1.2 m) tall. Upright, bushy. Needs protection from black spot. Winter hardy. Leaves light green, semiglossy.

Impatient, *p. 199*
(Warriner, 1984)

This recently introduced floribunda, which has blossoms like those of a hybrid tea, was an All-America Rose Selection for 1984.

Flowers
3 in. (7.5 cm) wide. Orange with yellow base. Double; 20–30 petals. Good midseason bloom with fair repeat bloom. Slight fragrance. Hybrid tea form; blooms singly and in small clusters.

Foliage
3–3½ ft. (90–105 cm) tall. Upright, vigorous, well branched. Disease resistant and winter hardy. Canes very thorny. Leaves dark green, semiglossy.

Intrigue, *p. 202*
(Warriner, 1984)

An All-America Rose Selection for 1984. There is another floribunda—a red one, by Kordes—that is also called Intrigue. Although Kordes' flower is sold mostly in

Europe, there are some of them in the U.S., and the confusion is unfortunate.

Flowers
3 in. (7.5 cm) wide. Medium purple. Double; 20–30 petals. Good midseason bloom with good repeat bloom. Very fragrant. High-centered form, blooming singly and in clusters.

Foliage
1 ft. (90 cm) tall. Upright, vigorous, well branched. Disease resistant, but not winter hardy without protection. Canes moderately thorny. Leaves dark green, glossy.

Ivory Fashion, *p. 185*
(Boerner, 1959)

This fragrant white floribunda was an All-America Rose Selection for 1959.

Flowers
3½ in. (9 cm) wide. Ivory white. Semidouble; 15–18 petals. Abundant midseason bloom with good repeat bloom. Fragrant. Open form, showing decorative yellow stamens. Blooms in clusters.

Foliage
3½–4 ft. (105–120 cm) tall. Upright, vigorous, well branched. Disease resistant and winter hardy. Canes smooth, with few thorns. Leaves medium green, leathery, semiglossy.

Lavender Pinocchio, *p. 189*
(Boerner, 1948)

These flowers are an unusual shade of lavender, intense and somewhat grayed, making Lavender Pinocchio an unforgettable rose.

Flowers
3–3½ in. (7.5–9 cm) wide. Deep lavender. Double; 25–30 petals. Good midseason bloom with fair repeat bloom. Fragrant. Loose, open, ruffled form in clusters.

Foliage
2½–3 ft. (75–90 cm) tall. Vigorous, bushy, compact. Disease resistant and winter hardy.

Canes moderately thorny. Leaves medium green, leathery.

Little Darling, *p. 192*
(Duehrsen, 1956)

Winner of the Portland Gold Medal in 1958 and the American Rose Society David Fuerstenberg Prize in 1964, this fragrant floribunda could be used as a shrub rose. Some rosarians consider that it makes a good hedge.

Flowers
2½–3 in. (6–7.5 cm) wide. Yellow and salmon-pink blend. Double; 24–30 petals. Abundant early to midseason bloom, followed by good repeat bloom all season. Spicy fragrance. Open, cupped form, blooming in clusters.

Foliage
2½–3½ ft. (75–105 cm) tall. Vigorous, bushy, spreading. Disease resistant and winter hardy. Leaves dark green, leathery, glossy.

Masquerade, *p. 196*
(Boerner, 1949)

Masquerade was a Royal National Rose Society Gold Medal winner in 1952. It is a "changing colors" rose; its hues deepen with exposure to sunlight.

Flowers
2½ in. (6 cm) wide. Yellow, turning salmon-pink and dark red. Semi-double; 12–20 petals. Profuse midseason bloom with good repeat bloom. Slight fragrance. High-centered form opening flat, revealing bright stamens. Blooms in clusters.

Foliage
2½–3 ft. (75–90 cm) tall. Vigorous, bushy, compact. Disease resistant and winter hardy. Canes moderately thorny. Leaves dark green, leathery.

Orangeade, *p. 197*
(McGredy, 1959)

Orangeade, with its abundant, bright orange blooms, claimed the Royal National Rose Society Gold Medal in 1959.

Flowers
3–3½ in. (7.5–9 cm) wide. Orange. Semidouble; 7–9 petals. Abundant midseason bloom, with good repeat. Slight fragrance. Open blooms in large clusters.

Foliage
2½–3 ft. (75–90 cm) tall. Vigorous, bushy, spreading. Disease resistant, but needs protection from mildew in cool, wet climates. Not winter hardy without protection. Leaves dark green, round, rather sparse.

Poulsen's Pearl, *p. 189*
(Poulsen, 1949)

A unique floribunda variety. Like all single roses, Poulsen's Pearl is very effective in garden display.

Flowers
3 in. (7.5 cm) wide. Light pink. Single; 5 petals. Midseason bloom with good repeat bloom. Fragrant. Bloom opens to become saucer shaped; its showy pink stamens are an unusual feature.

Foliage
2½–3 ft. (75–90 cm) tall. Upright, bushy. Disease resistant and winter hardy. Canes moderately thorny. Leaves light to medium green, semiglossy.

Redgold, *p. 197*
(Dickson, 1971)

Redgold was an All-America Rose Selection for 1971. The red color of the petal tips does not develop unless the flowers are exposed to strong sunlight. The cut flowers have a long vase life.

Flowers
2½–3 in. (6–7.5 cm) wide. Yellow, edged with red. Double; 25–30 petals. Good

midseason bloom, with fair repeat later in the season. Slight fruity fragrance. Hybrid tea form, opening to cup shape; blooms singly and in clusters.

Foliage
3–3½ ft. (90–105 cm) tall. Upright, vigorous, well branched. Disease resistant and winter hardy. Canes very thorny. Leaves medium green, semiglossy, and rather sparse.

___

Rose Parade, *p. 190*
(J. B. Billiams, 1975)

The vigorous Rose Parade, with its bright pink flowers, was an All-America Rose Selection for 1975.

Flowers
3½ in. (9 cm) wide. Rose-pink to coral-pink. Double; 30 petals. Abundant midseason bloom with good repeat bloom. Fragrant. Open, cupped blooms, in clusters.

Foliage
2½–3 ft. (75–90 cm) tall. Vigorous, bushy, compact. Disease resistant and winter hardy. Leaves large, dark green, glossy.

___

Sarabande, *p. 198*
(Meilland, 1957)

An All-America Rose Selection for 1960, Sarabande captured the Bagatelle Gold Medal, the Geneva Gold Medal, and the Rome Gold Medal in 1957, as well as the Portland Gold Medal in 1958. Sarabande is a spectacular rose that grows best in cool climates.

Flowers
2½ in. (6 cm) wide. Orange-red. Semidouble; 10–15 petals. Profuse midseason bloom with excellent repeat bloom. Slightly spicy fragrance. Form cupped to flat, showing bright yellow stamens, blooming in large clusters.

Foliage
2½ ft. (75 cm) tall. Vigorous, bushy. Disease resistant and winter hardy. Canes moderately thorny. Leaves medium green, semiglossy.

Saratoga, *p. 187*
(Boerner, 1963)

Saratoga's fragrant white blooms somewhat resemble gardenias. This rose was an All-America Rose Selection for 1964.

Flowers
4 in. (10 cm) wide. White. Double; 30–35 petals. Profuse midseason bloom, fair repeat. Very fragrant. Open blossoms, in clusters.

Foliage
4–4½ ft (120–135 cm) tall. Upright, well branched, vigorous. Disease resistant and winter hardy. Canes moderately thorny. Leaves light green, leathery, glossy.

Sea Pearl, *p. 193*
(Dickson, 1964)

This variety has never been given the publicity it deserves—yet it is nonetheless gaining in popularity each year.

Flowers
4½ in. (11.5 cm) wide. Light pink, reverse light apricot-yellow. Double; 24 petals. Profuse early to midseason bloom with good repeat bloom. Hybrid tea form; blooms singly and in clusters.

Foliage
3–3½ ft. (90–105 cm) tall. Upright, vigorous, well branched. Disease resistant and winter hardy. Canes moderately thorny. Leaves dark green, semiglossy.

Showbiz, *p. 201*
(Tantau, 1981)

Showbiz was an All-America Rose Selection for 1985. It is also known as Ingrid Weibull and Bernhard Daneke Rose.

Flowers
2½–3 in. (6–7.5 cm) wide. Medium red. Double; 28–30 petals. Good all-season bloom. Slight fragrance. Open, cupped form, with ruffled petals. Blooms in clusters.

Foliage
2½–3 ft. (75–90 cm) tall. Upright, vigorous,

spreading. Disease resistant and winter hardy.
Leaves dark green, glossy.

Simplicity, *p. 192*
(Warriner, 1979)

A good hedge rose, Simplicity has been
described as a pink version of Iceberg.

Flowers
3–4 in. (7.5–10 cm) wide. Medium pink.
Semidouble; 18–20 petals. Abundant
all-season bloom. Little or no fragrance.
Flower form opens to become cupped.
Blooms in clusters.

Foliage
2½–3½ ft. (75–105 cm) tall. Upright,
vigorous, bushy. Disease resistant and winter
hardy. Leaves medium green, semiglossy.

Summer Snow, *p. 187*
(Perkins, 1938)

In an unusual reverse, the climbing form of
Summer Snow was introduced in 1936, and
the bush form sported from it 2 years later.

Flowers
2½–3 in. (6–7.5 cm) wide. White.
Semidouble; 18–24 petals. Good all-season
bloom. Little or no fragrance. Cupped form;
blooms in clusters.

Foliage
2½–3 ft. (75–90 cm) tall. Upright, vigorous,
bushy. Disease resistant. Not winter hardy.
Canes moderately thorny. Leaves light green,
semiglossy. The climbing form achieves 8–10
feet and makes a good pillar rose.

Sun Flare, *p. 185*
(Warriner, 1983)

An All-America Rose Selection for 1983, Sun
Flare has an unusual, licoricelike fragrance.

Flowers
3 in. (7.5 cm) wide. Light to medium
yellow. Double; 27–30 petals. Good
all-season bloom. Slight licorice fragrance.

High centered, opening to become cupped. Blooms singly and in clusters.

Foliage
2–2½ ft. (60–75 cm) tall. Upright, vigorous, spreading. Disease resistant and winter hardy. Leaves light green, glossy.

Trumpeter, *p. 198*
(McGredy, 1977)

This hybrid tea–type floribunda produces an abundance of brilliant orange-red blooms.

Flowers
3½ in. wide. Orange-red. Double; 35–40 petals. Excellent midseason bloom with excellent repeat bloom. Slight fragrance. High-centered, classic hybrid tea bloom form. Blooms singly and in clusters.

Foliage
3½–4½ ft. (105–135 cm) tall. Upright, bushy, well branched. Disease resistant and winter hardy. Canes moderately thorny. Leaves dark green, glossy.

Vogue, *p. 193*
(Boerner, 1951)

An All-America Rose Selection for 1952, Vogue claimed the Portland Gold Medal and the Geneva Gold Medal in 1950.

Flowers
3½–4½ in. (9–11.5 cm) wide. Coral. Double; 25 petals. Good all-season bloom. Slight fragrance. High-centered form, blooming singly and in clusters.

Foliage
2½–3 ft. (75–90 cm) tall. Upright, vigorous, compact. Disease resistant and winter hardy. Canes moderately thorny. Leaves medium green, semiglossy.

Grandifloras

The year 1954 witnessed the inauguration of a new class of roses: the grandifloras. Intended to combine the long stems and beautiful blossoms of the hybrid teas with the hardiness and the clustered flowers of the floribundas, the grandifloras are still a small group, and only a few varieties within the class have come close to realizing these goals. But it is early days yet, and rose growers hope to achieve a great deal in the coming years.

First and Finest
It is interesting that the very first grandiflora—the one for which the new class was created—has also proven to be the finest. Queen Elizabeth, a variety introduced with much fanfare in the second year of that monarch's reign, has set the standard for all grandifloras. Queen Elizabeth was the progeny of Charlotte Armstrong (the seed parent and a hybrid tea) and Floradora (the pollen parent and a floribunda); the result of this union combined the best features of both classes. Queen Elizabeth has large, classic-shaped blossoms, usually occurring in small clusters. The robust, vigorous plant produces profuse blooms, with excellent repeat blooms throughout the growing season.

Permission from the Queen
Queen Elizabeth was hybridized by Dr. Walter E. Lammerts and introduced by Germain's, Inc. (Germain Seed and Plant Co.) of Los Angeles, California. Queen Elizabeth II granted Dr. Lammerts the right to use her name, and the British lawmakers formalized this permission in an act of Parliament. Germain's presented the very first Queen Elizabeth rose to Her Majesty in 1954.
Since that date, many other cultivars have been placed in the Grandiflora class, but no other rose has come up to the standard of Queen Elizabeth, and only a few—such as Comanche and Montezuma—have approached it.

A Difference of Opinion
Although the first rose in this class was named in honor of their queen, rose growers in Great Britain have never acknowledged the grandiflora class, classifying these cultivars instead as floribundas. In the United States, there are many varieties that cannot justifiably be placed in the grandiflora class; these roses are referred to as hybrid tea–type floribundas.

A Blend of Traits
In most respects, grandifloras display characteristics intermediate to those of its parent classes. Generally more vigorous than both floribundas and hybrid teas, they are only a little hardier than the latter, and thus cannot survive harsh winters.
Like floribundas, grandifloras produce abundant blooms, but the flowers themselves have the form and size of the hybrid teas.

Grandifloras exceed either parent, however, in height—most grow taller than members of these other two classes. Queen Elizabeth, for example, grows to a height of seven feet.

Making Use of Grandifloras
Because of their great height, grandifloras are well suited for use as hedges. They also make an excellent backdrop for other roses, or for all manner of different flowers in the garden. With their hybrid tea heritage, they produce wonderful long-stemmed blooms that are perfect for cutting and for use in a wide variety of arrangements.

Culture
You can grow your grandifloras much as you would hybrid teas, making allowances, of course, for their extra vigor and height. When pruning, be sure not to cut the canes back too far. Remember too that grandifloras are only a little hardier, on the whole, than hybrid teas, and certainly not as cold-tolerant as many floribunda varieties.

Future Considerations
As rose growers continue to perfect their techniques, the distinctions between certain classes of roses become smaller and smaller. This is what has happened with the floribundas, which have begun to resemble hybrid teas more and more; as grandiflora development becomes more advanced, the characteristics that set this class off may become less discernible. Until that time, modern rosarians will continue to produce better and better grandifloras.

Aquarius, *p. 209*
(Armstrong, 1971)

Aquarius was an All-America Rose Selection
for 1971. Its blooms can be large for the
grandiflora class, particularly when the plant
is disbudded. Flowers have a long vase life.

Flowers
3½–4½ in. (6–11.5 cm) wide. Medium pink
blended with cream. Double; 35–40 petals.
Good all-season bloom. Slight fragrance.
High-centered, evenly petaled form.

Foliage
4½–5 ft. (135–150 cm) tall. Upright,
vigorous, bushy. Disease resistant and winter
hardy. Leaves large, medium green, leathery.

Camelot, *p. 210*
(Swim & Weeks, 1964)

Camelot is particularly good for cutting, as
its flowers have a long vase life. It was an
All-America Rose Selection for 1965.

Flowers
3½–4 in. (9–10 cm) wide. Coral. Double;
40–55 petals. Good all-season bloom. Spicy
fragrance. Cupped form.

Foliage
5–5½ ft. (150–165 cm) tall. Upright,
vigorous, well branched. Disease resistant
and winter hardy. Leaves dark green,
leathery, glossy.

Comanche, *p. 207*
(Swim & Weeks, 1968)

This All-America Rose Selection for 1969 is
perhaps closer to the Grandiflora ideal than
many other cultivars in the class. It is long
lasting on the bush and as a cut flower.

Flowers
3–3½ in. (7.5–9 cm) wide. Orange-red.
Double; 35–40 petals. Abundant all-season
bloom. Slight fragrance. Form high centered
to cupped. Blooms singly and in clusters.

Foliage
4½–5 ft. (135–150 cm) tall. Upright, very

vigorous, bushy. Disease resistant and winter
hardy. Leaves medium green, leathery.

Gold Medal, *p. 206*
(Christensen, 1982)

Gold Medal has deep yellow blooms tipped
with red; they hold their form and color
well.

Flowers
3½ in. (9 cm) wide. Deep yellow, tipped
red. Double; 35–40 petals. Good all-season
bloom. Slight fruity, or tealike, fragrance.
Classic high-centered form. Blooms singly
and in clusters.

Foliage
4½–5½ ft. (135–165 cm) tall. Upright,
vigorous, bushy. Disease resistant, but needs
protection from black spot. Tender. Leaves
dark green, semiglossy.

Love, *p. 211*
(Warriner, 1980)

This All-America Rose Selection for 1980 is
a grandiflora that could just as easily be
considered a hybrid tea, as its blooms have
the classic, high-centered form.

Flowers
3½ in. (9 cm) wide. Red with white
reverse. Double; 24–30 petals. Good
continuous bloom throughout the season.
Very slight fragrance. High-centered, hybrid
tea–type form holds well before developing a
cupped form with confused center.

Foliage
3–3½ ft. (90–105 cm) tall. Upright,
moderately vigorous, sparsely branched.
Disease resistant and winter hardy. Very
thorny canes bear medium green, dull, rather
sparse leaves.

Montezuma, *p. 209*
(Swim, 1955)

Winner of the Geneva Gold Medal in 1955,
the Royal National Rose Society Gold Medal

in 1956, and the Portland Gold Medal in 1957, Montezuma comes very close to the grandiflora ideal.

Flowers
3½–4 in. (9–10 cm) wide. Deep coral. Double; 32–40 petals. Good all-season bloom. Slight fragrance. High-centered, classic form. Blooms singly and in small clusters.

Foliage
4½–5 ft. (135–150 cm) tall. Upright, very vigorous, compact, and well branched. Disease resistant and winter hardy. Canes moderately thorny. Leaves medium green, leathery, semiglossy.

Pink Parfait, *p. 210*
(Swim, 1960)

An All-America Rose Selection for 1961, Pink Parfait also claimed the Portland Gold Medal in 1959 and the Royal National Rose Society Gold Medal in 1962.

Flowers
3½–4 in. (9–10 cm) wide. Light to medium pink. Double; 20–25 petals. Abundant midseason bloom followed by good repeat bloom. Slight fragrance. Bloom high-centered to cupped. Blooms singly and in particularly fine clusters.

Foliage
3½–4½ ft. (105–135 cm) tall. Upright, vigorous, bushy. Disease resistant and winter hardy. Canes moderately thorny. Leaves medium green, leathery, semiglossy.

Prominent, *p. 206*
(Kordes, 1971)

Known as Korp in Europe, Prominent was an All-America Rose Selection for 1977 and the winner of the Portland Gold Medal that same year.

Flowers
3½ in. (9 cm) wide. Orange-red. Double; 30–35 petals. Excellent all-season bloom. Slight fragrance. Cupped form. Blooms singly and in clusters.

Foliage
3½–4½ ft. (105–135 cm) tall. Upright, well branched. Moderately vigorous. Disease resistant and winter hardy. Canes thorny. Leaves dull dark green, leathery.

Queen Elizabeth, *p. 208*
(Lammerts, 1955)

The prototype of the grandiflora class, Queen Elizabeth has proved itself second in popularity only to Peace in this century. In addition to being an All-America Rose Selection for the year of its introduction, this magnificent rose has captured top honors over the course of many years. It was the Royal National Rose Society Gold Medal winner in 1955, winner of the American Rose Society Gertrude M. Hubbard Gold Medal in 1957, recipient of the American Rose Society National Gold Medal Certificate in 1960, and the Golden Rose of The Hague in 1968. There is a climbing form.

Flowers
3½–4 in. (9–10 cm) wide. Medium pink. Double; 37–40 petals. Abundant midseason bloom followed by excellent repeat bloom. Fragrant. Blossom high centered to cupped. Blooms singly and in small clusters.

Foliage
5–7 ft. (1.5–2.1 m) tall. Upright, very vigorous, bushy. Disease resistant and winter hardy. Canes moderately thorny. Leaves dark green, leathery, glossy.

Shreveport, *p. 208*
(Kordes, 1982)

An All-America Rose Selection for 1982, Shreveport is named for the Louisiana city that is the home of the American Rose Center. This rose's cut flowers have a long vase life.

Flowers
3½–4 in. (9–10 cm) wide. Orange blend. Double; 24–30 petals. Fair all-season bloom. Slight fragrance. Cupped form.

Foliage
4½–5 ft. (135–150 cm) tall. Upright,

vigorous, bushy. Disease resistant and winter
hardy. Canes moderately thorny. Leaves dark
green, glossy.

Sundowner, *p. 207*
(McGredy, 1978)

An All-America Rose Selection for 1979.
Sundowner is a grandiflora of distinctive
color; it could perhaps fit as well into the
hybrid tea class.

Flowers
4 in. (10 cm) wide. Apricot to orange blend.
Double; 35 petals. Good all-season bloom.
Very fragrant. Cupped form. Blooms singly
and in clusters.

Foliage
4½–5½ ft.´ (135–165 cm) tall. Upright,
vigorous, well branched. Disease resistant,
but needs protection against mildew in cool,
wet climates. Winter hardy. Canes
moderately thorny. Leaves large, medium
green, leathery.

White Lightnin', *p. 211*
(Swim & Christensen, 1980)

This rose has rather small blossoms occurring
in small clusters. Nonetheless, White
Lightnin' is in many ways similar to the
hybrid teas, and could easily be classed with
them.

Flowers
3½–4 in. (9–10 cm) wide. White. Double;
26–32 petals. Good all-season bloom. Very
fragrant. Cupped form. Blooms singly and in
clusters.

Foliage
4½–5 ft. (135–150 cm) tall. Upright,
vigorous, bushy. Disease resistant and winter
hardy. Canes moderately thorny. Leaves dark
green, glossy.

Hybrid Teas

The year 1867 marks a watershed in the history of rose cultivation, for that year witnessed the introduction of La France, the variety generally recognized as the first hybrid tea of superlative distinction. In consequence, the American Rose Society has settled on this year as the dividing line between "old-fashioned" and "modern" roses. It is important to bear in mind, however, that this date is arbitrary, in one sense. It is simplistic to consider that hybrid teas did not exist before that time, because much development led up to the creation of La France. Indeed, in any class of roses, the true "firsts"—by genetic standards—probably resemble their forebears much more than they do the typical members of that class.

Origins of the Class
The hybrid tea class was developed in the late 19th and early 20th centuries by crossing two kinds of old garden roses—hybrid perpetuals and teas. Until the development of the hybrid teas, the hybrid perpetuals had been the most popular roses worldwide. Unfortunately, they were not reliable repeat-bloomers, which the teas (originating in China and other parts of Asia) were.

A Melding of Traits
Thus experimentation in blending these two sorts of roses was begun. The resulting flowers were a little smaller than the hybrid perpetuals, but a good deal more shapely than the teas. And although these new roses produced a first bloom that was less profuse than that of their progenitors, their repeat flowering was much more reliable. The plants were not as strong, sturdy, and winter hardy as the hybrid perpetuals, but much stronger, more upright, and hardier than the teas.

Early Adventures in Cross-Breeding
The first rose hybridizer known to have kept records of crosses was Henry Bennett, who introduced a series of "pedigreed roses" in the late 1800s. Before this time, the principles of cross-breeding were not well understood, and rose growers were apt to simply plant different roses next to each other; they could then wait and watch, hopeful that their plants would interbreed, and that some useful mixing of characteristics would take place.

Doubtless, this process had proved itself somewhat fruitful over time, but it was not an efficient way to develop new varieties. But in the late part of the 19th century, as the principles of genetic inheritance came to be elucidated and understood, tremendous advances became possible.

Marvelous New Colors
Until the beginning of the 20th century, roses had been grown in shades of white, pink, red, and mauve, but there were very few yellow roses. Joseph Pernet-Dicher began experimenting in the late

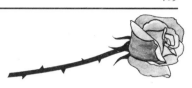

1800s with Persian Yellow (*Rosa foetida persiana,* the double form of the Austrian Briar). In the early 1900s he succeeded in introducing the first hybrid tea roses of a rich, pure, deep yellow.

The addition of this new color to the rose-grower's palette was of tremendous value, for it opened up a whole new world of color possibilities. At last, breeders had the ability to create brilliant, vibrant colors: flame reds, burning coppers, and other brilliant shades that had for so long been out of reach.

These early yellow and yellow blend hybrid teas were called "pernetianas" at the time, but through much interbreeding they soon became assimilated into the hybrid tea class. Unfortunately, this new group of roses also brought with them a susceptibility to black spot.

Tremendous Popularity

Today, the hybrid teas are the most popular of all roses. They also constitute a very large group, and new varieties are constantly being created. Grown in almost every part of the world, they bloom all season long, from spring to fall. With their elegant long-stemmed blooms, hybrid teas are well suited to formal rose gardens, but they also do nicely as shrubs in less formal settings.

American Pride, *p. 238*
(Warriner, 1978)

Its bright color and profuse blossoms make this healthy red rose a garden asset.

Flowers
4½–5½ in. (11.5–14 cm) wide. Bright medium to dark red. Double; 45–50 petals. Blooms best in early summer and fall. Little or no fragrance. High centered, becoming cupped with a confused center.

Foliage
5–5½ ft. (150–165 cm) tall. Upright, well branched. Disease resistant and winter hardy. Leaves large, dark green, semiglossy.

Bewitched, *p. 226*
(Lammerts, 1967)

An All-America Rose Selection and winner of the Portland Gold Medal in its year of introduction, Bewitched is a classic pink Hybrid Tea rose with a long vase life.

Flowers
5 in. (12.5 cm) wide. Even, medium pink. Double; 24–30 petals. Continuous all-season bloom. Medium to strong true-rose fragrance. Formal, high-centered form, opening gradually to show yellow stamens.

Foliage
7–9 ft. (2.1–2.7 m) tall. Upright and vigorous, somewhat willowy. Disease resistant, but needs protection against mildew in cool, wet climates. Winter hardy with some protection. Canes moderately thorny. Leaves large, medium green, semiglossy.

Blue Moon, *p. 225*
(Tantau, 1965)

Known as Mainzer Fastnacht in West Germany, this rose is very close to the blue side of lavender. It claimed the Rome Gold Medal in 1964.

Flowers
4½ in. (11.5 cm) wide. Mauve. Double; 40 petals. Good all-season bloom. Strong lemon

fragrance. Petals open evenly from a high
center, showing yellow stamens only when
fully expanded.

Foliage
4–5 ft. (1.2–1.5 m) tall. Upright, well
branched; of medium vigor. Disease resistant,
but not reliably winter hardy without
protection. Canes moderately thorny. Leaves
medium green, semiglossy.

Brandy, *p. 241*
(Swim & Christensen, 1982)

This All-America Rose Selection for 1982 is
popular for its outstanding color and
fruity fragrance.

Flowers
4–4½ in. (10–11.5 cm) wide. Apricot blend.
Double; 25–30 petals. Profuse all-season
bloom. Moderately strong, fruity fragrance.
Informal, loose form, opening quickly to
show bright golden stamens.

Foliage
4–5 ft. (1.2–1.5 m) tall. Upright, vigorous.
Disease resistant but needs protection from
black spot. Winter hardy with some
protection. Canes moderately thorny. Leaves
large, abundant, medium green, glossy.

Charlotte Armstrong, *p. 223*
(Lammerts, 1940)

An All-America Rose Selection for 1940,
Charlotte Armstrong was the winner of the
Portland Gold Medal in 1941. This rose is
noted for its beautiful, long, slender buds,
which open to an informal flower form, and
for its brilliant deep pink color. A climbing
form is available.

Flowers
3½–4½ in. (9–11.5 cm) wide. Deep cerise
pink. Double; 35 petals. Good early summer
bloom with moderate repeat bloom. Good
fragrance. Form rather loose and informal.

Foliage
4–5 ft. (1.2–1.5 m) tall. Upright, vigorous,
compact. Disease resistant; winter hardy with

some protection. Canes moderately thorny.
Leaves large, dark green, leathery.

Chicago Peace, *p. 219*
(Johnson, 1962)

This sport of Peace displays all of that
famous rose's good qualities in a deeper
color range.

Flowers
5–5½ in. (12.5–14 cm) wide. Deep pink
with strong yellow at base; some streaks and
patches of pink, yellow, and apricot. Double;
50–60 petals. Good all-season bloom. Some
fragrance. Form even and full but not high
centered.

Foliage
4½–5½ ft. (135–165 cm) tall. Upright,
vigorous, well branched. Disease resistant
and winter hardy. Canes moderately thorny.
Leaves large, leathery, glossy, dark green.

Christian Dior, *p. 236*
(Meilland, 1958)

An All-America Rose Selection for 1962, this
red hybrid tea won the Geneva Gold Medal
in 1958. The edges of the petals burn in hot,
dry settings, so it is advisable to plant
Christian Dior where it will receive some
afternoon shade.

Flowers
4–4½ in. (10–11.5 cm) wide. Medium red.
Double; 50–60 petals. Midseason bloom with
fair repeat bloom. Slight fragrance. Formal,
high-centered bloom opening to a cupped
form, full, well filled with petals.

Foliage
4–5 ft. (1.2–1.5 m) tall. Upright, vigorous,
well branched. Disease resistant but needs
protection from mildew. Not winter hardy
without protection. Canes have few thorns.
Leaves large, medium green, leathery,
semiglossy.

Chrysler Imperial, *p. 235*
(Lammerts, 1952)

An All-America Rose Selection in 1953, Chrysler Imperial won the Portland Gold Medal in 1951, the American Rose Society John Cook Medal in 1964, and the James Alexander Gamble Rose Fragrance Medal in 1965. This classic hybrid tea has proven popularity. A climbing form is available.

Flowers
4½–5 in. (11.5–12.5 cm) wide. Deep red. Double; 40–50 petals. Profuse midseason bloom, with good repeat. Very fragrant true-rose (damask) scent. High-centered form opening to a very full, evenly petaled bloom.

Foliage
4–5 ft. (1.2–1.5 m) tall. Upright, vigorous, compact. Disease resistant, but needs protection from mildew in cool, wet climates. Winter hardy. Canes moderately thorny; leaves dark green, semiglossy.

Color Magic, *p. 229*
(Warriner, 1978)

This All-America Rose Selection for 1978 is a "changing colors" variety; the deeper color spreads and intensifies as the petals are exposed to sunlight.

Flowers
5 in. (12.5 cm) wide. Ivory to deep pink. Double; 20–30 petals. Continuous all-season bloom. Slight fragrance. Very even, circular form, becoming cupped; blooms singly and in clusters.

Foliage
3½–4 ft. (105–120 cm) tall. Upright, well branched. Disease resistant, but not winter hardy without protection. Canes moderately thorny. Leaves large, dark green, semiglossy.

Crimson Glory, *p. 233*
(Kordes, 1935)

Crimson Glory claimed the Royal National Rose Society Gold Medal in 1936 and the James Alexander Gamble Rose Fragrance Medal in 1961. This classic hybrid tea is beloved for its fragrance, color, and petal texture. There is a very good climbing form.

Flowers
4–4½ in. (10–11.5 cm) wide. Deep, velvety crimson-red. Double; about 30 petals. Good all-season bloom. Very fragrant, with true damask rose scent. Classic form, but not extremely high centered.

Foliage
3½–4 ft. (105–120 cm) tall. Vigorous, spreading; needs judicious pruning to encourage a more upright habit. Disease resistant. Winter hardy. Moderately thorny. Leaves dark green, leathery, glossy.

Dainty Bess, *p. 223*
(Archer, 1925)

A Royal National Rose Society Gold Medal winner in 1925, this pink rose is the best-known and most widely grown of all the modern single roses. A climbing form is available.

Flowers
3½ in. (9 cm) wide. Medium to light pink. Single; 5 petals. Good all-season bloom. Fragrant. Petals open flat revealing maroon stamens. Blooms singly and in clusters.

Foliage
3½–4 ft. (105–120 cm) tall. Upright, well branched. Disease resistant and winter hardy. Canes very thorny. Leaves medium to dark green, leathery, semiglossy.

Dolly Parton, *p. 237*
(Winchel, 1983)

Very long lasting on the bush and as a cut flower, this bright red rose is strongly appealing for both color and fragrance.

Flowers
4½–5 in. (11.5–12.5 cm) wide. Vivid orange-red. Double; 30–35 petals. Good all-season bloom. Intensely fragrant. Classic, high-centered form.

Foliage
4–5 ft. (1.2–1.5 m) tall. Upright, well

branched, vigorous. Disease resistant. Young leaves dark red, maturing to dark green; glossy.

Double Delight, *p. 228*
(Swim & Ellis, 1977)

This All-America Rose Selection for 1977 is a "changing colors" hybrid tea. It is popular for its color, form, and fragrance. Cut flowers have a long vase life.

Flowers
5½ in. (14 cm) wide. Creamy white with red edge, becoming red. Double; 35–45 petals. Excellent all-season bloom. Spicy fragrance. High-centered, classic form.

Foliage
3½–4 ft. (105–120 cm) tall. Upright, spreading, very bushy. Disease resistant, but needs protection from mildew in cool, wet climates. Winter hardy. Leaves a dull medium green.

Duet, *p. 220*
(Swim, 1960)

This pink blend was an All-America Rose Selection for 1961. Its flowers—a light pink and deeper pink bicolor—have a long vase life.

Flowers
4 in. (10 cm) wide. Light pink with deeper pink reverse. Double; 25–35 petals. Good midseason bloom with excellent repeat. Fragrant. Classic high-centered hybrid tea form.

Foliage
4½–5½ ft. (135–165 cm) tall. Upright, vigorous, well branched. Disease resistant and winter hardy. Leaves large, medium green, leathery.

Eclipse, *p. 242*
(Nicolas, 1935)

This rose was named to commemorate the solar eclipse that took place on August 31,

1932. The rose has received top honors: the Portland Gold Medal and Rome Gold Medal in 1935; the Bagatelle Gold Medal in 1936; and the American Rose Society David Fuerstenberg Prize in 1938.

Flowers
3½–4 in. (9–10 cm) wide. Medium yellow. Double; 25–30 petals. Profuse midseason bloom, with fair repeat bloom. Slight fragrance. Bloom form rather open and loose.

Foliage
3½–4 ft. (105–120 cm) tall. Upright, vigorous, bushy. Disease resistant. Not reliably winter hardy without protection. Leaves dark green, leathery.

Electron, *p. 232*
(McGredy, 1970)

Called Mullard Jubilee in Europe, this All-America Rose Selection in 1973 is popular for its rich color and fragrance.

Flowers
5 in. (12.5 cm) wide. Deep pink. Double; 32 petals. Very fragrant. Abundant all-season bloom. Classic hybrid tea form.

Foliage
2½–3½ ft. (75–105 cm) tall. Upright, vigorous, stocky. Disease resistant and winter hardy. Canes moderately thorny. Leaves medium green, leathery.

First Prize, *p. 230*
(Boerner, 1970)

An All-America Rose Selection in 1970 and winner of the American Rose Society Gertrude M. Hubbard Gold Medal in 1971. This fragrant hybrid tea is a popular exhibition variety, and the cut flowers have a long vase life.

Flowers
5–5½ in. (12.5–14 cm) wide. Medium pink, center blended with ivory. Double; 30–35 petals. Good midseason bloom and good repeat bloom. Fragrant. Classic high-centered hybrid tea form.

Foliage
5 ft. (150 cm) tall. Vigorous, spreading.
Disease prone; requires protection against
black spot and mildew. Very tender. Leaves
dark green, leathery.

***

Fragrant Cloud, *p. 238*
(Tantau, 1963)

Fragrant Cloud received the Royal National
Rose Society Gold Medal in 1963, the
Portland Gold Medal in 1967, and the James
Alexander Gamble Rose Fragrance Medal in
1969. Called Duftwolke in West Germany, it
is popular for its intense fragrance. Its
coral-red color is somewhat grayed, but not
unpleasing.

Flowers
5 in. (12.5 cm) wide. Coral-red. Double;
25–30 petals. Good all-season bloom. Intense
fragrance, true rose (damask) scent. High-
centered form opens to full, evenly petaled
bloom.

Foliage
4–5 ft. (1.2–1.5 m) tall. Upright, vigorous,
well branched. Disease resistant and winter
hardy. Leaves dark green, glossy.

***

Fred Edmunds, *p. 242*
(Meilland, 1943)

This All-America Rose Selection for 1944
won the Portland Gold Medal in 1942. A
climbing form is available.

Flowers
5–5½ in. (12.5–14 cm) wide. Copper-orange.
Double; 20–30 petals. Good all-season
bloom. Very spicy fragrance. Cupped bloom
opens to showy golden stamens.

Foliage
2½–3 ft. (75–90 cm) tall. Bushy, open
habit. Disease resistant and winter hardy.
Canes moderately thorny. Leaves medium
green, leathery, glossy.

Friendship, *p. 228*
(Lindquist, 1978)

All-American Rose Selection for 1979, this
is a typical pink hybrid tea. There are a
greater number of roses in the pink and pink
blend color classes than any other color; thus
those that appear on the market are more
carefully monitored than roses in other color
classes. Friendship has a long vase life.

Flowers
5½ in. (14 cm) wide. Medium to deep pink.
Double; 25–30 petals. Good all-season
bloom. Very fragrant. Classic high-centered
hybrid tea form.

Foliage
5–6 ft. (1.5–1.8 m) tall. Upright, vigorous.
Disease resistant and winter hardy. Leaves
large, medium green, glossy.

Garden Party, *p. 216*
(Swim, 1959)

An All-America Rose Selection in 1960 and
winner of the Bagatelle Gold Medal in 1959,
Garden Party is a popular exhibition variety.

Flowers
5–5½ in. (12.5–14 cm) wide. White with
light pink edge. Double; 25–30 petals.
Profuse midseason bloom followed by good
repeat. Fragrant. Classic high-centered form.

Foliage
5–6 ft. (1.5–1.8 m) tall. Upright, vigorous.
Disease resistant but needs protection from
mildew. Winter hardy. Leaves large, long,
medium green, semiglossy.

Granada, *p. 218*
(Lindquist, 1963)

Winner of the James Alexander Gamble
Rose Fragrance Medal in 1968, Granada
presents a pleasing blend of colors and a
spicy fragrance. It is a prolific bloomer.

Flowers
4–5 in. (10–12.5 cm) wide. Blend of pink,
orange-red, and light yellow. Double; 18–25
petals. Excellent all-season bloom. Spicy

fragrance. Classic high-centered form. Blooms singly and in clusters.

Foliage
5–6 ft. (1.5–1.8 m) tall. Upright, vigorous, bushy. Disease resistant, but needs protection from mildew. Not reliably winter hardy without protection in severe climates. Canes rather thorny. Leaves dark green, leathery.

Gypsy, *p. 236*
(Swim & Weeks, 1972)

An All-America Rose Selection for 1973, Gypsy has particularly brilliant orange-red flowers.

Flowers
4–4½ in. (10–11.5 cm) wide. Orange-red. Double; 30–35 petals. Good all-season bloom. Slight fragrance. Flower form tulip-shaped, well filled with petals. Blooms singly and in clusters.

Foliage
4–5 ft. (1.2–1.5 m) tall. Upright, vigorous, well branched. Disease resistant and winter hardy. Canes moderately thorny. Leaves large, dark green, leathery, glossy.

Helen Traubel, *p. 221*
(Swim, 1951)

An All-America Rose Selection for 1952 and winner of the Rome Gold Medal in 1951. Many roses are named for famous people, but few turn out to have the staying power of this consistently popular classic, which was named for a famous opera singer. Reputedly very difficult to propagate, this rose has nonetheless endured, although it is known among some professionals as "Hell 'n' Trouble."

Flowers
4½–5 in. (11.5–12.5 cm) wide. Pink to apricot blend. Double; 20–25 petals. Good all-season bloom. Moderate fragrance. High-centered, becoming cup shaped. Blooms singly and in clusters.

Foliage
5–5½ ft. (150–165 cm) tall. Upright,

vigorous, bushy. Disease resistant and winter hardy. Canes moderately thorny. Leaves medium green, leathery, semiglossy.

Honor, *p. 214*
(Warriner, 1980)

An All-America Rose Selection for 1980, Honor produces fragrant white blooms all season long. Cut flowers have a long vase life.

Flowers
4–5 in. (10–12.5 cm) wide. White. Double; 20–22 petals. Good all-season bloom. Slight fragrance. Form high centered to open, loose. Blooms singly and in clusters.

Foliage
5–5½ ft. (150–165 cm) tall. Upright, vigorous, well branched. Disease resistant. Not winter hardy without protection. Canes moderately thorny. Leaves large, dark green, leathery.

Irish Gold, *p. 244*
(Dickson, 1966)

Called Grandpa Dickson in Europe, Irish Gold won the Royal National Gold Medal in 1965, The Hague Gold Medal in 1966, and the Golden Rose of The Hague in 1966. Its outer petals quill when the bloom is fully expanded, giving the flower a star-shaped outline.

Flowers
6–7 in. (15–17.5 cm) wide. Light yellow with faint pink edge. Double; 34 petals. Good all-season bloom. Light, sweet fragrance. Classic hybrid tea form with petals unfurling evenly from a high center.

Foliage
4–4½ ft. (120–135 cm) tall. Upright, vigorous, bushy. Disease resistant, but not reliably winter hardy without protection. Leaves dark green, leathery, glossy.

John F. Kennedy, *p. 245*
(Boerner, 1965)

The green tint at the center of the bloom
makes this hybrid tea unique. As the bloom
matures, the green shading disappears.

Flowers
5–5½ in. (12.5–14 cm) wide. White with
green in center. Double; 45–50 petals. Good
all-season bloom. Fragrant. Classic high-
centered form. Blooms singly and in clusters.

Foliage
3–4 ft. (90–120 cm) tall. Upright,
moderately vigorous, compact. Disease
resistant. Not winter hardy without
protection. Canes moderately thorny. Leaves
medium green, leathery, semiglossy.

Kaiserin Auguste Viktoria, *p. 214*
(Lambert, 1891)

Sometimes called K. A. Viktoria, this is one
of the early hybrid teas and is still widely
grown. A climbing form is available.

Flowers
4–4½ in. (10–11.5 cm) wide. Creamy white.
Very double; 100 petals. Lavish early to
midseason bloom, fair repeat bloom. Very
fragrant. Flower form classic, very full, very
evenly petaled.

Foliage
5–7 ft. (1.5–2.1 m) tall. Upright, vigorous,
bushy. Disease resistant and winter hardy.
Leaves dull, dark green.

Keepsake, *p. 233*
(Kordes, 1981)

Also known as Esmeralda, this very fragrant
Hybrid Tea blooms well all season.

Flowers
5 in. (12.5 cm) wide. Deep pink with a
lighter pink reverse. Double; perhaps 30–35
petals. Good all-season bloom. Very fragrant.
Classic high-centered form. Blooms singly
and in clusters.

Foliage
5–6 ft. (1.5–1.8 m) tall. Upright, vigorous,
bushy. Disease resistant and winter hardy.
Canes moderately thorny. Leaves light green,
glossy.

King's Ransom, *p. 243*
(Morey, 1961)

An All-America Rose Selection for 1962.
King's Ransom has held its own over the
years in spite of its faults. It is prone to
mildew and somewhat tender, and its
blooms do not quite achieve the classic
hybrid tea form.

Flowers
5–6 in. (12.5–15 cm) wide. Deep yellow.
Double, 35–40 petals. Profuse midseason
bloom, good repeat bloom. Fragrant.
Blossoms somewhat loose and cup shaped.
Blooms singly and in clusters.

Foliage
4½–5 ft. (135–150 cm) tall. Upright,
vigorous, well branched. Disease resistant,
but needs protection from mildew.
Somewhat tender in severe winter climates.
Canes moderately thorny. Leaves light green,
glossy.

Kölner Karneval, *p. 225*
(Kordes, 1964)

Also known as Cologne Carnival and Blue
Girl, Kölner Karneval sometimes appears on
the market under other names as well. It is
perhaps the most reliable variety in its color
range.

Flowers
5½ in. (14 cm) wide. Mauve. Double; 40
petals. Good all-season bloom. Slight
fragrance. Good hybrid tea form, although
not high centered. Blooms singly and in
clusters.

Foliage
2½–3 ft. (75–90 cm) tall. Upright, vigorous,
bushy. Disease resistant and winter hardy.
Canes moderately thorny. Leaves dark green,
leathery, glossy.

Kordes' Perfecta, *p. 218*
(Kordes, 1957)

This very fragrant hybrid tea was a Royal National Rose Society Gold Medal winner in 1957 and winner of the Portland Gold Medal in 1958.

Flowers
4½–5 in. (11.5–12.5 cm) wide. Cream, with red suffusing from petal edges. Very double; 65–70 petals. Good all-season bloom. Very fragrant. High centered; rather loosely petaled, considering its high petal count. Blooms singly and in clusters.

Foliage
4–5 ft. (1.2–1.5 m) tall. Upright, vigorous, well branched. Disease resistant and winter hardy. Canes very thorny. Leaves dark green, leathery, glossy.

La France, *p. 217*
(Guillot Fils, 1867)

One of the early hybrid teas, La France is considered by many to be the prototype of the class. A climbing form is available.

Flowers
4–4½ in. (10–11.5 cm) wide. Silvery pink with bright pink reverse. Very double; 60 petals. Profuse early to midseason bloom; good repeat, particularly in the fall. Very fragrant. High centered, evenly petaled.

Foliage
4–5 ft. (1.2–1.5 m) tall. Upright, well branched. Moderately vigorous. Disease resistant and winter hardy. Leaves medium size, medium green, semiglossy.

Lady X, *p. 224*
(Meilland, 1966)

The very tall and stately Lady X produces blooms that tend toward the pink side of mauve.

Flowers
4½–5 in. (11.5–12.5 cm) wide. Mauve. Double; perhaps 30–35 petals. Good all-season bloom. Fragrant. Classic,

high-centered form. Blooms mostly singly, few clusters.

Foliage
5-7 ft. (1.5-2.1 m) tall. Upright, well branched, vigorous. Disease resistant and winter hardy. Very thorny canes bear sparse, medium green, leathery, semiglossy leaves.

Medallion, *p. 220*
(Warriner, 1973)

An All-America Rose Selection for 1973, Medallion is a variable hybrid tea rose, changing with climatic conditions. It grows best in mild, cool weather. Cut flowers have a long vase life.

Flowers
5-5½ in. (12.5-14 cm) wide. Light apricot. Double; 25-35 petals. Profuse midseason bloom followed by good repeat bloom. Fruity fragrance. Bloom form loose, tuliplike.

Foliage
4½-5½ ft. (135-165 cm) tall. Upright, vigorous, well branched. Disease resistant, but not reliably winter hardy without protection. Leaves medium green, large, leathery.

Michèle Meilland, *p. 221*
(Meilland, 1945)

This classic light pink hybrid tea has held its place on the market and in gardens against the influx of new varieties that eclipse older—and often better—roses. It has great staying power, on the bush and cut.

Flowers
3½-4 in. (9-10 cm) wide. Light pink. Double; perhaps 30-35 petals. Excellent all-season bloom. Slight fragrance. Classic hybrid tea form. Blooms singly and in clusters.

Foliage
3-4 ft. (90-120 cm) tall. Upright, well branched, compact; moderately vigorous. Disease resistant and winter hardy. Canes moderately thorny. Leaves medium green, semiglossy.

Mirandy, *p. 234*
(Lammerts, 1945)

This classic hybrid tea was an All-America
Rose Selection for 1945. Its velvety, dark red
petals tend to hold their color instead of
developing purple tones.

Flowers
4½–5 in. (11.5–12.5 cm) wide. Very dark
red. Double; 40–50 petals. Good all-season
bloom. Very strong true-rose (damask)
fragrance. Classic hybrid tea form; high
centered, very full.

Foliage
4–5 ft. (1.2–1.5 m) tall. Upright, vigorous,
well branched. Disease resistant and winter
hardy. Canes moderately thorny. Leaves
medium green, leathery, semiglossy.

Miss All-American Beauty, *p. 239*
(Meilland, 1965)

An All-America Rose Selection for 1968, this
rose is called Maria Callas in Europe.

Flowers
5 in. (12.5 cm) wide. Deep pink. Very
double; 50–60 petals. Abundant midseason
bloom with good repeat bloom. Very
fragrant. Classic high-centered form. Blooms
singly and in clusters.

Foliage
4–5 ft. (1.2–1.5 m) tall. Upright, vigorous,
bushy. Disease resistant. Winter hardy. Canes
moderately thorny. Leaves medium green,
leathery.

Mister Lincoln, *p. 235*
(Swim & Weeks, 1964)

Perhaps the most popular hybrid tea in its
color range, Mister Lincoln was an All-
America Rose Selection for 1965.

Flowers
5–5½ in. (12.5–14 cm) wide. Dark red.
Double, 30–40 petals. Good all season
bloom. Very fragrant. Classic high-centered
bloom becomes somewhat cupped, well filled
with petals.

Foliage
4½–5½ ft. (135–165 cm) tall. Upright,
vigorous, well branched. Disease resistant
and winter hardy. Leaves dark green,
leathery, semiglossy.

Mojave, *p. 241*
(Swim, 1954)

An All-America Rose Selection for 1954 and
winner of the Bagatelle Gold Medal and the
Geneva Gold Medal in 1953. The beautiful
blend of colors in this rose call to mind
sunsets in the Mojave Desert.

Flowers
4–4½ in. (10–11.5 cm) wide. Apricot-
orange, tinted red. Double; 25 petals.
Fragrant. Good all-season bloom. Classic,
high-centered form. Blooms singly and in
clusters.

Foliage
4–5 ft. (1.2–1.5 m) tall. Upright, vigorous,
well branched. Disease resistant and winter
hardy. Canes moderately thorny. Leaves
medium green, glossy.

Mon Cheri, *p. 229*
(Christensen, 1982)

An All-America Rose Selection for 1982. A
"changing colors" variety, Mon Cheri has
bright pink blossoms that slowly deepen to
red with exposure to sunlight. Its fragrance
may not be detected in the garden, but a
vase of cut flowers will perfume a room.

Flowers
4½ in. (11.5 cm) wide. Pink-edged red,
becoming red. Double; 30–35 petals. Good
all-season bloom. Moderate fragrance. Classic
hybrid tea form, but not particularly high
centered.

Foliage
2½–3 ft. (75–90 cm) tall. Upright, compact.
Disease resistant and winter hardy. Canes
moderately thorny. Leaves dark green, glossy.

New Day, *p. 245*
(Kordes, 1977)

Known as Mabella in Europe. If grown in partial shade, New Day will retain the depth of its color as the bloom matures.

Flowers
4–5 in. (10–12.5 cm) wide. Medium to deep yellow. Double; 25–35 petals. Abundant midseason bloom, followed by good repeat bloom. Very spicy fragrance. Classic hybrid tea form, with petals unfurling evenly from a high center. Long vase life.

Foliage
4 ft. (1.2 m) tall. Upright, vigorous, well branched. Disease resistant and winter hardy. Canes moderately thorny. Leaves large, light gray-green.

Oklahoma, *p. 232*
(Swim & Weeks, 1964)

This is the deepest hybrid tea in color; it retains a pure, deep maroon-red in most climates, without developing violet or purple shadings. A climbing form is available.

Flowers
4–5½ in. (10–14 cm) wide. Maroon. Double; 40–55 petals. Abundant all-season bloom. Very fragrant. Classic high-centered hybrid tea form.

Foliage
5–6 ft. (1.5–1.8 m) tall. Upright, vigorous, well branched. Disease resistant and winter hardy. Canes moderately thorny. Leaves dull green, leathery.

Olympiad, *p. 237*
(McGredy, 1984)

This All-America Rose Selection for 1984 has particularly velvety petals. Olympiad's bright color holds extremely well, and cut flowers have a long vase life.

Flowers
4–4½ in. (10–11.5 cm) wide. Brilliant medium red. Double; 24–30 petals. Good all-season bloom. Slight fragrance. Classic,

high-centered hybrid tea form. Blooms
mostly singly, few clusters.

Foliage
4–5 ft. (1.2–1.5 m) tall. Upright, vigorous,
compact. Disease resistant and winter hardy.
Canes very thorny. Leaves medium green,
semiglossy.

Oregold, *p. 243*
(Tantau, 1975)

Named Miss Harp in Europe, this deep
yellow hybrid tea was an All-America Rose
Selection in 1975.

Flowers
4½–5 in. (11.5–12.5 cm) wide. Deep yellow.
Double; 35–40 petals. Abundant midseason
bloom, with fair repeat. Slight fragrance.
High centered bloom, becoming cup-shaped.

Foliage
3½–4 ft. (105–120 cm) tall. Upright, well
branched. Moderately vigorous. Disease
resistant, but needs protection from black
spot and mildew. Not reliably winter hardy
without protection. Canes moderately
thorny. Leaves large, dark green, glossy.

Paradise, *p. 230*
(Weeks, 1978)

This hybrid tea, with its classically formed,
red-edged blooms, was an All-America Rose
Selection for 1979. Cut flowers have a long
vase life.

Flowers
3½–4½ in. (9–11.5 cm) wide. Mauve, edged
with red. Double; 26–30 petals. Good all-
season bloom. Fragrant. Classic high-centered
hybrid tea form with petals unfurling
evenly.

Foliage
4–4½ ft. (120–135 cm) tall. Upright,
vigorous, well branched. Disease resistant,
but needs protection from mildew in cool,
wet climates. Winter hardy. Canes
moderately thorny. Leaves dark green, glossy.

Pascali, *p. 215*
(Lens, 1963)

An All-America Rose Selection for 1969,
Pascali won The Hague Gold Medal in 1963
and the Portland Gold Medal in 1967. This
medium-size hybrid tea may be the most
popular variety in its color class.

Flowers
4–4½ in. (10–11.5 cm) wide. Creamy white.
Double; 30 petals. Very slight fragrance.
Excellent all-season bloom. Classic hybrid tea
form.

Foliage
3½–4 ft. (105–120 cm) tall. Upright,
vigorous, well branched. Disease resistant.
Winter hardy. Canes moderately thorny.
Leaves dark green, semiglossy.

Peace, *p. 217*
(Meilland, 1945)

Peace is the rose of the century. Without
doubt the most popular hybrid tea of all.
All-America Rose Selection for 1946 and
winner of the Portland Gold Medal in 1944,
the American Rose Society National Gold
Medal Certificate in 1947, the Royal
National Rose Society Gold Medal in 1947,
and the Golden Rose of The Hague in 1965.
The climbing form is one of the finest and
most beautiful of hybrid tea climbers,
although it requires a few years to become
well established and blooms somewhat
sparsely until then. The variety is known as
Madame Antoine Meilland in France, Gloria
Dei in Germany, and Gioia in Italy.

Flowers
5½–6 in. (14–15 cm) wide. Yellow, edged
pink. Double; 40–45 petals. Good all-season
bloom. Slight fragrance. Classic, high-
centered Hybrid Tea blossoms often open
to confused or divided centers.

Foliage
5–6 ft. (1.5–1.8 m) tall. Upright, vigorous,
branching. Disease resistant and winter
hardy. Canes moderately thorny. Leaves large,
dark green, leathery, glossy.

Perfume Delight, *p. 226*
(Weeks, 1973)

An All-America Rose Selection for 1974, Perfume Delight has a variable fragrance.

Flowers
4–4½ in. (10–11.5 cm) wide. Deep pink. Double; 30–35 petals. Abundant midseason bloom, with fair repeat. Fragrance varies. Cupped form. Blooms singly and in clusters.

Foliage
4–4½ ft. (120–135 cm) tall. Upright, vigorous, well branched. Disease resistant; needs protection from black spot, mildew, and cold. Canes rather thorny. Leaves large, medium green, leathery.

Pink Favorite, *p. 231*
(Van Abrams, 1956)

Winner of the Portland Gold Medal in 1957, Pink Favorite has bright, glossy leaves.

Flowers
3½–4 in. (9–10 cm) wide. Medium pink. Double; 21 to 28 petals. Profuse midseason bloom and good repeat. Slight fragrance. Loose, cupped form, singly and in clusters.

Foliage
4–4½ ft. (120–135 cm) tall. Upright, bushy, vigorous. Disease resistant; hardy. Canes moderately thorny. Leaves green, very glossy.

Pink Peace, *p. 227*
(Meilland, 1959)

Pink Peace claimed the Geneva Gold Medal and the Rome Gold Medal in 1959.

Flowers
4½–6 in. (11.5–15 cm) wide. Medium to deep pink. Very double; 50–65 petals. Good all-season bloom. Very fragrant. Classic form, very full, very evenly petaled.

Foliage
4½–5½ ft. (135–165 cm) tall. Upright, vigorous, bushy. Disease resistant and winter hardy. Canes moderately thorny. Leaves medium green, leathery, glossy.

Precious Platinum, *p. 234*
(Dickson, 1974)

Precious Platinum is an extremely prolific
bloomer. Its cut flowers have a long vase life.

Flowers
3½ in. (9 cm) wide. Medium red. Double;
35–40 petals. Abundant all-season bloom.
Slight fragrance. Typical hybrid tea form, but
not very high centered. Blooms singly and in
clusters.

Foliage
4 ft. (1.2 m) tall. Upright, vigorous, well
branched. Disease resistant and winter hardy.
Canes moderately thorny. Leaves dark green,
leathery, glossy.

Princesse de Monaco, *p. 219*
(Meilland, 1981)

Also called Princess Grace, Princesse de
Monaco is very much like Pristine, but has a
wider band of deeper pink edging.

Flowers
4½ in. (11.5 cm) wide. White with pink
edge. Double; probably 35–40 petals. Sparse
midseason bloom, followed by fair repeat
bloom. Fragrant. Classic high-centered hybrid
tea form.

Foliage
4–4½ ft. (120–135 cm) tall. Upright,
vigorous, well branched. Disease resistant.
Leaves medium green, semiglossy.

Pristine, *p. 216*
(Warriner, 1978)

In a fully expanded bloom, one or more of
Pristine's outer petals drop down below the
others.

Flowers
4½–6 in. (11.5–15 cm) wide. White with
pink edge. Double; 30–35 petals. Good
all-season bloom. Slight fragrance. Classic
hybrid tea form. Blooms mostly singly.

Foliage
4–4½ ft. (120–135 cm) tall. Upright,

moderate vigor, slender habit. Disease
resistant. Winter hardy. Canes smooth with
few thorns. Leaves very large, dark green,
glossy.

Royal Highness, *p. 222*
(Swim & Weeks, 1962)

This All-America Rose Selection for 1963
won the Portland Gold Medal in 1960, the
Madrid Gold Medal in 1962, and the
American Rose Society David Fuerstenberg
Prize in 1964.

Flowers
5–5½ in. (12.5–14 cm) wide. Light pink.
Double; 40–45 petals. Good all-season
bloom. Very fragrant. Classic high-centered
hybrid tea form.

Foliage
4½–5 ft. (135–150 cm) tall. Upright,
vigorous, bushy. Disease resistant. Not
winter hardy. Canes moderately thorny.
Leaves light green, leathery, glossy.

Seashell, *p. 231*
(Kordes, 1976)

An All-America Rose Selection for 1976.
Seashell's color is much deeper than its name
might suggest.

Flowers
4–5 in. (10–12.5 cm) wide. Coral to apricot
blend. Double; 35–40 petals. Fair all-season
bloom. Fragrant. Classic hybrid tea form.
Blooms singly and in clusters.

Foliage
3½–4 ft. (105–120 cm) tall. Upright,
moderately vigorous, well branched. Disease
resistant and winter hardy. Canes moderately
thorny. Leaves dark green, glossy.

Sterling Silver, *p. 224*
(Fisher, 1957)

The first of the lavender or mauve hybrid
teas, this is still one of the best for bloom
form and color. There is a climbing form.

Flowers
3½ in. (9 cm) wide. Mauve. Double; 30
petals. Fair all-season bloom. Very fragrant,
lemon scent. Classic hybrid tea form. Blooms
mostly singly, some clusters.

Foliage
2½–3 ft. (75–90 cm) tall. Upright, well
branched. Very little vigor. Disease resistant,
but needs protection from black spot and
mildew. Winter hardy. Canes quite smooth.
Leaves medium green, leathery, semiglossy.

Summer Sunshine, *p. 244*
(Swim, 1962)

This is a dependable yellow hybrid tea, and
one of the best in its color range for disease
resistance. It needs protection in severe
winter climates.

Flowers
3½–5 in. (9–12.5 cm) wide. Deep yellow.
Double; 25 petals. Excellent all-season
bloom. Slight fragrance. Form high centered
to cupped. Blooms singly and in clusters.

Foliage
4–5 ft. (1.2–1.5 m) tall. Upright, vigorous,
well branched. Disease resistant. Somewhat
tender. Canes moderately thorny. Leaves
gray-green, leathery.

Sutter's Gold, *P. 240*
(Swim, 1950)

An All-America Rose Selection for 1950,
Sutter's Gold claimed the Portland Gold
Medal in 1946, the Bagatelle Gold Medal in
1948, the Geneva Gold Medal in 1949, and
the James Alexander Gamble Rose Fragrance
Medal in 1966. It is the most strongly
fragrant of the fruit-scented hybrid teas.

Flowers
4–5 in. (10–12.5 cm) wide. Yellow, overlaid
and veined with orange-gold, and tipped red.
Double; 30–35 petals. Good all-season
bloom. Very fragrant, fruity scent. Classic
hybrid tea form.

Foliage
4–4½ ft. (120–135 cm) tall. Upright,

vigorous, well branched. Disease resistant. Fairly winter hardy. Canes moderately thorny. Leaves dark green, leathery, semiglossy.

Sweet Surrender, *p. 227*
(Weeks, 1983)

This fragrant pink hybrid tea was an All-America Rose Selection for 1983.

Flowers
3½–4½ in. (9–11.5 cm) wide. Medium pink. Double; 40–44 petals. Fair all-season bloom. Very fragrant. Very evenly petaled form opens rather flat.

Foliage
3½–5 ft. (105–150 cm) tall. Upright, compact. Not reliably winter hardy. Leaves large, dull, medium green.

Tiffany, *p. 222*
(Lindquist, 1954)

One of the most popular hybrid teas, Tiffany was an All-America Rose Selection for 1955. It also captured the David Fuerstenberg Prize in 1957 and the James Alexander Gamble Rose Fragrance Medal in 1962. There is a climbing form.

Flowers
4–5 in. (10–12.5 cm) wide. Medium pink to deep pink blend. Double; 25–30 petals. Good all-season bloom. Very fragrant. Classic high-centered form. Blooms singly and in clusters.

Foliage
4–4½ ft. (120–135 cm) tall. Upright, very vigorous, bushy. Disease resistant and winter hardy. Canes moderately thorny. Leaves dark green, glossy.

Tropicana, *p. 239*
(Tantau, 1960)

Called Super Star in Europe, Tropicana was an All-America Rose Selection for 1963. It was the first pure fluorescent orange rose, and still the best in its color range—as evidenced by the 7 gold medals it has captured. Tropicana is the third-biggest-selling rose in this century. A climbing form is available.

Flowers
5 in. (12.5 cm) wide. Orange. Double; 30–35 petals. Excellent all-season bloom. Very fragrant. fruity scent. High-centered form, becoming cup-shaped.

Foliage
4–5 ft. (1.2–1.5 m) tall. Upright, vigorous, well branched. Disease resistant and winter hardy. Canes moderately thorny. Leaves dark green, leathery, glossy.

White Masterpiece, *p. 215*
(Boerner, 1969)

This exhibition hybrid tea has large white blossoms that are unfortunately rather sparse.

Flowers
5–5½ in. (12.5–14 cm) wide. White. Very double, 50–60 petals. Sparse all-season bloom. Slight fragrance. Classic high-centered form.

Foliage
3 ft. (90 cm) tall. Upright, moderate vigor, compact. Disease resistant. Needs winter protection. Leaves medium green, semiglossy.

Yankee Doodle, *p. 240*
(Kordes, 1976)

An All-America Rose Selection for 1976. Yankee Doodle is a dependable hybrid tea, and an extremely prolific bloomer.

Flowers
4 in. (10 cm) wide. Yellow with pink edge and apricot shadings. Very double; 75 petals. Excellent all-season bloom. Slight fragrance. Very full, very evenly petaled, but not high centered.

Foliage
4–4½ ft. (120–135 cm) tall. Upright, vigorous, bushy. Disease resistant and winter hardy. Canes moderately thorny. Leaves dark green, glossy.

Miniatures

Present-day rose growers display a tremendous amount of enthusiasm for miniature roses. These little plants are at the forefront of interest, and new varieties are constantly being created. This was not always the case, however. In times past, rose growers were apt to discard weak varieties; thus many true miniatures have probably turned up, only to be roughly excluded from the nursery bed. Miniatures were considered a curiosity until recent times, when rose breeders began to find an eager market for them.

In the second quarter of this century, there were only a handful of well-known miniature varieties. However, the promise of these little plants was apparent, and some breeders—among them, Jan de Vink and Ralph Moore—set about creating new cultivars. There are now many more rose breeders who are busily creating all manner of miniature varieties.

Miniatures have been crossed with nearly every other class of roses, yielding still more miniature varieties. Drawing on the traits of many of the larger roses in cultivation, breeders have developed compact little bushes and sprawling miniatures that make excellent ground cover—all in a rainbow of colors. There are even climbing miniatures, a few of which may grow as high as five feet, although they retain other class characteristics.

What Makes a Mini?

Miniature roses range in height from about 3 inches to 18 inches, with the average being about a foot. Their stature alone does not entirely justify their classification, as they have other determining characteristics: The well-formed buds and closely spaced foliage are extremely small, the canes are thin, and the plants are very free-flowering and comparatively hardy.

Miniature roses are extremely adaptable. They can be grown in rock gardens, in containers, and along borders; they also hold their own when grown indoors in pots during the winter. Miniatures are a big favorite of city dwellers, who brighten their window ledges with these colorful little plants. These roses are also perfect for small yards; the small size and compact habit of many varieties enable the ambitious rose-grower who has limited space to fill the garden with a wonderful bounty of blossoms.

Uncertain Origins

The miniature rose class is probably derived from *Rosa roulettii* (which is generally believed to be identical to *Rosa chinensis minima,* an ancient Chinese dwarf rose). Cultivated perhaps as far back as 1815, *Rosa rouletti* was first brought to public attention by one Colonel Roulet, who discovered the plant in a Swiss village at about the turn of the century and was quick to recognize its potential. Pompon de Paris, another ancient miniature rose, has been cultivated since about 1839; it was sold in the markets of 19th-century Paris as a pot plant. Some authorities hold that these

varieties are identical, but the descriptions that exist from the early 19th century do not support this view. (Such uncertainty illustrates one problem common to all very old varieties—namely, knowing whether a plant has always been properly labeled. Thus some varieties have been known by different names at different times in history, contributing to the confusion.)

Culture
You should be sure to plant your miniatures where they will receive plenty of sunlight—although small, they need as much sunshine as their larger relatives.

Considering their size, these plants are surprisingly hardy—a little more so than the hybrid teas. In areas with very mild winters, they will survive with little or no protection; in colder regions, mulching should provide the shelter they require.

Miniature roses are very easy to hybridize and work with. They root readily from cuttings, and this is the accepted method of propagation, since these roses lose their miniature status when budded onto a vigorous understock.

Pruning
Like the larger roses, miniatures will lose the energy they need to produce flowers if they are not pruned carefully. Be sure to clear away deadwood and any canes that are weak and spindly. Pruning will help to keep pests and diseases at bay and allow the plant to concentrate on producing vibrant blooms.

Growing Miniatures Indoors
Although miniature roses will grow indoors, they nonetheless need plenty of sunlight—a commodity that is in short supply in most houses or apartments. A southern exposure, unobscured by buildings or trees, will be your best bet.

You can also make use of supplemental artificial light, in the form of fluorescent bulbs, to help your minis to grow indoors. In recent years, growing miniatures indoors under lights has become very popular.

Angel Darling, *p. 267*
(Moore, 1976)

Excellent for bedding and borders, this mauve miniature is good for container planting. It is important when planting miniature roses in containers always to keep them well watered.

Flowers
1½ in. (4 cm) wide. Mauve. Nearly single; 10 petals. Midseason bloom with good repeat bloom. Slight fragrance. Bloom form open, cup shaped, with bright yellow stamens.

Foliage
12–18 in. (30–45 cm) tall. Vigorous, upright, well branched. Disease resistant, but may need protection from black spot and mildew. Winter hardy. Leaves dark green, glossy, leathery.

Antique Rose, *p. 272*
(Moore, 1980)

This miniature looks like an old garden rose of the Bourbon type. Excellent for bedding, borders, or containers, Antique Rose is also good in pots under grow-lights or in a sunny window sill during winter.

Flowers
1¾ in. (4.5 cm) wide. Medium to deep pink. Double; 35–45 petals. Midseason bloom with good repeat bloom. Slight fragrance. Blossom globular.

Foliage
14–16 in. (35–40 cm) tall. Vigorous, upright, spreading, well branched. Disease resistant and winter hardy. Leaves dark green, semiglossy.

Avandel, *p. 256*
(Moore, 1977)

An American Rose Society Award of Excellence winner in 1978, Avandel is good for borders, edgings, miniature garden beds, and also for growing in pots indoors.

Flowers
1–1½ in. (2.5–4 cm) wide. Yellow, blended

with peach and pink. Double; 20–25 petals. Excellent midseason bloom with good repeat. Very fragrant, fruity. Bloom form open, cupped.

Foliage
12 in. (30 cm) tall. Upright, bushy. Disease resistant and winter hardy. Leaves medium to dark green, leathery.

Baby Betsy McCall, *p. 249*
(Morey, 1960)

This light pink rose is excellent for edgings and borders, rock gardens, and special miniature beds. It also grows well in pots indoors during the winter.

Flowers
1–1½ in. (2.5–4 cm) wide. Light pink. Double; 20–24 petals. Midseason bloom with good repeat bloom. Fragrant. Bloom form cupped.

Foliage
12–18 in. (30–45 cm) tall. Upright, bushy, compact. Disease resistant and winter hardy. Leaves light green, leathery.

Baby Cheryl, *p. 262*
(E. D. Williams, 1965)

Excellent for rock gardens, miniature rose beds, and edgings, Baby Cheryl also does well in pots during the winter, under lights or in a sunny window. Most miniatures will grow indoors, but they will not bloom well unless under strong light. They must never be allowed to dry out.

Flowers
1¼ in. (3 cm) wide. Light pink with lighter reverse. Double; 24–30 petals. Midseason bloom with good repeat bloom. Spicy fragrance. Bloom form cupped.

Foliage
8–12 in. (20–30 cm) tall. Bushy, very vigorous, very compact. Disease resistant and winter hardy. Leaves medium green, semiglossy.

Baby Masquerade, *p. 255*
(Tantau, 1956)

A miniature rose showing the China rose
influence, Baby Masquerade blooms yellow
but changes through shades of pink and
coral to medium or deep red where touched
by sunlight. There is a climbing form.

Flowers
1½ in. (4 cm) wide. Yellow, aging red.
Double; 20–24 petals. Midseason bloom
followed by good repeat bloom. Slight, fruity
fragrance. Bloom form cupped, with petals
quilling to form a star shape upon full
expansion.

Foliage
10–14 in. (25–35 cm) tall. Upright, bushy,
spreading. The climbing form will reach up
to 24 in. Disease resistant and winter hardy.
Leaves medium green, semiglossy.

Beauty Secret, *p. 284*
(Moore, 1965)

Winner of the American Rose Society
Award of Excellence in 1975, this fragrant
miniature is good for garden beds and
borders, edgings, and containers. It also
grows well in pots indoors over the winter.

Flowers
1½ in. (4 cm) wide. Medium red. Double;
24–30 petals. Excellent midseason bloom
with excellent repeat bloom. Very fragrant.
Bloom form classic hybrid tea type in
miniature.

Foliage
10–18 in. (25–45 cm) tall. Upright,
vigorous, well branched. Disease resistant
and winter hardy. Leaves medium green,
semiglossy.

Bit O' Magic, *p. 270*
(E. D. Williams, 1979)

Excellent for garden display, Bit O' Magic is
also a popular exhibition variety.

Flowers
1½ in. (4 cm) wide. Pink blended with

deep pink. Very double; 50 petals. Excellent midseason bloom with good repeat bloom. Slight fragrance. Bloom form classic hybrid tea type, with petals unfurling evenly from a high center.

Foliage
12-14 in. (30-35 cm) tall. Vigorous, compact and spreading. Disease resistant and winter hardy. Leaves dark green, glossy.

Bonny, *p. 277*
(Kordes, 1974)

This deep pink "micro-mini" is good for bedding and edgings and excellent in miniature gardens and rock gardens. It is suitable for containers and pots.

Flowers
¾ in. (2 cm) wide. Deep pink. Double; perhaps 35-45 petals. Midseason bloom with excellent repeat bloom. Slight fragrance. Bloom form full, cupped.

Foliage
6-8 in. (15-20 cm) tall. Bushy, compact. Disease resistant and winter hardy. Leaves medium green, semiglossy.

Carol-Jean, *p. 282*
(Moore, 1977)

A miniature rose that is excellent for garden display in miniature rose beds and edgings, rock gardens, and containers in patios. As a young plant, Carol-Jean does well indoors, either under lights or in a sunny window.

Flowers
1 in. (2.5 cm) wide. Deep pink. Double; 20-25 petals. Midseason bloom with good repeat bloom. Slight fragrance. Bloom form cupped.

Foliage
10-18 in. (25-45 cm) tall. Vigorous, upright, well branched. Disease resistant and winter hardy. Leaves dark green, semiglossy.

Center Gold, *p. 250*
(Saville, 1981)

Center Gold won an American Rose
Society Award of Excellence for 1982. The
medium to deep yellow bloom occasionally
sports to near white, so don't be surprised to
see a white flower among all the yellow
ones.

Flowers
1½ in. (4 cm) wide. Medium to deep
yellow. Double; 25–35 petals. Midseason
bloom with good repeat bloom. Little or no
fragrance. Bloom form classic hybrid tea
type, with petals unfurling evenly from a
high center.

Foliage
14–18 in. (35–45 cm) tall. Vigorous,
upright, well branched. Disease resistant and
winter hardy. Leaves medium green,
semiglossy.

Charmglo, *p. 275*
(E. D. Williams, 1980)

Excellent for bedding and borders, rock
gardens, edgings, and container planting,
Charmglo is also good in pots indoors over
winter.

Flowers
1½ in. (4 cm) wide. Pink blend. Double;
35 petals. Midseason bloom with good repeat
bloom. Slight fragrance. Bloom form high
centered to cupped.

Foliage
10–14 in. (25–35 cm) tall. Vigorous, bushy,
compact. Disease resistant and winter hardy.
Leaves dull, dark green.

Chattem Centennial, *p. 278*
(Betty Jolly, 1979)

This orange-red miniature rose is
particularly prolific—outstanding even
among a class known for its abundant
flowering. Excellent for garden display, and
also very good in a pot indoors over the
winter.

Flowers
1½ in. (4 cm) wide. Orange-red. Double; 35 petals. Excellent midseason bloom with very good repeat bloom. Slight fruity fragrance. High-centered or cupped blossoms.

Foliage
10 in. (25 cm) tall. Upright, bushy, compact. Disease resistant and winter hardy. Leaves dark green, glossy.

Chipper, *p. 268*
(Meilland, 1966)

A miniature rose that has remained popular despite the creation of thousands of new varieties, Chipper is excellent for garden display and also good in a pot indoors over winter.

Flowers
1¼ in. (3 cm) wide. Salmon pink. Double; 24–30 petals. Good midseason bloom and excellent repeat bloom. Slight fragrance. Bloom form cupped.

Foliage
10–14 in. (25–35 cm) tall. Vigorous, upright, well branched. Disease resistant and winter hardy. Leaves medium to dark green, leathery, glossy.

Choo-Choo Centennial, *p. 261*
(Betty Jolly, 1980)

This profuse bloomer is excellent for bedding, borders, edgings, container plantings; like many miniatures, it does well indoors over winter.

Flowers
1½ in. (4 cm) wide. Light pink. Very double; 65 petals. Profuse midseason bloom with good repeat bloom. Slight fragrance. Bloom form high centered to cupped, well filled with petals.

Foliage
10–18 in. (25–45 cm) tall. Vigorous, bushy, compact. Disease resistant and winter hardy. Leaves dull, light green.

Cinderella, *p. 258*
(de Vink, 1953)

This classic miniature rose is one of the most popular varieties of all time. One of the very petite "micro-minis," Cinderella is especially good for growing in miniature rose beds and rock gardens and indoors over winter. Its creator, Jan de Vink, was the first breeder of modern miniatures.

Flowers
¾ in. (2 cm) wide. Light pink, fading to white. Very double; 45 petals. Excellent midseason bloom and excellent repeat bloom. Very spicy fragrance. Bloom cupped, tightly filled with even rows of petals.

Foliage
8–10 in. (20–25 cm) tall. Upright, vigorous, compact. Disease resistant and winter hardy. Leaves medium green, semiglossy.

Cricket, *p. 279*
(Christensen, 1978)

Excellent for planting in garden beds and borders, Cricket is also good for container planting and patio display.

Flowers
1¼ in. (3 cm) wide. Orange, blended with yellow. Double; 25 petals. Midseason bloom with good repeat bloom. Slight fragrance. Bloom high centered to cupped.

Foliage
14 in. (35 cm) tall. Upright, bushy. Disease resistant. Winter hardy. Leaves dark green, semiglossy.

Cuddles, *p. 283*
(Schwartz, 1978)

A winner of the American Rose Society Award of Excellence in 1979, this deep coral pink miniature rose is good for bedding and borders and container plantings. Young plants do very well indoors over the winter.

Flowers
1¼ in. (3 cm) wide. Deep coral pink. Very double; 55–60 petals. Excellent midseason

bloom with good repeat bloom. Slight fragrance. Bloom form classic hybrid tea type, with petals unfurling evenly from a high center.

Foliage
14–16 in. (35–40 cm) tall. Vigorous, bushy, compact. Disease resistant and winter hardy. Leaves medium green, semiglossy.

Cupcake, *p. 264*
(Spies, 1981)

This miniature is very full petaled, yet classic in form. Hybridized by an amateur, Cupcake is a big hit with everyone who sees it.

Flowers
1½ in. (4 cm) wide. Medium pink. Very double; 50 petals. Midseason bloom with good repeat bloom. Little or no fragrance. Classic hybrid tea–type form, with petals unfurling evenly from a high center.

Foliage
12–14 in. (30–35 cm) tall. Vigorous, bushy, compact. Disease resistant. Winter hardy. Leaves medium green, semiglossy.

Darling Flame, *p. 279*
(Meilland, 1971)

This orange-red rose is good for bedding and borders, edgings, and containers for patio display. In winter, Darling Flame does well under lights or in a sunny window.

Flowers
1½ in. (4 cm) wide. Orange-red. Double; 25 petals. Midseason bloom with good repeat bloom. Fragrant, fruity. Bloom form globular.

Foliage
10–14 in. (25–35 cm) tall. Bushy, well branched. Disease resistant, but needs protection from black spot and mildew. Winter hardy. Leaves dark green, glossy.

Dreamglo, *p. 274*
(E. D. Williams, 1978)

Excellent for bedding and borders, Dreamglo
is a popular exhibition miniature as well.

Flowers
1 in. (2.5 cm) wide. Red, blended with
white at base. Very double; 50 petals.
Excellent midseason bloom with good repeat
bloom. Slight fragrance. Very full, classic
hybrid tea type, with petals unfurling
evenly from a high center.

Foliage
18–24 in. (45–60 cm) tall. Vigorous,
upright, well branched. Disease resistant and
winter hardy. Leaves medium to dark green,
semiglossy.

Dwarfking, *p. 285*
(Kordes, 1957)

Called Zwergkönig in Europe, this is one of
the early miniatures, and still popular in
spite of the influx of thousands of varieties
since its introduction. Dwarfking is quite
petite—perhaps not a "micro-mini," but very
close to it.

Flowers
1¼ in. (3 cm) wide. Dark red. Double;
20–30 petals. Midseason bloom with good
repeat bloom. Slight fragrance. Bloom form
cupped.

Foliage
8–10 in. (20–25 cm) tall. Dwarf, compact.
Disease resistant and winter hardy. Leaves
dark green, glossy.

Fairlane, *p. 256*
(Schwartz, 1981)

Excellent for garden display, Fairlane also
makes a popular exhibition miniature.

Flowers
1½ in. (4 cm) wide. Yellow blended with
pink and cream. Double; 20 petals.
Midseason bloom with good repeat bloom.
Fragrant. Classic hybrid tea–type form, with
petals unfurling evenly from a high center.

Foliage
10–12 in. (25–30 cm) tall. Bushy, compact.
Disease resistant and winter hardy. Leaves
medium green, glossy.

Fire Princess, *p. 278*
(Moore, 1969)

Fire Princess is excellent for bedding and
borders. Good also for container planting, it
can even be trained on a small trellis.

Flowers
1½ in. (4 cm) wide. Orange-red. Double; 24
petals. Excellent midseason bloom with good
repeat bloom. Little or no fragrance. Bloom
form cupped.

Foliage
12–14 in. (30–35 cm) tall. Very vigorous,
bushy. Disease resistant and winter hardy.
Leaves medium green, leathery, glossy.

Galaxy, *p. 287*
(Moore, 1980)

This dark red miniature rose is good for
garden display in beds, borders, and edgings.
Like most minis, it does well indoors during
the winter, given enough light.

Flowers
1½ in. (4 cm) wide. Dark red. Double; 25
petals. Midseason bloom with good repeat
bloom. Little or no fragrance. Bloom form
high centered to cupped.

Foliage
12 in. (30 cm) tall. Upright, well branched,
compact. Disease resistant and winter hardy.
Leaves medium green, semiglossy.

Gold Coin, *p. 252*
(Moore, 1967)

This classic miniature rose maintains its
popularity year after year. Gold Coin was
originated by Ralph Moore, who has
hybridized more miniatures than any other
breeder, and is sometimes referred to as
"Mister Miniature Rose."

Flowers
1½ in. (4 cm) wide. Deep yellow. Double;
24–30 petals. Excellent midseason bloom
with good repeat bloom. Fragrant. Bloom
form cupped.

Foliage
8–12 in. (20–30 cm) tall. Vigorous, low,
bushy, compact. Disease resistant and winter
hardy. Leaves medium green, semiglossy.

Green Ice, *p. 251*
(Moore, 1971)

A miniature rose with extra-long, lax, canes,
Green Ice can be trained as a climber but is
just perfect for a hanging basket. The pink
buds open to whitish pink blooms,
becoming light green as they age, with a
very pleasing effect.

Flowers
1¼ in. (3 cm) wide. White changing to
green. Double; 30 petals. Midseason bloom
with good repeat bloom. Slight fragrance.
Bloom form classic hybrid tea type, with
petals unfurling evenly from a high center.

Foliage
8 in. (20 cm) tall, and 16 in. (40 cm) wide.
Vigorous, dwarf, bushy, spreading. Disease
resistant and winter hardy. Leaves medium
green, leathery, glossy.

Heidi, *p. 263*
(Christensen, 1978)

This miniature moss variety is suitable for
beds and borders, edgings, rock gardens, and
containers. It does very well indoors in pots
over the winter.

Flowers
1¼ in. (3 cm) wide. Medium pink. Double;
35 petals. Midseason bloom with good repeat
bloom. Very sweet fragrance. Bloom form
high centered to cupped, well filled with
petals.

Foliage
12 in. (30 cm) tall. Very vigorous, bushy.
Disease resistant. Winter hardy. Leaves
medium to dark green, glossy.

Helen Boehm, *p. 261*
(Christensen, 1983)

A popular exhibition variety, this is
especially good in miniature beds and rock
gardens, and for container display. Like many
miniatures, it grows very nicely indoors in
winter.

Flowers
1½ in. (4 cm) wide. Light pink and cream.
Double; 25 petals. Midseason bloom with
good repeat bloom. Slight fragrance. Classic
hybrid tea form, with petals unfurling
evenly from a high center.

Foliage
10–12 in. (25–30 cm) tall. Bushy, well
branched, compact. Disease resistant and
winter hardy. Leaves medium green,
semiglossy.

Hokey Pokey, *p. 257*
(Saville, 1980)

Excellent for garden display in beds, borders,
and edgings, Hokey Pokey is also fine for
container planting and for planting in pots
indoors over winter.

Flowers
1½ in. (4 cm) wide. Apricot to orange
blend. Semidouble; perhaps 20 petals.
Midseason bloom with good repeat. Little
or no fragrance. Bloom form cupped,
opening flat.

Foliage
12–14 in. (30–35 cm) tall. Vigorous, bushy,
compact. Disease resistant and winter hardy.
Leaves medium green, semiglossy.

Holy Toledo, *p. 280*
(Christensen, 1979)

Winner of the American Rose Society
Award of Excellence in 1980. Suitable for
bedding and borders, Holy Toledo is also a
popular exhibition miniature.

Flowers
1¾ in. (4.5 cm) wide. Orange with yellow
at base. Double; 25 petals. Midseason bloom

with good repeat bloom. Slight fragrance.
Classic hybrid tea-type form, with petals
unfurling evenly from a high center.

Foliage
15–18 in. (37.5–45 cm) tall. Vigorous,
bushy, well branched. Disease resistant and
winter hardy. Leaves dark green, glossy.

Honest Abe, *p. 285*
(Christensen, 1978)

A popular exhibition variety, this miniature
moss is not a "micro-mini," but very close to
it. Its dark red blooms add a nice touch to
special miniature rose beds, edgings, rock
gardens, and container planting and it is
good indoors under lights or in a sunny
window over winter.

Flowers
1¼ in. (3 cm) wide. Dark red. Double;
30–35 petals. Very sweet fragrance. Hybrid
tea form with petals unfurling evenly from a
high center.

Foliage
12 in. (30 cm) tall. Very vigorous, bushy,
compact. Disease resistant and winter hardy.
Medium to dark green leaves, leathery and
glossy.

Hot Shot, *p. 280*
(Bennett, 1982)

An American Rose Society Award of
Excellence winner in 1984. Suitable for
garden display as well as exhibition, Hot
Shot is excellent in special miniature rose
beds.

Flowers
1¾ in. (4.5 cm) wide. Orange-red. Double;
35 petals. Midseason bloom with excellent
repeat bloom. Very slight fragrance. Classic
hybrid tea-type form, with petals unfurling
evenly from a high center.

Foliage
8–10 in. (20–25 cm) tall. Very dense, bushy,
rounded. Disease resistant and winter hardy.
Leaves medium green, semiglossy.

Hotline, *p. 272*
(Christensen, 1984)

This miniature moss rose variety is suitable for garden display in beds and borders but perhaps too vigorous for container displays. All the mossy miniature roses have a pine fragrance.

Flowers
1½ in. (4 cm) wide. Medium red. Semidouble; 20 petals. Midseason bloom with good repeat bloom. Hybrid tea form, becoming cupped. Flower has little or no fragrance.

Foliage
15–18 in. (37.5–45 cm) tall. Very vigorous and strong growing, yet compact. Disease resistant. Winter hardy. Leaves medium green, semiglossy.

Hula Girl, *p. 281*
(E. D. Williams, 1975)

Winner of the American Rose Society Award of Excellence in 1975. Hula Girl is a popular exhibition variety and outstanding for garden display. It performs well in beds and borders, edgings, rock gardens, container displays, and even indoors in winter.

Flowers
1¼ in. (3 cm) wide. Orange. Double; 24–30 petals. Fruity fragrance. Midseason bloom with good repeat bloom. High-centered bloom form.

Foliage
12 in. (30 cm) tall. Upright, well branched. Disease resistant and winter hardy. Leaves medium green, semiglossy.

Humdinger, *p. 281*
(Schwartz, 1976)

Winner of the American Rose Society Award of Excellence in 1978, Humdinger is so small that it is almost a "micro-mini." Excellent for garden display and also very good in containers and pots, it is often seen in exhibitions.

Flowers
1 in. (2.5 cm) wide. Orange-red. Very double; 50 petals. Midseason bloom with excellent repeat bloom. Classic hybrid tea-type form, with petals unfurling evenly from a high center.

Foliage
8–10 in. (20–25 cm) tall. Dwarf, bushy, compact. Disease resistant and winter hardy. Leaves dark green, glossy.

Jean Kenneally, *p. 252*
(Bennett, 1984)

This apricot-colored rose is excellent for garden display in beds, borders, edgings, and container plantings. A popular exhibition variety, it is good for growing in pots indoors over the winter.

Flowers
1½ in. (4 cm) wide. Apricot blend. Double; 24–30 petals. Midseason bloom with excellent repeat bloom. Slight fragrance. Classic hybrid tea–type form.

Foliage
10–14 in. (25–35 cm) tall. Upright, well branched, bushy. Disease resistant and winter hardy. Leaves medium green, semiglossy.

Jet Trail, *p. 248*
(Moore, 1964)

This fragrant white rose is good for miniature rose beds and borders and excellent in edgings and rock gardens. It is also suitable for indoor pots over winter.

Flowers
1¼ in. (3 cm) wide. White. Double; 24–30 petals. Midseason bloom with good repeat bloom. Fragrant. Bloom high centered to cupped.

Foliage
10–14 in. (25–35 cm) tall. Bushy, compact. Disease resistant and winter hardy. Leaves medium green, leathery, glossy.

Judy Fischer, *p. 269*
(Moore, 1968)

This popular exhibition variety won an
American Rose Society Award of Excellence
in 1975. Excellent for garden display, it is
perhaps too vigorous for containers and pots.

Flowers
1½ in. (4 cm) wide. Medium pink. Double;
24–30 petals. Midseason bloom with
excellent repeat bloom. Moderate fragrance.
Classic hybrid tea-type form, with petals
unfurling evenly from a high center.

Foliage
18–24 in. (45–60 cm) tall. Upright,
vigorous, well branched. Disease resistant
and winter hardy. Leaves medium green,
semiglossy.

Julie Ann, *p. 276*
(Saville, 1984)

Julie Ann won an American Rose Society
Award of Excellence in 1984. Excellent for
gardens or containers and pots, it is a variety
often encountered at rose shows.

Flowers
1½ in. (4 cm) wide. Orange-red. Double;
24–30 petals. Midseason bloom with good
repeat bloom. Fragrant. Classic hybrid
tea-type bloom form.

Foliage
10–14 in. (25–35 cm) tall. Upright, bushy,
well branched. Disease resistant. Winter
hardy. Leaves medium green, semiglossy.

Kara, *p. 273*
(Moore, 1972)

This little miniature moss variety is a
"micro-mini." It is excellent for special
miniature rose beds and edgings, rock
gardens, and growing in containers.

Flowers
1 in. (2.5 cm) wide. Medium pink. Single;
5 petals. Midseason bloom with excellent
repeat bloom. Fragrant. Bloom form flat,
with showy stamens.

Foliage
6–8 in. (15–20 cm) tall. Dwarf; dense, compact, rounded. Disease resistant and winter hardy. Leaves dark green, semiglossy.

Kathy, *p. 282*
(Moore, 1970)

A miniature rose variety that has proven staying power. Because of its spreading habit, Kathy is especially suitable for pots and hanging baskets.

Flowers
1½ in. (4 cm) wide. Medium red. Double; 24–30 petals. Midseason bloom with excellent repeat bloom. Fragrant. Classic hybrid tea form.

Foliage
8–10 in. (20–25 cm) tall. Spreading growth; vigorous yet compact. Disease resistant and winter hardy. Leaves medium to dark green, leathery, semiglossy.

Kathy Robinson, *p. 271*
(E. D. Williams, 1968)

An excellent variety for garden display and a popular exhibition variety, Kathy Robinson has been a favorite for many years.

Flowers
1½ in. (4 cm) wide. Pink blend with buff reverse. Double; 24–30 petals. Midseason bloom with excellent repeat bloom. Very slight fragrance. High-centered blossoms.

Foliage
14 in. (35 cm) tall. Upright, bushy, well branched. Disease resistant and winter hardy. Leaves medium green, semiglossy.

Lavender Jewel, *p. 264*
(Moore, 1978)

With its very rich tone of lavender or lilac, this mini is second only to Lavender Lace in popularity in its color class. It is good for container growing and makes an excellent hanging basket.

Flowers
1½ in. (4 cm) wide. Mauve. Semidouble;
12–20 petals. Midseason bloom with good
repeat bloom. Slight fragrance. Open, cupped
form.

Foliage
10–15 in. (25–37.5 cm), with long,
spreading canes. Disease resistant and winter
hardy. Leaves dark green, semiglossy.

Lavender Lace, *p. 265*
(Moore, 1968)

Winner of the American Rose Society
Award of Excellence in 1975, this mauve
variety has remained the most popular
miniature rose in its color class. The
climbing form is a favorite for hanging
baskets.

Flowers
1½ in. (4 cm) wide. Mauve. Double; 24–30
petals. Midseason bloom with good repeat
bloom. Slight fragrance. Classic, high-
centered to cupped blossom.

Foliage
8–12 in. (20–30 cm) tall. Bushy, compact.
The climbing form may reach 3 ft. (90 cm).
Disease resistant and winter hardy. Leaves
medium green, semiglossy.

Lemon Delight, *p. 255*
(Moore, 1978)

This yellow miniature moss is very delicate
and compact, almost a "micro-mini." Good
for special miniature rose beds and edgings,
and excellent for containers and pots.

Flowers
1¼ in. (3 cm) wide. Medium yellow.
Almost single to semidouble; 7–10 petals.
Midseason bloom with good repeat bloom.
Slight, sweet fragrance. Blossoms cupped to
saucer shaped.

Foliage
12 in. (30 cm) tall. Bushy, well branched,
compact. Disease resistant and winter hardy.
Leaves medium green, semiglossy.

Little Jackie, *p. 266*
(Saville, 1982)

Winner of the American Rose Society
Award of Excellence in 1984, this fragrant
miniature rose is suitable for bedding and
borders. It is a popular show variety.

Flowers
1½ in. (4 cm) wide. Orange blended with
pink and yellow. Double; 24–30 petals. Very
fragrant. Classic hybrid tea–type form.

Foliage
14–18 in. (35–45 cm) tall. Upright,
vigorous, bushy, well branched. Disease
resistant and winter hardy. Leaves medium
green, semiglossy.

Loveglo, *p. 265*
(E. D. Williams, 1983)

Excellent for beddings and borders, this
variety is a little too vigorous for containers
and pots. It is often seen in exhibitions.

Flowers
1½ in. (4 cm) wide. Coral salmon. Double;
35 petals. Midseason bloom with good
repeat. Fragrant. Classic hybrid tea–type
bloom form.

Foliage
12–18 in. (30–45 cm) tall. Vigorous,
upright, well branched. Disease resistant and
winter hardy. Leaves dark green, glossy.

Magic Carrousel, *p. 274*
(Moore, 1972)

Winner of the American Rose Society
Award of Excellence in 1975. Suitable for
bedding and borders, it is an eye-catcher in
the garden, and a popular show variety.

Flowers
1¾–2 in. (4.5–5 cm) wide. White with red
edges. Semidouble; 12–20 petals. Midseason
bloom with good repeat bloom. Little or no
fragrance. Open blossoms, cup-shaped to flat.

Foliage
15–18 in. (37.5–45 cm) tall; sometimes

reported up to 30 in. (75 cm) tall. Very vigorous, spreading. Disease resistant and winter hardy. Leaves medium green, semiglossy.

Mary Marshall, *p. 267*
(Moore, 1970)

Mary Marshall received the American Rose Society Award of Excellence in 1975. It is excellent for garden display and popular in exhibitions. There is a climbing form available.

Flowers
1½ in. (4 cm) wide. Deep coral; yellow-orange tones quite pronounced at certain seasons. Double; 24–30 petals. Midseason bloom followed by good repeat bloom. Slight fragrance. Classic hybrid tea–type bloom form.

Foliage
10–14 in. (25–35 cm) tall; climbing form reported to reach 5 ft. (1.5 m). Upright, bushy, well branched. Disease resistant and winter hardy. Leaves medium green, semiglossy.

Nancy Hall, *p. 257*
(Moore, 1972)

This popular exhibition variety is excellent for bedding and borders, edgings, and container planting. It does well potted indoors in winter.

Flowers
1¼ in. (3 cm) wide. Pink blend. Double; 24–30 petals. Midseason bloom with good repeat bloom. Fragrant. Classic hybrid tea–type bloom form, with petals unfurling evenly from a high center.

Foliage
10–14 in. (25–35 cm) tall. Upright, bushy, compact. Disease resistant and winter hardy. Leaves medium green, semiglossy.

Over the Rainbow, *p. 275*
(Moore, 1972)

Over the Rainbow won the American Rose Society Award of Excellence in 1975. As with all bicolor roses, it is a real eye-catcher. There is a climbing form.

Flowers
1¼–1½ in. (3–4 cm) wide. Red blended with yellow. Double; 28–35 petals. Midseason bloom with excellent repeat bloom. Little or no fragrance. Full blossom with pointed petals.

Foliage
12–14 in. (30–35 cm) tall; climbing form reported to attain 5–6 ft. (1.5–1.8 m). Upright, vigorous, well branched. Disease resistant and winter hardy. Leaves dark green, semiglossy.

Party Girl, *p. 253*
(Saville, 1979)

Winner of the American Rose Society Award of Excellence in 1981, Party Girl is suitable for beds, borders, edgings, and rock gardens as well as containers and indoor pots in winter. It is a popular exhibition variety.

Flowers
1¼ in. (3 cm) wide. Apricot yellow blended with salmon pink. Double; 25 petals. Midseason bloom with good repeat bloom. Sweet, spicy fragrance. Classic hybrid tea-type bloom form.

Foliage
12–14 in. (30–35 cm) tall. Bushy, compact. Disease resistant and winter hardy. Leaves medium to dark green, semiglossy.

Peaches 'n' Cream, *p. 266*
(Woolcock, 1976)

Peaches 'n' Cream was awarded the American Rose Society Award of Excellence in 1977. Suitable for bedding and borders, it is also popular for exhibition.

Flowers
1½ in. (4 cm) wide. Pink and cream blend.

Double; 50 petals. Midseason bloom with good repeat bloom. Slight fragrance. Classic hybrid tea bloom form.

Foliage
15–18 in. (37.5–45 cm) tall. Vigorous, upright, well branched. Disease resistant and winter hardy, with dark green, semiglossy leaves.

Peachy Keen, *p. 260*
(Bennett, 1979)

Excellent for beds, borders, edging, rock gardens, and container plantings, Peachy Keen is also good for growing in pots indoors over winter.

Flowers
1–1¼ in. (2.5–3 cm) wide. Apricot blend. Semidouble to double; about 20 petals. Midseason bloom with good repeat bloom. Slight fragrance. Classic hybrid tea–type bloom form.

Foliage
8–12 in. (20–30 cm) tall. Compact, bushy, spreading. Disease resistant and winter hardy. Leaves medium green, semiglossy.

Peachy White, *p. 258*
(Moore, 1976)

This white variety is good for beds, borders, edgings, rock gardens, and container planting. In winter, it grows well in pots indoors.

Flowers
1½ in. (4 cm) wide. White with pink or peach shadings. Double; 24–30 petals. Midseason bloom with good repeat bloom. Slight fragrance. Bloom form high centered to cupped.

Foliage
10–14 in. (25–35 cm) tall. Upright, bushy, well branched. Disease resistant and winter hardy. Leaves medium green, leathery.

Persian Princess, *p. 268*
(Moore, 1970)

All miniature rose varieties are extremely floriferous, but Persian Princess is outstanding in that regard. It is excellent for garden display.

Flowers
1¾ in. (4.5 cm) wide. Orange-red. Double; 35–45 petals. Midseason bloom with excellent repeat. Slight fragrance. High-centered to cupped blossoms.

Foliage
12–18 in. (30–45 cm) tall. Upright, bushy, well branched. Disease resistant and winter hardy. Leaves dark green, glossy.

Petite Folie, *p. 269*
(Meilland, 1968)

This orange-blend variety is good for bedding, borders, edging, and container plantings. It also grows well in pots indoors over winter, under lights, or in a sunny window.

Flowers
1¼ in. (3 cm) wide. Orange blend. Double; 24–30 petals. Midseason bloom with good repeat bloom. Slight fragrance. Bloom form high centered to cupped.

Foliage
10–14 in. (25–35 cm) tall. Upright, bushy. Disease resistant and winter hardy. Leaves light to medium green, semiglossy.

Pink Petticoat, *p. 259*
(Strawn, 1979)

This pink and white Miniature was awarded an American Rose Society "E" for Excellence in 1980.

Flowers
1¼–1½ in. (3–4 cm) wide. Creamy white with coral-pink edges. Double; 30 petals. Good continuous bloom in midseason, with excellent repeat when planted outdoors. Slight fragrance. Classic hybrid tea form.

Foliage
14–16 in. (35–40 cm) tall. Upright,
vigorous, bushy. Disease resistant and winter
hardy, with dark green, glossy leaves.

Poker Chip, *p. 286*
(Saville, 1979)

A popular exhibition variety, this red-and-
gold miniature rose is excellent for bedding,
borders, and edgings.

Flowers
1½ in. (4 cm) wide. Red blended with gold.
Double; 25 petals. Midseason bloom with
good repeat bloom. Very sweet fragrance.
Classic hybrid tea bloom form.

Foliage
15–18 in. (37.5–45 cm) tall. Vigorous, well
branched. Disease resistant and winter hardy.
Leaves dark green, glossy.

Pompon de Paris, *p. 260*
(1839)

Some authorities believe this is the same as
Rosa roulettii, although the descriptions do
vary slightly. The problem is compounded
when plants are sent out under the wrong
name, as can happen with any variety.

Flowers
¾ in. (2 cm) wide. Deep pink. Double; 65
petals. Midseason bloom with good repeat.
Little or no fragrance. Bloom full, cupped.

Foliage
8–10 in. (20–25 cm) tall. Very bushy.
Disease resistant and winter hardy. Leaves
medium green, glossy.

Popcorn, *p. 249*
(Morey, 1973)

Excellent for beds, borders, edgings, rock
gardens, and container plantings, this
honey-fragrant variety is one of the most
popular in its color class. The clusters of
little white flowers look like popcorn—hence
the name.

Flowers
¾ in. (2 cm) wide. White. Single; 5 petals, with yellow stamens showing. Midseason bloom with excellent repeat bloom. Honey fragrance. Blossom cupped; blooms in clusters.

Foliage
12–14 in. (30–35 cm) tall. Vigorous, compact. Disease resistant and winter hardy. Leaves medium green, glossy.

Puppy Love, *p. 277*
(Schwartz, 1978)

This multicolored miniature rose won an American Rose Society Award of Excellence in 1979. It is well suited both to garden display and exhibition.

Flowers
1½ in. (4 cm) wide. Orange blended with pink and yellow. Double; 24–30 petals. Midseason bloom with good repeat bloom. Little or no fragrance. Classic hybrid tea bloom, with petals unfurling evenly from a high center.

Foliage
12–15 in. (30–37.5 cm) tall. Upright, bushy, compact. Disease resistant and winter hardy. Leaves medium green, semiglossy.

Rainbow's End, *p. 254*
(Saville, 1984)

Excellent in beds, borders, and edgings, and suitable for container plantings, this yellow-blend miniature rose is good for growing in pots indoors over winter.

Flowers
1½ in. (4 cm) wide. Yellow blend. Double; 24–30 petals. Midseason bloom with good repeat bloom. Little or no fragrance. Classic hybrid tea–type bloom form.

Foliage
10–14 in. (25–35 cm) tall. Upright, bushy, well branched. Disease resistant and winter hardy. Leaves dark green, glossy.

Red Beauty, *p. 284*
(E. D. Williams, 1981)

Red Beauty adds color to beds, borders, edgings, rock gardens, and container plantings; this dark red rose is also suited to indoor pots in winter. It is a popular exhibition variety.

Flowers
1½ in. (4 cm) wide. Dark red. Double; 35 petals. Midseason bloom with good repeat bloom. Slight fragrance. Classic hybrid tea form, with petals unfurling evenly from a high center.

Foliage
10–12 in. (25–30 cm) tall. Bushy, compact. Disease resistant and winter hardy. Leaves dark green, glossy.

Red Cascade, *p. 286*
(Moore, 1976)

This climbing miniature won the American Rose Society Award of Excellence in 1976. It is suitable for training on a low trellis and excellent for hanging baskets.

Flowers
1½ in. (4 cm) wide. Dark red. Double; 35 petals. Excellent midseason bloom with good repeat bloom. Little or no fragrance. Bloom form cupped, well filled with petals.

Foliage
2–6 in. (60–180 cm) long canes. Dense, spreading. Disease resistant, but needs protection from mildew in some climates. Winter hardy. Leaves dark green, semiglossy.

Rise 'n' Shine, *p. 254*
(Moore, 1977)

Winner of the American Rose Society Award of Excellence in 1978, this yellow miniature is outstanding in its color class. It is well suited to beds, borders, edgings, and container plantings, and it is a popular show variety.

Flowers
1½–1¾ in. (4–4.5 cm) wide. Medium yellow.

Double; 35 petals. Midseason bloom with good repeat bloom. Slight fragrance. Classic hybrid tea bloom form.

Foliage
10–14 in. (25–35 cm) tall. Upright, bushy, rounded. Disease resistant and winter hardy. Leaves dull, medium green.

Rosa roulettii p. 263
(1815)

Also known as *Rosa chinensis minima,* this pink miniature is thought by some authorities to be the same as Pompon de Paris, which is reported to be a more double rose. Some experts favor classifying this rose with the Chinas rather than with the miniatures.

Flowers
¾–1 in. (2–2.5 cm) wide. Deep pink. Double; 20–30 petals. Midseason bloom with good repeat bloom. Little or no fragrance. Bloom form cupped.

Foliage
15–18 in. (37.5–45 cm) tall. Upright, bushy, well branched. Disease resistant and winter hardy. Leaves medium green, glossy.

Rosmarin, *p. 262*
(Kordes, 1965)

Rosmarin is an outstanding variety for beds, borders, and edgings. It blooms abundantly and is notably winter hardy in a class that is known for this quality.

Flowers
1½ in. (4 cm) wide. Pink and white blend. Double; 35 petals. Midseason bloom with excellent repeat bloom. Fragrant. Bloom form full, cupped.

Foliage
15–18 in. (37.5–45 cm) tall. Very vigorous, strong, upright, well branched. Disease resistant and very winter hardy. Leaves medium green, semiglossy.

Seabreeze, *p. 259*
(Lemrow, 1976)

This pink miniature is good for bedding, borders, and edgings. It is a prolific bloomer.

Flowers
1¼ in. (3 cm) wide. Medium pink. Double; 26 petals. Excellent midseason bloom with excellent repeat bloom. Little or no fragrance. Bloom form cupped.

Foliage
10–14 in. (25–35 cm) tall; reportedly can spread to 20 in. (50 cm). Very bushy, dense. Disease resistant and winter hardy. Leaves dull, medium green.

Shooting Star, *p. 276*
(Meilland, 1972)

This star-shaped miniature is excellent for beds, borders, and containers; it also performs well indoors in pots over winter.

Flowers
1½ in. (4 cm) wide. Yellow blend with red petal tips. Double; 24–30 petals. Slight fragrance. High-centered or cupped blossoms; when fully open, outer petals quill, creating a star outline.

Foliage
10–12 in. (25–35 cm) tall. Bushy, compact. Disease resistant and winter hardy. Leaves medium green, semiglossy.

Simplex, *p. 248*
(Moore, 1961)

Perhaps the most popular of the single rose varieties, Simplex is good for beds and borders. Under glass and in cool, cloudy weather, this white rose produces pink blossoms.

Flowers
1¼ in. (3 cm) wide. White; occasionally pink. Single; 5 petals. Bloom opens flat with showy yellow stamens.

Foliage
15–18 in. (37.5–45 cm) tall. Very vigorous,

upright, well branched. Disease resistant and winter hardy. Leaves light to medium green, semiglossy.

Starglo, *p. 250*
(E. D. Williams, 1973)

Winner of the American Rose Society Award of Excellence in 1975, this white miniature is excellent for beds, borders, edgings, and container plantings around patios. It is also good for growing indoors in pots over winter.

Flowers
1¾ in. (4.5 cm) wide. White. Double; 35 petals. Midseason bloom with good repeat bloom. Very fragrant. Classic hybrid tea blossoms.

Foliage
10–14 in. (25–35 cm) tall. Upright, bushy, well branched. Disease resistant and winter hardy. Leaves medium green, semiglossy.

Starina, *p. 283*
(Meilland, 1965)

Perhaps the most popular exhibition miniature rose of all, Starina is without a doubt the most widely sold of any variety. It is the standard against which other miniature rose varieties in its color class are judged in the public mind.

Flowers
1½ in. (4 cm) wide. Orange-red. Double; 35 petals. Midseason bloom with excellent repeat bloom. Little or no fragrance. Classic hybrid tea–type bloom form.

Foliage
12–16 in. (30–40 cm) tall. Upright, bushy, dense, compact. Disease resistant and winter hardy. Leaves dark green, semiglossy.

Stars 'n' Stripes, *p. 270*
(Moore, 1975)

One of the first of the Ralph Moore striped miniatures, and still perhaps the most popular. Stars 'n' Stripes performs well in the garden in a hanging basket, and in shows.

Flowers
1¾ in. (4.5 cm) wide. Red and white stripes. Semidouble; 14 petals. Midseason bloom with good repeat bloom. Little or no fragrance. Bloom form cupped, open.

Foliage
10–14 in. (25–35 cm) tall. Upright, spreading; canes can attain 36 in. (105 cm) in length. Disease resistant and winter hardy. Leaves medium to dark green, semiglossy.

Summer Butter, *p. 253*
(Saville, 1979)

Good for garden display and excellent in containers and pots, this yellow variety is very fragrant.

Flowers
1½ in. (4 cm) wide. Medium to deep yellow. Double; 20 petals. Midseason bloom with good repeat bloom. Very fragrant, spicy, sweet. Bloom cupped, becoming flat.

Foliage
10–14 in. (25–35 cm) tall. Vigorous, compact. Disease resistant and winter hardy. Leaves medium green, very glossy.

Toy Clown, *p. 271*
(Moore, 1966)

An American Rose Society Award of Excellence winner in 1975 and a popular exhibition variety, Toy Clown grows well both outdoors and indoors, in containers, beds, and borders.

Flowers
1½ in. (4 cm) wide. White edged in red. Semidouble; 12–20 petals. Midseason bloom with good repeat bloom. Little or no fragrance. Bloom form cupped, becoming flat.

Foliage
10–14 in. (25–35 cm) tall. Upright, spreading. Disease resistant and winter hardy. Leaves dull, dark green.

Valerie Jeanne, *p. 273*
(Saville, 1980)

An American Rose Society Award of Excellence winner in 1983, this deep pink miniature is suitable for bedding, borders, and edgings. Valerie Jeanne is also a popular show variety.

Flowers
1¾ in. (4.5 cm) wide. Deep pink. Double; 55 petals. Midseason bloom followed by good repeat bloom. Slight fragrance. Classic hybrid tea-type blossoms in miniature, with petals unfurling evenly from a high center.

Foliage
15–18 in. (37.5–45 cm) tall. Upright, very vigorous, well branched. Disease resistant and winter hardy. Leaves medium to dark green, very glossy.

Yellow Doll, *p. 251*
(Moore, 1962)

A small plant with rather large flowers for its size. This light yellow miniature is good in beds, borders, edgings, rock gardens, and containers. There is also a climbing form available.

Flowers
1½ in. (4 cm) wide. Light yellow. Double; 24–30 petals. Midseason bloom with good repeat bloom. Slight fragrance. Blossom form classic hybrid tea type in miniature, with petals unfurling evenly from a high center.

Foliage
8–10 in. (20–25 cm) tall; climbing form reported to reach 4 ft. (1.2 m). Low, rounded, compact in bush form. Disease resistant and winter hardy. Leaves dark green, leathery.

Zinger, *p. 287*
(Schwartz, 1978)

Zinger's semidouble red blooms give the effect of small single roses in the garden landscape. This miniature makes a pleasant garden addition, suitable for bedding, borders, and edgings.

Flowers
1½ in. (4 cm) wide. Medium red. Semidouble; 12–18 petals. Midseason bloom with good repeat bloom. Little or no fragrance. Bloom opens flat with showy yellow stamens.

Foliage
14–18 in. (35–45 cm) tall. Upright, vigorous, well branched. Disease resistant and winter hardy. Leaves medium to dark green, glossy.

Arranging Cut

Arrangers call the rose the "complete flower" because it provides all stages of bloom for a complete arrangement. The rose is adaptable to every occasion: It can be formal when used for weddings, in churches, and at formal teas and showers; and it can be informal any place at home, on the porch or patio, and on the office desk. Moreover, roses are suitable for all types and styles of containers; the old rule that roses should be arranged only in silver or crystal was discarded long ago. People now realize that roses are for everyone and for any setting, which has made them the most popular flower worldwide.

Gathering Roses

Before cutting roses, select the container that will hold them, and try to decide where you will be placing it. If you are a beginner, select a low bowl or horizontal container; one that is about ten inches in diameter and two inches deep will do nicely. You will want to cut your roses early in the morning or after sundown in the evening. They will keep longer if the plants are thoroughly watered one-half day before cutting; make sure to water the soil deeply around the bushes.

Take a pail of cold water with you into the garden. Using sharp rose pruners, cut the stems on a slant, selecting the proper stem length for the container you will be using. Choose strong stems, some with tight buds, some one-quarter open, and the remaining ones one-half and two-thirds open. Clean the foliage with a damp paper napkin or soft cloth (not nylon), and then dry it. Place the roses in a cool place, preferably in a refrigerator at 38° to 40° F.—they will keep for days in there. If you have an old refrigerator, you are in luck—the new, self-defrosting models will remove moisture from flowers and thus cause early aging.

In these early stages of rose preparation, remove most thorns and some foliage, especially thorns and foliage below the water line. Rose foliage may be added later if the arrangement calls for it.

Beginning the Arrangement

To establish the proper proportion from the start, choose a stem that is 50 percent longer than your bowl; if your bowl is 8 inches long, your stem should be 12 inches. Using a sharp needlepoint secured with floral clay, place the first stem upright, toward the left side of the bowl. Choose a second stem, approximately three-fourths the length of the first, with the bloom one-fourth to one-third open. Put it firmly in the needlepoint, slanted to the left at an angle of about 45 degrees. The third stem should be about three-fourths the length of the second stem, with the bloom two-thirds or three-fourths open. The third stem shoud be at a 60-degree angle to the right and in front, with the bloom lower than the bloom on the second stem. This solid, three-stem, three-position, triangular design serves as a basic foundation for a completed arrangement. You may use other

Roses

lengths of roses or other foliage or flowers to fill in areas and to complete the plan.

Make certain that all your containers, water, and plant material are clean. You may use oasis for arrangements (well soaked before using) if you do not expect the arrangement to last more than one day. If you want to use oasis for a longer period, you must recut the stems (on a slant) and add more cold water. Be sure to use good sharp needlepoints large enough to provide adequate space for the foliage stems and flowers. If some stems are too short, try using florists' picks (vials filled with water).

A word of caution: Never place cut roses in hot water, since they will not last. Clean cold water in clean containers is all you need to preserve the roses and all plant materials. (Flower preservatives seem to help the arranger more than the flowers themselves.) Change the water and cut the stems a little each day; otherwise, the stems may become clogged and decay. Keep cut roses out of the sun. With this care, cut roses will last a week or longer.

Design Tips

Distinction is the quality all good designers strive for. It may be the result of imagination, originality, beauty, or the use of usual materials in an unusual manner. But one factor common to all distinctive designs is good grooming—that is, attention to detail in handling and preparing roses.

Learn to master mechanical techniques, keeping in mind that, in the final analysis, simplicity is a key concept. "When in doubt, leave it out" is an old but excellent rule for new and advanced arrangers alike. Don't use too much plant material; don't feel that you must put in all the flowers and foliage that you have on hand. Many times it is wise to make the arrangement, leave it for a while, then return to look at it. You will often then see some changes to be made, and most of the time you'll remove or change some of the flowers. Looking at the design through the lens of a camera is often a good way to get a fresh idea of what your arrangement needs. Other factors to consider in your choice of arrangement style or design are the kinds and sizes of other plant materials and your containers. You will also want to think about color values (lightness or darkness) and other qualities such as shapes, silhouettes, contours, and textures.

Consider also the space the arrangement will occupy. For example, if the arrangement is for a mantel, complete the design at that height in order to visualize everything from that vantage point. If it will be placed on a table, work on the design at a table or at the same height. If it is an arrangement for a church or auditorium, sit down at the far end of a room to look at your finished design. By seeing the design from the vantage point from which others will ultimately see it, you will often find ways to improve the design or placement of your arrangement.

Arranging Cut Roses

Color

Be sure the colors of your flowers do not clash, but blend and complement each other. Remember that some colors—such as mauve, blue, and purple—recede. Use bold, bright tones in a large area. White is lovely in a church and in some auditoriums, but it needs a suitable background to be fully enjoyed. A polychromatic scheme is often appropriate for mass arrangements, whereas a monochromatic one, or a design with variations of one hue, is suitable when particular subtlety or elegance is needed.

The Influence of Geometry

Certain visual elements create certain moods. Horizontal lines suggest peace and tranquillity; vertical lines produce a sense of energy; and diagonal lines are dynamic, restless, and forceful—use these lines with restraint. A circle or oval conveys a restful or passive mood; triangles create a sense of stability. Curved lines are gracious and flexible, but avoid drooping curves, which imply instability and weakness. Bear in mind, of course, that these geometric patterns are merely a way of classifying designs. A good design does not necessarily follow a geometric pattern.

Matching Design and Placement

If the arrangement is to be placed on a dining table, be sure to finish the arrangement on both sides, front and back. Never make a table arrangement that will block a person's view. If the arrangement is for a buffet table, it may be seen from only one side, so it is not necessary to finish the back; however, you may want to use large leaves or foliage to add depth to the arrangement, as depth is important to the completeness of any design.

Healthy Roses Make Good Arrangements

Remember that good culture pays off. No matter how exquisite your arrangement, if your roses have been neglected or improperly cared for, they will not do justice to your design. It is vital to put the same effort into cultivation—proper planting, pruning, watering, and fertilizing—that you do into arranging your roses once they are cut.

Buying Containers and Vases

If you are going to purchase containers for arrangements, consider the colors and types of roses and other plant material that you will often be using. Soft, subdued pottery in a neutral color is always a fine choice. For arrangements that will look well in a gray container, use something made of lead, pewter, or silver. For yellow flowers, try gold, bronze, or brass. To bring out the orange, go with copper. Baskets are good, too, and interestingly shaped bottles lend themselves to exciting arrangements. Wooden and woven trays also suit many types of arrangements. Vases and containers with unexpected potential may be found at flea markets, Goodwill shops, thrift shops, and garage sales. Once you start arranging, you will find unusual containers for all types of designs.

Flowers and Foliages for Arrangements
Many flowers and foliages go very well with roses. Try the following: daisies, gerberas, snapdragons, love-in-a-mist (*Nigella*), larkspur, delphinium (all colors), lilies (be sure they are in proportion with the size of roses you are using), gladiolas, lupine, tritoma, and veronica. Dried allium blossoms sprayed with gold or silver are like tiny stars on the stem and make beautiful arrangements with roses at Christmastime; place some holly at the base of the arrangement for a lovely holiday touch. You will find many other interesting flowers for arranging with roses.

Line Materials in Arrangements
In arranging roses, it is important to use materials that serve to extend or enhance the line within the arrangement. Line materials include: equistum (a horse tail rush); mullein (flower or seed stem); corn stalks (green or brown); forsythia (green or brown); okra stalks (green or mature); sea oats; pampas grass plumes; wild grasses; Scotch broom; wheat; *spuria* iris foliage; dried burdock; cattails; sanseveria; yucca; and Queen Anne's lace (wild carrot).
Vines can often be used when a free-flowing or loose line is needed. Some vines that can be used are: ivy (English, glacier, curly, porcelain, and grape); honeysuckle; grapevine (remove the foliage); wisteria (dried and peeled, with leaves recently removed; it will add a lovely white to an arrangement); white hemlock or circuta (dried); bittersweet; and clematis (with seed pods).
Some large leaves, including the following, are used quite frequently in mass or line arrangements: hosta, canna, calla lily, saxifrage, hydrangeas (dried), and fantail willow (*Salix*). Hydrangea blossoms may also be used; try blue hydrangea blooms with blue-red roses.
Some arrangements call for branches from trees and shrubs, such as: Japanese quince; holly (Chinese or American); red plum; Japanese maple; Japanese fantail willow; tamarix (gives roses an airy feeling); pussy willow; white pine; cork bark (*Euonymus alatus*); highbush cranberry (*Viburnum americana*); and nandina. Trim excess leaves from branches. With some branches, such as cork bark or fantail willow, you can remove all foliage from the branches in order to reveal interesting lines, forms, colors, and textures.

Other Ideas for Arrangements
You can create distinctive rose arrangements by using feathers (especially pheasant or grouse), interesting stones or rocks, dried fungi, and unusual pieces of weathered wood or driftwood. Once you start arranging, you will find beauty in the out-of-doors that you have never really seen or noticed before.

Pests & Diseases

Plant diseases, insects, and other pests are a fact of life for a gardener. No matter what you grow or how large your garden, it is helpful to become familiar with the common problems in your area and to learn how to control them. Since the general symptoms of plant problems—yellowing of leaves, death or disappearance of plant parts, stunting, poor growth, and wilting—can be caused by a multitude of diseases or pests, some experience is needed to determine which culprit is attacking your roses.

Diseases
Fungi and bacteria cause a variety of diseases, ranging from leaf spots and wilts to root rot, but bacterial diseases usually make the affected plant tissues appear wetter than fungi do. Viruses and mycoplasma are microorganisms too small to be seen with an ordinary microscope. They are often transmitted by insects, such as aphids and leafhoppers, and cause mottled yellow or deformed leaves and stunted growth. Nematodes are microscopic roundworms that usually live in association with plant roots; they cause stunting and poor growth, and sometimes produce galls on leaves. The way a particular disease organism has spread to your roses influences the control measures you may need to take.

Insects and Other Pests
Roses attract many different kinds of insects. Sap-sucking insects—including aphids, leafhoppers, and scale insects—suck plant juices, leaving the victim yellow, stunted, and misshapen. They also produce honeydew, a sticky substance that attracts ants and sooty mold fungus. Thrips and spider mites scrape plant tissue and suck the juices that well up in the injured areas. Beetles and caterpillars consume leaves, whole or in part. Borers tunnel into shoots and stems, where they deposit their eggs; the larvae that hatch feed on plant tissue. Some insects, such as grubs and maggots, are rarely seen above ground. They are destructive nonetheless, because they feed on roots, weakening or killing the plant.

Environmental Stresses
Some plant injuries are caused by severe weather conditions, salt toxicity, rodents, nutritional deficiencies or excesses, pesticides, or damage from lawnmowers. You can avoid many of these injuries by being aware of potential dangers and taking proper precautions.

Methods of Control
Controlling plant pests and diseases is not as overwhelming a task as it may seem. Many of the measures, performed on a day-to-day basis, are preventive, so that you don't have to rely on pesticides that may not be very effective once a culprit has attacked your roses. Observe plants each week for signs of trouble. That way you can prevent or limit a disease or infestation in the early stages.

Your normal gardening routine should include preventive measures. By cultivating the soil regularly, you expose insect and disease-causing organisms to the sun and thus lessen their chances of survival. In the fall, destroy infested and diseased canes, remove dead leaves and flowers, and clean up plant debris. Do not add diseased or infested material to the compost pile. Spray plants with water to dislodge insects and remove suffocating dust. Pick off larger insects by hand. To discourage fungal leaf spots and blights, water plants in the morning and allow leaves to dry off before nightfall. For the same reason, provide adequate air circulation around leaves and stems by giving plants sufficient space.

Always buy healthy, certified, disease-free plants. Check leaves and canes for dead areas and for off-color and stunted tissue. Make sure that your roses are properly cared for.

Insecticides and Fungicides

Weeds provide a home for insects and diseases, so pull them up or use herbicides. Be careful near roses, however, since they are very sensitive to weed-killers. Herbicide injury may cause elongated, straplike, or downward-cupping leaves. Do not apply herbicides, including "weed-and-feed" lawn preparations, too close to flower beds. Spray weed-killers only when there is little air movement, but not on a very hot, dry day.

To protect plant tissue from damage done by insects and diseases, you may choose from among the many insecticides and fungicides that are available. However, few products control diseases that result from bacteria, viruses, and mycoplasma.

Pesticides are usually either "protectant" or "systemic" in nature. Protectants ward off insects or disease organisms from uninfected foliage, while systemics can move through the plant and provide therapeutic or eradicant action as well as protection. Botanical insecticides such as pyrethrum and rotenone have a shorter residual effect on pests, but are considered generally safer for the user and the environment than inorganic chemical insecticides.

Biological control through the use of organisms like *Bacillus thuringiensis* (a bacterium toxic to moth and butterfly larvae) is effective and safe. Recommended pesticides may vary to some extent from region to region, so consult your local Agricultural Experiment Station or plant professional about the appropriate material to use. Always read the pesticide label to be sure that it is registered for use on roses and on the pest with which you are dealing. Follow the label recommendations regarding safety precautions, dosage, and frequency of application. Learn about the life cycle of the pest, so that you know when to begin—and when to stop—spraying.

Learning to recognize the most common insects and diseases that plague roses is a first step toward controlling them. The following chart describes the most common pests and diseases that attack roses, the damage they cause, and measures you can take to control them.

Pest or Disease

Aphids

Black Spot

Borers

Bristly Roseslugs

Cankers

Description	Damage	Controls
Tiny green, brown, or reddish, pear-shaped, soft-bodied insects in clusters on buds, shoots, and undersides of leaves.	Suck plant juices, causing stunted or deformed blooms and leaves. Some transmit plant viruses. Secretions attract ants.	Spray with malathion, Orthene, or rotenone. Encourage natural predators such as ladybugs.
Round, fringed, black spots on leaves. Usually detected during humid or wet weather.	Leaves may turn yellow near spots and drop off prematurely.	Water at soil-line or early in day. Remove diseased leaves and clean up debris. Spray with phaltan or triforine.
Several kinds of wormlike, legless, cream-colored larvae tunneling in canes.	Swollen bands on canes indicate presence within. Girdling causes dieback of canes and shoots.	Remove and destroy infested canes, pruning several inches below swelling. Fertilize and water to increase plant vigor.
Hairy, greenish-white, ½-inch-long sawfly larvae; present on undersides of leaves.	Make holes in leaves by feeding from underside.	Rid garden debris of cocoons in fall. Spray undersides of leaves with malathion or carbaryl.
Fungal disease causing spots and dead areas on canes. Black dots of fungal spores in dead areas.	Red to purple spots on canes. Spots enlarge, becoming light or dark and dry. Shoots wilt and canes die back.	Prune and destroy infected canes. Avoid wounding healthy canes in wet weather. Spraying with maneb or chlorothalonil may help.

Pests & Diseases

Pest or Disease

Crown Gall

Leaf-feeding Beetles

**Leaf-feeding
Caterpillars**

Nematodes

Powdery Mildew

Description	Damage	Controls
Soil-borne bacterial disease, forming cancerlike growths on plant stems and roots.	Rounded growths on stem near soil-line. May also be present on roots and occasionally on canes.	Remove and destroy infected plants. Buy only healthy, certified disease-free bushes. Plant in uninfested soil.
Hard-shelled, oval to oblong insects on leaves, stems, and flowers. Common species including Japanese, Fuller, rose chafer, and curculio.	Chew plant parts, leaving holes. Larvae of some species feed on roots.	Pick off and destroy. Spray with malathion, rotenone, or pyrethroids.
Soft-bodied, wormlike crawling insects with several pairs of legs. May be smooth, hairy, or spiny. Adults are moths or butterflies.	Consume part or all of leaves. Flowers and shoots may also be eaten.	Pick off and destroy. Spray with *Bacillus thuringiensis*, carbaryl, or malathion.
Microscopic roundworms, usually associated with roots that cause various diseases.	Stunted, off-color plants that do not respond to water or fertilizer. Minute galls may be present on roots.	Remove and destroy badly affected plants. Nematocides are available for use around valuable plants.
Powdery, white fungal disease on aerial plant parts.	Powdery fungal growth. Leaves may become distorted and drop off. Stems, buds, and flowers also affected.	Remove badly infected leaves. Increase air circulation. Spray with triforine, benomyl, or sulfur.

Pests & Diseases

Pest or Disease

Rust

Scale

Spider Mites

 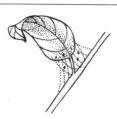

Thrips

Viruses

Description	Damage	Controls
Fungus causing powdery orange spots on lower sides of leaves.	Leaves, stems, and sepals may be attacked. Infected leaves may drop.	Remove and destroy infected leaves. Clean up rose debris in fall. Spray with ferbam or zineb.
Small, waxy, soft or hard-bodied stationary insects on shoots and leaves. May be red, white, brown, black, or gray.	Suck plant juices, causing stunted, off-color plants. May cover large portion of cane.	Spray with malathion or Orthene when crawlers are present, or use a dormant oil spray in early spring before growth begins.
Tiny golden, red, or brown arachnids on undersides of leaves. Profuse, fine webs seen, with heavy infestations.	Scrape leaves and suck plant juices. Leaves become pale and dry. Plant may be stunted.	Spray leaves with water or use a miticide, Kelthane or Vendex, on undersides of leaves.
Small, brown, elongated insects with feathery wings. Black frass or droppings on affected plant tissue.	Scrape plant tissue and suck juices. Leaves and blossoms are tannish and dry.	Spray with Orthene or dust with diatomaceous earth.
Various diseases, including mosaics, that cause off-color, stunted plants. May be transmitted by aphids or by using infected grafting tools.	Crinkled, mottled, deformed leaves, stunted plants, and poor growth.	Remove and destroy infected plants. Control the insect vector (aphids), if present, and use a clean grafting knife. Buy only healthy, certified plants.

Glossary

Anchor root
A large root serving mainly to hold a plant in place in the soil.

Anther
The terminal part of a stamen, containing one or more pollen sacs.

Basal cane
One of the main canes of a rose bush, originating from the bud union.

Bud eye
A dormant bud in the axil of a leaf, used for propagation in bud-grafting. Also called an eye.

Bud union
The junction, usually swollen, between the understock and the top variety grafted to it, at or near soil level.

Budded
Propagated from a bud eye.

Button center
A round center in a rose blossom, formed by unexpanded petaloids in the very double roses.

Calyx
Collectively, the sepals of a flower.

Calyx tube
A tubed formed partly by the united bases of the sepals and partly by the receptacle.

Confused center
A flower center whose petals are disorganized, not forming a pattern.

Corolla
Collectively, the petals of a flower.

Crown
The region of the bud union, the point near soil level where the top variety and the understock are joined.

Cultivar
An unvarying plant variety, maintained by vegetative propagation or by inbred seed.

Cupped form
In a rose bloom, having an open center, with the stamens visible.

Deadheading
Removal of old flowers during the growing season to encourage the development of new flowers.

Disbudded
Having the side buds removed to encourage the growth of the flower at the tip of the stem.

Double
Having 24 to 50 petals.

Eye
See Bud eye.

Feeder root
One of the numerous small roots of a plant, through which moisture and nutrients are absorbed from the soil.

Filament
The threadlike lower portion of a stamen, bearing the anther.

Floriferous
Blooming profusely.

Guard petals
The outer petals of a rose, especially when these are larger than the inner petals and enclose them.

High-centered
Having the central petals longest; the classic hybrid tea rose form.

Hip
The closed and ripened receptacle of a rose, containing the seeds, and often brightly colored.

Lateral cane
A branch of a basal cane.

Leaf axil
The angle between a petiole and the stem to which it is attached.

Leaflet
One of the leaflike parts of a compound leaf.

Main shoot
A basal cane or a strong lateral cane.

Muddled center
A flower center whose petals are disorganized, not forming a pattern. A term applied to old garden roses.

Ovary
The swollen base of a pistil, in which one or more seeds develop.

Peduncle
The stalk of an individual flower.

Petal
One of a series of flower parts lying within the sepals and outside the stamens and pistils; in roses, the petals are large and brightly colored. Collectively termed the corolla.

Petaloids
Small, very short petals located near the center of a flower.

Petiole
The stalk of a leaf.

Pistil
The female reproductive organ of a flower, consisting of an ovary, a style, and a stigma.

Quartered
Having the petals arranged in three, four, or five radial segments.

Receptacle
The terminal part of a peduncle, bearing the flower parts, and in roses enfolding the developing ovaries to form a hip.

Retentive sepals
Sepals that remain attached to the apex of the receptacle after it has ripened into a hip.

Rhachis
The central axis of a compound leaf, to which the leaflets are attached.

Root stock
See Understock.

Rugose
Having the leaf veins deeply etched into the upper surface of the leaf.

Semidouble
Having 12 to 24 petals.

Single
Of flowers, having 5 to 12 petals. Of varieties, having only one bloom per stem.

Sport
An abrupt, naturally occurring genetic change resulting in a branch that differs in appearance from the rest of the plant, or, a plant derived by propagation from such a genetically changed branch. Also called a mutation.

Stamen
The male reproductive organ of a flower, consisting of a filament and a pollen-bearing anther.

Stem
A branch of a cane, emerging from a bud eye and bearing leaves and at least one flower.

Stigma
The terminal portion of a pistil, consisting of a sticky surface to which pollen grains adhere during pollination.

Stipule
A small, leaflike appendage at the base of the petiole of a leaf.

Style
The columnar portion of a pistil, extending between the ovary and the stigma.

Sucker
A young cane emerging below the bud union and therefore representing the variety of the understock rather than the top variety.

Top variety
The variety bud-grafted to the understock, and thus the variety that will be represented by the flowers.

Understock
The plant providing the root system to which the top variety is attached in bud-grafting. Also called a root stock.

Very double
Having more than 50 petals.

Photo Credits

The letter after each page number refers to the position of the color plates. A represents the picture at the top and B the picture at the bottom. Some are also in the Color and Visual Keys. Photographs reproduced with permission. Compilation © 1986 Houghton Mifflin Company.

Walter H. Hodge
182–183, 196B, 197B, 198A, 198B, 199A, 199B, 200B, 201B, 212–213, 216A, 220B, 222B, 226A, 242A, 245A

Doug Wechsler
103A, 196A, 209B, 217B, 219B, 222A, 226B, 239A, 239B, 241B, 242B

Sonja Bullaty and Angelo Lomeo
80B, 82B, 123A, 126A, 130B, 132–133, 158A, 227A, 227B

Derek Fell
100B, 118A, 161A, 169B, 195A, 218B, 243A

Ann Reilly
81B, 102A, 173A, 187B, 190A, 267A

Peggy Wingood/Courtesy of The Bermuda Rose Society
134A, 143A, 158B, 159B, 174A

Al Medino
186A, 224A, 238A, 264B, 265B

Armstrong Roses
279B, 280A

Al Bussewitz, PHOTO/NATS
85B

The Conard-Pyle Co.
268A

Judy Goldman
209A

John A. Lynch
105A

Nurseries

AGM Miniature Roses, Inc.
P.O. Box 6056, Monroe, LA 71211
American Beauty Roses, Spring Hill Nurseries
P.O. Box 1758, Peoria, IL 61656 (alternate address: 6523 North
Galena Road, Peoria, IL 61632)
Anderson's Nursery
3630 Highway 60 E, Bartow, FL 33830
(miniature roses)
The Antique Rose Emporium
Route 5, Box 143, Brenham, TX 77833
BDK Nursery
P.O. Box 628, Apopka, FL 32704
Buckley Nursery Garden Center
646 North River Road, Buckley, WA 98321
Burgess Seed & Plant Company
905 Four Seasons Road, Bloomington, IL 61701
W. Atlee Burpee Company
Warminster, PA 18974
Carroll Gardens, Inc.
P.O. Box 310, 444 East Main Street, Westminster, MD 21157
Donovan's Roses
P.O. Box 37800, Shreveport, LA 71133
ROSES by Fred Edmunds
6235 S.W. Kahle Road, Wilsonville, OR 97070
Emlong Nurseries, Inc.
Stevensville, MI 49127
Farmer Seed and Nursery Company
Faribault, MN 55021
Ferbert Garden Center
806 South Belt Highway, St. Joseph, MO 64507
Earl Ferris Nursery
Hampton, IA 50441
Henry Field Seed & Nursery Company
Shenandoah, IA 51602
Flowers 'n' Friends Greenhouse
9590 100th Street S.E., Alto, MI 49302
Gloria Dei Nursery
36 East Road, High Falls Park, High Falls, NY 12440
Greenmantle Nursery
3010 Ettersburg Road, Garberbille, CA 95440
Gurney Seed & Nursery Co.
Yankton, SD 57079
Harrison's Antique & Modern Roses
P.O. Box 527, Canton, MS 39046
Heritage Rose Gardens
16831 Mitchell Creek Road, Fort Bragg, CA 95437

Hershey Nursery
621 Park Avenue, Hershey, PA 17033
High Country Rosarium
1717 Downing Street, Denver, CO 80218
Historical Roses
1657 West Jackson Street, Painesville, OH 44077
John Hoverman & Sons, Inc.
Route 17, Rochelle Park, NJ 07662
Inter-State Nurseries, Inc.
Hamburg, IA 51640
Jackson & Perkins
Medford, OR 97501
J.W. Jung Seed Co.
Randolph, WI 53957
Justice Miniature Roses
5947 S.W. Kahle Road, Wilsonville, OR 97070
Kelly Bros. Nurseries, Inc.
650 Maple Street, Dansville, NY 14437
Krider Nurseries, Inc.
Box 29, Middlebury, IN 46540
Lakeland Nurseries Sales
Unique Merchandise Mart Building 4, Hanover, PA 17333
A.M. Leonard, Inc.
6665 Spiker Road, Piqua, OH 45356
Liggett's Rose Nursery
1206 Curtiss Avenue, San Jose, CA 95125
Limberlost Roses
7304 Forbes Avenue, Van Nuys, CA 91406
Lowe's Own Root Rose Nursery
6 Sheffield Road, Nashua, NH 03062
Earl May Seed & Nursery Company
Shenandoah, IA 51603
MB Farm Miniature Roses, Inc.
Jamison Hill Road, Clinton Corners, NY 12514
McDaniel's Miniature Roses
7523 Zemco Street, Lemon Grove, CA 92045
Mellinger's, Inc.
2310 West South Range, North Lima, OH 44452
Mike's Roses
6807 Smithway Drive, Alexandria, VA 22307
The Miniature Rose Company
200 Rose Ridge, Greenwood, SC 29647
The Mini Farm
Route 1, Box 501, Bon Aqua, TN 37025
Mini-Roses (Ernest D. Williams)
P.O. Box 4255 Station A, Dallas, TX 75208

Nurseries

Miniature Plant Kingdom
4125 Harrison Grade Road, Sebastopol, CA 95472
Moore Miniature Roses (Sequoia Nursery)
2519 East Noble Avenue, Visalia, CA 93277
Nor'East Miniature Roses
58 Hammond Street, Rowley, MA 01969
L. L. Olds Seed Company
Madison, WI 53707
Oregon Miniature Roses, Inc.
8285 S.W. 185th Street, Beaverton, OR 97007
Port Stockton Nursery
2910 East Main Street, Stockton, CA 95205
Richard Owen Nursery
2300 East Lincoln Street, Bloomington, IL 61701
Pixie Treasures Miniature Rose Nursery
4121 Prospect Avenue, Yorba Linda, CA 92686
Rose Acres
6641 Crystal Boulevard, Diamond Springs, CA 95619
Rosehill Farm
Gregg Neck Road, Box 406, Galena, MD 21635
Roses of Yesterday & Today (formerly Tillotson's)
802 Brown's Valley Road, Watsonville, CA 95076
Roseway Nurseries
P.O. Box 50, Route 1, Box 42B, La Center, WA 98629
Spring Hill Nurseries
110 West Elm Street, Tipp City, OH 45371 (alternate address: 6523
North Galena Road, Peoria, IL 61656)
Stanek's Garden Center
East 2929 27th Avenue, Spokane, WA 99203-4494
Stark Bro's Nurseries
Louisiana, MO 63353
Stocking Rose Nursery
785 North Capitol Avenue, San Jose, CA 95133
Tate Nursery
Route 20, Box 436, Tyler, TX 75708
Thomasville Nurseries, Inc.
P.O. Box 7, Thomasville, GA 31799
Tiny Petals Nursery
489 Minot Avenue, Chula Vista, CA 92010
Wayside Gardens
Hodges, SC 29695

Index

Numbers in boldface
type refer to pages on
which color plates
appear.

Chanticleer Staff

Publisher: Paul Steiner
Editor-in-Chief: Gudrun Buettner
Executive Editor: Susan Costello
Managing Editor: Jane Opper
Series Editor: Mary Beth Brewer
Senior Editor: Ann Whitman
Assistant Editors: David Allen,
Leslie Ann Marchal
Production: Helga Lose, Gina Stead
Art Director: Carol Nehring
Art Associate: Ayn Svoboda
Picture Library: Edward Douglas
Natural History Editor: John Farrand, Jr.
Drawings: Sarah Pletts, Alan D. Singer,
Mary Jane Spring

Design: Massimo Vignelli